THE
PLANTING PLANNER

Graham Rice trained in horticulture at Kew.
He is now Gardening Editor of the *Daily Mail* and contributes
to *BBC Gardener's World* and to *Practical Gardening*
and *Garden News* magazines.
He has also written a number of books,
including *The Complete Small Garden,*
Plants for Problem Places, Hardy Perennials, Perfect Plants and,
with Christopher Lloyd,
Garden Flowers from Seed.

THE
PLANTING
PLANNER

Thousands of plants with hundreds of uses, that take
the guesswork out of choosing what will grow in *your* garden

Graham Rice

MACMILLAN

First published 1996 by Macmillan
an imprint of Macmillan General Books
25 Eccleston Place, London SW1W 9NF
and Basingstoke

Associated companies throughout the world

ISBN 0–333-600665

A CIP catalogue record for this book is available from the British Library

Photoset by Parker Typesetting Service, Leicester
Printed and bound by Mackays of Chatham plc, Chatham, Kent

CONTENTS

PART ONE
SOLVING PROBLEMS

─────── PART TWO ───────
USING PLANTS

PART THREE
CHOOSING PLANTS

PLANNING PLANTING

The single most important factor in the creation of a beautiful garden is putting the right plant in the right place. Gardens, after all, are about plants and when plants languish in the wrong conditions or look out of place the whole garden is disappointing.

Choosing the right plants is crucial, but they must be right in two ways. First of all, they must suit the conditions in which they're expected to grow and this is the first area where this book will help. You can't expect plants which like shade to thrive in the sun, or plants which like Mediterranean conditions to grow in wet soil by the pond. So here I give lists of plants for a range of garden sites and soils so you can make a selection from those which are most suitable and which are most likely to grow well.

Secondly, of course, it is important to grow plants which you actually like. A plant may thrive, it may fulfil the purpose for which it is intended, but if you don't enjoy it then instead of bringing pleasure it will bring constant irritation. So I also give lists of plants with different characteristics to provide a choice in every possible style from specimen trees to annuals for containers.

However, the book is called *The Planting Planner*, and planning is important to the success of any garden. It's so easy for enthusiasm to take over from judgement and forethought; we need both. By planning I don't mean drawing scale plans on graph paper – that's for the professionals. I mean thinking first and planting later so that the choices you make are not rushed and the right plant really does go in the right place.

Plants must also be considered as part of the whole planting and of the whole garden. Looking at plants without considering their relationship to each other will often result in nothing more than a series of individuals which do not make a coherent display. So the lists of plants with different features, be it flower colour or leaf colour or plant habit, should be used to help choose varieties which look well together – just like furnishing the house, the colours must blend or contrast well. So that when you look out of the kitchen window or walk up the front path, never again will your heart sink as you look at your own garden.

USING *THE PLANTING PLANNER*

This book is broken up into three sections. The first two sections cover plants for different sites and situations, and the contents pages will guide you to the lists which you will find most helpful for the conditions in your own particular garden. The third part of the book concerns plants with different features, and here too the contents pages are set out to show the breakdown of each section so that each list is easy to find. Finally, there is a section of other useful lists and sources of information which fit nowhere else.

I have also included some extra guidance on especially good plants. Those marked ♀ had gained the Award of Garden Merit (AGM) at the time the book was completed. This award is given by the Royal Horticultural Society to plants of special merit for general garden planting and is constantly being expanded as new plants are assessed. It turns out that many of the plants featured in this book have gained the AGM, although I did not actually check this until after the lists had been compiled.

In addition, I have picked one plant from each list as my own special recommendation and this is marked *. These are plants which I have found particularly beautiful or adaptable, or which are especially appropriate to the heading under which they occur.

This is a pragmatic book so that while the lists generally contain ten plants each, I have given important choices a list of twenty plants. At the same time when there are very few plants which match a particular choice they have sometimes been amalgamated with another list. In general the different types of subjects (for example, the various flower colours) tend to appear in the same order each time but there are a few occasions when a slight rearrangement of the order has helped save space.

CHOOSING THE PLANTS FOR THIS BOOK

Many of the plants included in this book have been selected as a result of my own experience of growing them but it would hardly be possible for me to grow them all. I have therefore also relied on my observations of plants both in both private and public gardens and on the advice of specialists on different plants and different planting situations.

The Royal Horticultural Society have provided valuable help and their advice leaflets, available free but only to members, have also been most useful. All the plants chosen are available from nurseries in the UK at the time of writing, and all have been checked in the most recent edition of *The Plant Finder*, which also lists the nurseries which stock each one. *The Plant Finder* does not cover annuals and bedding plants, so I have checked these in all the most recent catalogues to ensure availability.

It is true, however, that many of the plants I have included are not to be found in garden centres. The range of varieties stocked in garden centres is generally rather narrow, and readers will usually have to turn to specialist nurseries, either those open to callers or those which operate by mail order, to obtain many of the plants.

The situation is similar with annuals and other seed-raised varieties. Garden centres usually stock a limited range, while the mail order seed catalogues list a far wider selection. Mail order seed catalogues are usually available free of charge; nurseries often charge for their catalogues and details are given in *The Plant Finder*.

The Plant Finder has also been the basis for the choice of names for the plants. The fact that developing botanical research necessitates the changing of some plant names is understandably irritating to gardeners and I hesitate to go into the reasons here. However, it is never done without careful debate and consideration and changes always fall within the guidelines of the appropriate international agreements.

I have, however, occasionally shortened a name where it would otherwise leave no room for descriptive notes and where confusion will not arise. In one or two cases I have ignored the very latest changes of names in favour of names which are more familiar. And to help familiarize readers with new names I have included a list of those which have been used in this book along with their older and sometimes more familiar equivalents.

Finally, I should say that simply planting one of my recommended plants in the right place is not *quite* enough. The soil must be prepared well first, and the plants looked after in the succeeding seasons. Then they will thrive.

PART ONE

SOLVING PROBLEMS

PROBLEM SITUATIONS

PROBLEM SOILS

PROBLEM SITES

PROBLEM SITUATIONS†

PROBLEM SOILS

Clay soil

Even plants which enjoy clay soil benefit from having their sites improved with organic matter like garden compost before planting.

TREES

Many of these trees, especially the *Carpinus*, *Eucalyptus* and *Populus*, can be kept to a more modest size by careful pruning.

- ♀ *Acer campestre* Native maple; wonderful autumn colour. 18ft (5.4m)
- *Alnus incana 'Latifolia'* Slender alder with finely cut leaves. 18ft (5.4m)
- ♀ *Carpinus betulus 'Fastigiata'* Upright habit; autumn colour. 20ft (6m)
- ♀ *Eucalyptus gunnii* Unusually vigorous; pretty grey leaves. 45ft (13.5m)
- ♀ *Laburnum* × *watereri 'Vossii'* Yellow flowers in late spring. 20ft (6m)
- ♀* *Malus 'Golden Hornet'* Yellow fruited crab; good for jelly. 15ft (4.5m)
- *Populus* × *candicans 'Aurora'* Green, pink and white foliage. 30ft (9m)
- ♀ *Prunus 'Spire'* Pink flowers; fiery autumn colour; slender. 25ft (7.5m)
- ♀ *Salix babylonica 'Tortuosa'* Contorted willow; twisted stems. 30ft (9m)
- ♀ *Sorbus aucuparia 'Sheerwater Seedling'* Flat white heads. 18ft (5.4m)

SHRUBS

This is but a small selection of the many shrubs which will thrive on heavy soil; but like trees they appreciate improved conditions.

- ♀ *Abelia* × *grandiflora* Pink and white flowers all summer. 4ft (1.2m)
- ♀ *Brachyglottis 'Sunshine'* Silver leaves; yellow flowers; lax. 3ft (90cm)
- ♀ *Corylus maxima 'Purpurea'* Rich purple foliage for months. 8ft (2.4m)
- *Escallonia 'Slieve Donard'* Pink summer flower; arching habit. 6ft (1.8m)
- ♀ *Hamamelis mollis 'Pallida'* Yellow, scented, winter flowers. 6ft (1.8m)
- *Lonicera fragrantissima* Cream, sweet scented, winter flowers. 6ft (1.8m)
- ♀ *Philadelphus 'Manteau d'Hermine'* Double white, scented. 3ft (90cm)

---

† My other book, *Plants for Problem Places*, will also be helpful.

ANNUALS & BEDDING PLANTS

The use of annuals which are only in place for a single season gives an opportunity to improve clay soils between plantings.

Amaranthus caudatus Love-lies-bleeding; long red tassels. 2ft (60cm)
Digitalis purpurea Foxglove; purple or white spikes; biennial. 5ft (1.5m)†
* *Helianthus 'Giant Single'* Sunflower; roots break up clay. 8ft (2.4m)
Impatiens 'Expo' Vigorous, large-flowered busy lizzie mix. 9in (23cm)
🏆 *Limnanthes douglasii* Poached egg plant; yellow-eyed white. 9in (23cm)
🏆 *Lobelia 'Crystal Palace'* Classic blue lobelia; bronzed leaves. 6in (15cm)
Mimulus Magic Series Twelve colours; flowers in eight weeks. 9in (23cm)
Myosotis 'Marine' Traditional blue forget-me-not; very neat. 8in (20cm)†
Reseda odorata Sweet-scented mignonette in reddish cream. 1ft (30cm)
Zea mays Ornamental maize varieties; deep roots break clay. 4ft (1.2m)

Chalky soil

In this section I particularly have in mind relatively shallow, rocky, well-drained, chalky and limestone soils rather than limy clay.

TREES

Digging a planting hole can be tricky on chalky soil, a mattock and crowbar may be useful! Be especially diligent with the watering.

🏆 *Acer griseum* Delightful peeling bark; superb autumn colour. 15ft (4.5m)
Acer negundo 'Elegans' Yellow-edged foliage; vigorous. 20ft (6m)
🏆 *Cercis siliquastrum* Judas tree; purple flowers in spring. 10ft (3m)
🏆 *Crataegus laevigata 'Paul's Scarlet'* Double red flowers. 15ft (4.5m)
🏆 *Fagus sylvatica 'Dawyck'* Tall slender beech; good specimen. 18ft (5.4m)
🏆 *Morus nigra* Mulberry; slow, but fruits temptingly delicious. 9ft (2.7m)
* *Populus alba 'Richardii'* Pretty, silver-backed, yellow leaves. 15ft (4.5m)
🏆 *Pyrus salicifolia 'Pendula'* Small, weeping silver-leaved tree. 10ft (3m)
🏆 *Sophora japonica* Cream flowers in late summer and autumn. 15ft (4.5m)
🏆 *Sorbus aria 'Lutescens'* Whitebeam; silvery-yellow leaves. 18ft (5.4m)

---

† These are actually biennials; sow in summer to flower the next spring.

SHRUBS

Many other shrubs will grow well on chalk if the soil above it is sufficiently
deep and generously enriched with organic matter.

♀ *Buxus sempervirens* The best evergreen hedge for chalk. 9in-15ft
    (23cm–4.5m)
    Cistus 'Silver Pink' Pink flowers; grey, evergreen leaves. 3ft (90cm)
    Daphne mezereum Purple winter flowers; red berries later. 3ft (90cm)
♀ *Euonymus alatus* Spectacular pinkish red autumn colour. 4ft (1.2m)
♀ *Laurus nobilis* Bay tree; essential kitchen herb; clip to shape. 7ft (2.1m)
♀ *Mahonia aquifolium 'Apollo'* Gold flowers; spreads well. 2ft (60cm)
    Rosa pimpinellifolia Spiny dwarf rose; many good forms. 4ft (1.2m)
♀ *Sambucus nigra 'Guincho Purple'* Purple-leaved elderberry. 10ft (3m)
♀ *Ulex europaeus 'Flore Pleno'* Double-flowered gorse; spiny. 5ft (1.5m)
* *Viburnum opulus 'Sterile'* Snowball tree; white flowers. 8ft (2.4m)

CLIMBERS AND WALL SHRUBS

Shrubs and climbers planted on south-facing walls or trained through trees
are especially prone to drying out in their early years.

♀ *Buddleia fallowiana 'Alba'* Sweet white flowers; grey leaves. 8ft (2.4m)†
♀ *Ceanothus 'Puget Blue'* Clouds of dark blue, spring flowers. 10ft (3m)
    Clematis tangutica Vigorous, yellow climber; feathery seeds. 20ft (6m)
♀ *Escallonia 'Iveyi'* Large white flowers; glossy foliage; sun. 8ft (2.4m)
    Forsythia 'Weekend' Yellow; the most floriferous forsythia. 6ft (1.8m)
♀ *Fremontodendron 'California Glory'* Spectacular yellow. 15ft (4.5m)
♀ *Indigofera heterantha* Purple flowers in summer and autumn. 5ft (1.5m)
♀ *Lathyrus latifolius* Perennial pea; red, pink or white; no scent. 6ft (1.8m)
    Romneya 'White Cloud' Huge, white, fragrant, flowers. 5ft (1.5m)
♀* *Spartium junceum* Spanish broom; bright yellow flowers. 8ft (2.4m)

---

†   This variety is less tough than the more familiar buddleias.

PERENNIALS

Many perennials are adapted to chalk soil and their roots run widely in the shallow surface layer. Others delve into cracks.

    Campanula glomerata Bold purplish-blue flowers; invasive. 2ft (60cm)

    Clematis integrifolia Reflexed blue flowers; herbaceous type. 2ft (60cm)

*   *Dianthus Garden Pinks* Many colours; many well scented. 1ft (30cm)†

    Eremurus robustus Dramatic 4ft (1.2m) spikes of pink flowers. 8ft (2.4m)

    Iris Bearded Forms Tall, medium, dwarf; every colour. 1–2½ ft (30-75cm)

    Knautia macedonica Crimson pincushion flowers all summer. 2ft (60cm)

    Linaria purpurea 'Canon Went' Tall, slender, pink spikes. 3ft (90cm)

    Paeonia Double Hybrids Many colours; prepare soil well. 2–3ft (60-90cm)

    Primula veris Cowslips; natural chalk-lovers; not just yellow. 9in (23cm)

    Scabiosa 'Butterfly Blue' Pale blue flowers all summer. 18in (45cm)

GROUND COVER PLANTS

Some of these run out over the soil surface, rooting as they go; some sucker enthusiastically; others spread out from a tight crown.

♆ *Bergenia 'Bressingham White'* White flowers; vigorous. 18in (45cm)

♆ *Campanula portenschlagiana* Blue flowers but rampageous. 9in (23cm)

♆ *Ceratostigma willmottianum* Blue flowers; autumn colour. 2ft (60cm)

    Coreopsis verticillata Bright yellow daisies; feathery leaves. 2ft (60cm)

    Cotoneaster microphyllus var. cochleatus Flat; red berries. 1ft (30cm)

♆ *Euonymus 'Emerald 'n' Gold'* The name describes the leaves. 1ft (30cm)

♆ *Hebe pinguifolia 'Pagei'* Neat silver leaves; white flowers. 9in (23cm)

    Helianthemum Wisley Series Silver leaves; various flowers. 15in (38cm)

    Sarcococca humilis Hummocky growth; sweet white flowers. 18in (45cm)

♆* *Vinca minor 'Argenteo-variegata'* Variegated leaves. 9in (23cm)

---

†   Many garden pinks have been given the Award of Garden Merit.

ALPINES

Many alpines are ideally suited to chalky soils as they appreciate the good drainage; but they dislike starvation and also need full sun.

♀ *Anthemis punctata ssp. cupaniana* Silver leaf; white daisies. 1ft (30cm)

♀ *Aurinia saxatilis* Clouds of foamy yellow spring flowers. 1ft (30cm)

♀ *Campanula cochlearifolia* Dainty blue bells; can be invasive. 4in (10cm)

♀ *Geranium 'Ballerina'* Silvery leaves; lilac and purple flowers. 6in (15cm)

♀ *Gypsophila repens* Grey leaves, pink flowers; creeping habit. 3in (7.5cm)

Helichrysum bellidioides White everlasting flowers; prostrate. 3in (7.5cm)

♀* *Pulsatilla vulgaris* Purple bells; pretty feathery seed heads. 10in (25cm)

♀ *Saponaria ocymoides* Pink flowers in spring; easy trailer. 6in (15cm)

♀ *Saxifraga 'Gregor Mendel'* Yellow flowers; tight hummocks. 4in (10cm)

Thymus serpyllum Creeping thyme; magenta, pink or white. 2in (5cm)

BULBS

Shallow soils over chalk suit many bulbs, which enjoy the good drainage, but they appreciate liquid feeding after flowering.

♀ *Allium moly* Heads of bright yellow flowers in spring. 9in (23cm)

Anemone blanda Creeping anemone in blues, pinks and white. 9in (23cm)

Crocus chrysanthus Many colours and patterns; very dainty. 4in (10cm)

♀ *Galanthus elwesii* The best snowdrop for chalk; broad leaves. 9in (23cm)

Galtonia candicans Open heads of white bells in summer. 3–4ft (90cm–1.5m)

Hermodactylus tuberosus Unusual green and black flowers. 9in (23cm)

♀ *Iris reticulata* Small iris in blue and purple; also good in pots. 4in (10cm)

♀ *Iris unguicularis* Scented winter iris; purple, blue or white. 1ft (30cm)†

♀* *Lilium candidum* Classic white summer lily; loves chalk. 3–4ft (90cm–1.5m)

♀ *Tulipa tarda* Wild tulip; yellow-centred white flowers. 9in (23cm)

---

† Protect from slugs, which can eat the buds before they open.

ANNUALS AND BEDDING PLANTS

Many annuals grow naturally on chalky and well-drained soils and there are many more apart from these which will be suitable.

*   *Antirrhinum 'Sonnet'* Early, prolific; nine-colour mix. 18in (45cm)

    Cheiranthus 'Harlequin' Wallflower in sparkling colours. 18in (45cm)

    Chrysanthemum 'Tricolor Mixed' Fiery tricolor mixture. 2ft (60cm)

♈ *Convolvulus 'Royal Ensign'* White-throated blue trumpets. 1ft (30cm)

♈ *Dianthus 'Princess Mixed'* Six colours; single-flowered mix. 9in (23cm)

    Echium 'Blue Bedder' Dark blue, long season; bees love it. 1ft (30cm)

    Linaria 'Fairy Bouquet' Cheerful mixture of pretty bicolours. 9in (23cm)

    Salvia sclarea Pinky white flowers; bold rosette; stout biennial. 3ft (90cm)

    Verbascum 'Silver Lining' Spectacular silver rosette; biennial. 5ft (1.5m)

    Viscaria 'Rose Angel' Vivid pink flowers on wiry stems. 1ft (30cm)

——————————— Wet soil ———————————

Wet or badly-drained soil is usually less of a problem for the plants than for the gardener – as long as the right varieties are chosen.

TREES

Trees vary in their tolerance of wet conditions. A few thrive in shallow water, some at the water's edge, some in damp garden soil.

    Alnus incana Alder; some have especially attractive leaves. 20ft (6m)

    Mespilus germanica Medlar; makes a good lawn specimen. 15ft (4.5m)

♈ *Metasequoia glyptostroboides* Elegant deciduous conifer. 15ft (4.5m)

♈* *Nyssa sylvatica* Superb autumn colour; best in open site. 12ft (3.6m)

    Populus 'Aurora' Startling pink and white young foliage. 30ft (9m)†

♈ *Pterocarya fraxinifolia* Elegant specimen for watersides. 25ft (7.5m)

    Pyrus communis White flowers; casts only light shade. 15ft (4.5m)

♈ *Salix babylonica 'Tortuosa'* Spiralled and twisted stems. 25ft (7.5m)

    Sorbus aucuparia Mountain ash; berries in many colours. 20–25ft (6cm–7.5m)

♈ *Taxodium distichum* Deciduous conifer for the water's edge. 15ft (4.5m)

—————————————————————————————————

†   'Aurora' can also be pruned each spring and grown as a shrub.

SHRUBS

This selection includes some shrubs which especially like damp conditions, and some adaptable shrubs which grow well there.

♀ *Amelanchier lamarckii* White spring flowers; autumn colour. 15ft (4.5m)

Clethra alnifolia Fluffy spikes of white flowers; hates lime. 4ft (1.2m)

Cornus alba Many forms with coloured stems; prune hard. 3ft (90cm)

♀ *Hippophaë rhamnoides* Silver foliage; orange fruits; suckers. 10ft (3m)†

♀ *Physocarpus opulifolius 'Dart's Gold'* Bright yellow leaves. 6ft (1.8m)

♀ *Pleioblastus auricomus* Yellow striped bamboo; best in sun. 4ft (1.2m)

Salix alba Many with coloured stems; prune hard in spring. 3ft (90cm)

♀* *Sambucus 'Guincho Purple'* Bronze leaves; pink flowers. 10ft (3m)

Sasa veitchii Green leaves with unique parchment edges. 3ft (90cm)

Symphoricarpus 'Mother of Pearl' White fruits; neat growth. 4ft (1.2m)

PERENNIALS AND BULBS

Some perennials demand a moist soil, others are more adaptable and will also grow in drier conditions. Few bulbs like soggy soil.

♀ *Anaphalis margaritacea var. yedoensis* Pretty silver leaves. 2ft (60cm)

♀ *Astilbe 'Rheinland'* Dense plumes of clear pink flowers. 2ft (60cm)

Fritillaria meleagris Purple or white chequered bells; bulb. 15in (38cm)

* *Iris pseudacorus 'Variegata'* Dramatic yellow striped foliage. 3ft (90cm)

♀ *Iris sibirica 'Cambridge'* Pale blue flowers on elegant plants. 3ft (90cm)

♀ *Leucojum 'Gravetye Giant'* Like a huge summer snowdrop. 15in (38cm)

♀ *Lobelia 'Queen Victoria'* Beetroot foliage and scarlet flowers. 3ft (90cm)

Monarda didyma 'Adam' Aromatic foliage; scarlet flowers. 3ft (90cm)

Primula japonica 'Miller's Crimson' Tiers of red flowers. 2ft (60cm)

♀ *Trollius europaeus 'Superbus'* Elegant cool yellow bowls. 2ft (60cm)

---

† Ask the garden centre to give you females and a male (page 276).

GROUND COVER PLANTS

Ground cover plants are especially useful in damp soils as weeding can be difficult. But beware, some may become weeds themselves.

♀ *Ajuga reptans 'Burgundy Glow'* Dark pink and grey leaves. 9in (23cm)
♀ *Caltha palustris 'Flore Pleno'* Bright yellow double buttons. 1ft (30cm)
♀ *Darmera peltata* Large leaves like umbrellas; pink flowers. 3ft (90cm)
♀ *Filipendula purpurea* Foamy cerise spikes; bold, dark foliage. 4ft (1.2m)
♀ *Gunnera manicata* Like a vast rhubarb; for large gardens only. 6ft (1.8m)
♀ *Ligularia dentata 'Desdemona'* Purplish leaves; orange daisies. 4ft (1.2m)
♀* *Persicaria bistorta 'Superba'* Pink spikes; spreads well. 3ft (90cm)
   Persicaria campanulata Pink bells; can be rather invasive. 3ft (90cm)
   Petasites japonica Bold foliage; scented flowers; very invasive. 3ft (90cm)
   Symphytum 'Hidcote Blue' Blue flowers; rough foliage. 2ft (60cm)

ANNUALS AND BEDDING PLANTS

Many annuals and bedding plants do not thrive on wet sites, but more can be grown by building up the soil to improve drainage.

   Amaranthus caudatus Long red tassels; self-sows freely. 2ft (60cm)
   Cosmos 'Sonata Mixed' Dwarf mixture in four colours. 2ft (60cm)
   Impatiens glandulifera Pink policeman's-helmet flowers. 3ft (90cm)
♀ *Impatiens Super Elfin Series* Eighteen colours and two mixes. 6in (15cm)
♀ *Limnanthes douglasii* Poached egg plant; white, yellow eye. 6in (15cm)
   Mimulus Magic Series Twelve sparkling colours and a mix. 8in (20cm)
* *Mimulus 'Viva'* Large yellow flowers with bold red spots. 15in (38cm)
   Nemophila menziesii Soft blue flowers; dislikes drought. 6in (15cm)†
   Ricinus 'Impala' Castor oil plant; large bronzey red leaves. 3ft (90cm)
   Tagetes 'Lemon Gem' Masses of small yellow flowers. 1ft (30cm)

---

† Nemophilas in black, and in white with spots are also now available.

PROBLEM SITES

───────────────── Dry shade ─────────────────

Dry shade is one of the most difficult sites for plants, as neither moisture nor light, the two things plants need most, are available.†

SHRUBS

When planting dig a 2–3ft (60–90cm) hole, cut off any tree roots and low branches, add plenty of compost and water well until thriving.

     Aucuba japonica 'Rozannie' Bad reputation, excellent plant. 5ft (1.5m)

♀   *Berberis* × *stenophylla* Orange sprays; spiny; good hedge. 4ft (1.2m)

♀   *Cotoneaster 'Cornubia'* Arching evergreen; scarlet berries. 10ft (3m)

♀   *Danae racemosa* Very tough evergreen; orange berries. 2ft (60cm)

     Euonymus japonicus 'Aureus' Evergreen leaf, splashed yellow. 4ft (1.2m)

♀*   *Ilex 'Golden Milkboy'* Yellow-splashed leaves; purple stems. 4ft (1.2m)

♀   *Mahonia aquifolium 'Apollo'* Yellow suckering evergreen. 4ft (1.2m)

     Ruscus aculeatus Red berries in autumn; spiny evergreen. 3ft (90cm)

♀   *Skimmia japonica 'Rubella'* Red buds, scented pink flowers. 3ft (90cm)

     Symphoricarpos 'White Hedge' White berries; good hedge. 6ft (1.8m)

CLIMBERS AND WALL SHRUBS

On walls which receive no sun and are sheltered from the rain, or on tree trunks, there are plants which will put up a good show.

     Chaenomeles varieties Spring flowers in red, pink or white. 4–6ft (1.2-1.8m)

♀*   *Euonymus 'Silver Queen'* Silver variegated and self clinging. 3ft (90cm)

♀   *Fallopia baldshuanica* Rampageous – but tolerates anything. 30ft

     Garrya elliptica Greyish evergreen foliage; pale olive catkins. 6ft (1.8m)

♀   *Hedera helix 'Glacier'* Silvered ivy; brightens dark corners. 10ft (3m)

♀   *Hydrangea anomala ssp. petiolaris* White; self clings well. 10ft (3m)

♀   *Jasminum nudiflorum* Yellow flowers on bare green stems. 10ft (3m)

♀   *Kerria japonica 'Pleniflora'* Double yellow flowers in spring. 6ft (1.8m)

♀   *Lonicera* × *americana* Creamy scented flowers in summer. 15ft (4.5m)

     Rubus 'Betty Ashburner' Ground cover which climbs trees. 8ft (2.4m)

───

†   No trees are listed, they only make the problem worse.

PERENNIALS

Dry soil in shade can be made more suitable for perennials by raising the level and adding organic matter for extra moisture.

Acanthus mollis 'Latifolius' Bold, glossy foliage; few flowers. 4ft (1.2m)

♡ *Alchemilla mollis* Yellow-green foamy flowers; good leaves. 1ft (30cm)

Campanula latifolia Violet-blue or white spikes in summer. 3ft (90cm)

Carex pendula Arching spikes of green flowers; evergreen. 4ft (1.2m)

♡* *Dryopteris filix-mas* Pretty lacy foliage; toughest of ferns. 3–4ft (90cm–1.5m)

♡ *Euphorbia amygdaloides var. robbiae* Bright green flowers. 2ft (60cm)

Helleborus foetidus Red-tipped bells; divided evergreen leaves. 3ft (90cm)

Lamium maculatum Red, pink or white; silvered leaf. 1ft (30cm)

♡ *Liriope muscari* Violet autumn spikes; thin evergreen leaves. 1ft (30cm)

♡ *Polystichum setiferum* Luxuriant fern; happy in drought. 3ft (90cm)

GROUND COVER PLANTS

Resilient ground cover can be the most effective way of dealing with dry shade. Plant in the lightest spot and prepare the soil well.

♡ *Berberis wilsoniae* Coral berries; good autumn colour; spiny. 4ft (1.2m)

Epimedium × *versicolor* Delicate yellow flowers; evergreen. 1ft (30cm)

♡ *Hedera hibernica* The best ground cover ivy; very dark. 9in (23cm)†

Lamium galeobdolon Bright yellow spring flowers; spreads. 1ft (30cm)

Lonicera pileata Neat, spreading evergreen shrub; no flowers. 2ft (60cm)

Rubus tricolor Glossy leaves on bristly, rusty coloured stems. 6in (15cm)

Trachystemon orientalis Big heart-shaped leaf; blue flowers. 1ft (30cm)

♡* *Vinca major 'Variegata'* Yellow-variegated blue periwinkle. 15in (38cm)

Vinca minor 'Aureovariegata' Neater variegated periwinkle. 1ft (30cm)

Waldsteinia ternata Dark green mats; yellow spring flowers. 4in (10cm)

---

† The trick is to plant ivy in the sun then guide it into the shade.

BULBS

Most bulbs and bulb-like plants will thrive more heartily if dry soils are improved with organic matter and mulched in autumn.

    Allium ursinum White spring flowers; smells of garlic. 1ft (30cm)

♀ *Anemone nemorosa* Blue or white; needs improved soil. 6–9in (15–23cm)

♀ *Arum italicum 'Marmoratum'* White-veined winter leaves. 15in (38cm)

    Arum maculatum Orange berries in summer; good leaves. 15in (38cm)

♀ *Cyclamen hederifolium* Pink or white flowers; silvery leaves. 6in (15cm)

    Hyacinthoides non-scripta Bluebell; self-sows once settled. 1ft (30cm)

* *Iris foetidissima* Evergreen leaves; orange berries in winter. 2ft (60cm)†

    Iris foetidissima 'Variegata' Variegated evergreen leaves. 2ft (60cm)

♀ *Polygonatum × hybridum* The toughest solomon's seal. 2ft (60cm)

    Speirantha convallarioides Delicate, scented white stars. 1ft (30cm)

Damp shade

Moist shade is more an opportunity than a problem as it suits a very wide range of plants, providing the shade is not too dense.

SHRUBS

Many of the shrubs which thrive in moist shade are evergreen, many flower in winter or spring and many are also fragrant.

    Acer 'Dissectum Atropurpureum' Finely cut purple leaves. 4ft (1.2m)

♀ *Cercidiphyllum japonicum* Spring and autumn leaves pink. 15ft (4.5m)

    Cornus alba varieties Purple, red or yellow winter stems. 4ft (1.2m)

    Daphne 'Margaret Mathew' Fragrant yellow winter flowers. 2ft (60cm)

♀ *Fothergilla major* Fragrant tufts in spring; good autumn colour. 4ft (1.2m)

♀* *Hamamelis 'Jelena'* Orange winter flowers; autumn colour. 6ft (1.8m)

♀ *Osmanthus × burkwoodii* Fragrant, white spring flowers. 6ft (1.8m)

♀ *Pieris 'Debutante'* Prolific, white spring flowers; hates lime. 3ft (90cm)

    Rhododendron All will thrive if the soil is acid; evergreen. 2–10ft (90–3m)

♀ *Sarcococca confusa* Powerfully scented, white winter flowers. 2ft (60cm)

----

†   Probably the best of all plants for dry shade, there are four forms.

CLIMBERS AND WALL SHRUBS

The range of climbers and wall shrubs is fairly extensive, but the soil at the
foot of shady walls may be drier than you think.

    Camellia × *williamsii forms* Reds, pinks and white; acid soil. 8ft (2.4m)

    Clematis forms In shade, will climb towards the light. 6–15ft

    Eleagnus × *ebbingei 'Limelight'* Yellow-splashed leaves. 10ft (3m)

    Ercilla volubilis Pink flowers in spring; rare self-clinger. 8ft (2.4m)†

♈* *Hedera helix 'Buttercup'* Yellow leaves; good on tree trunks. 8ft (2.4m)

♈ *Lathyrus latifolius 'White Pearl'* Perennial pea, pure white. 8ft (2.4m)

    Lonicera japonica 'Aureoreticulata' Yellow-veined foliage. 8ft (2.4m)

♈ *Osmanthus delavayi* Dark leaves; fragrant white flowers; slow. 2ft (60cm)

    Rosa 'Madame Alfred Carrière' Best rose for shady walls. 6ft (1.8m)

    Schizophragma hydrangeoides White lacecaps; self-clinging. 9ft (2.7m)

PERENNIALS

There is a wonderful variety of woodland plants suitable for moist shade, and
they include some of the most lovely of all perennials.

♈ *Epimedium grandiflorum* Red, white or pink spidery flowers. 1ft (30cm)

♈ *Gentiana asclepiadea* Blue flowers in autumn; slender shoots. 3ft (90cm)

* *Helleborus Orientalis Hybrids* Winter flowers in all colours. 18in (45cm)

    Primula vulgaris forms Primroses in singles and doubles. 6in (15cm)

♈ *Ramonda myconi* Blue spring flowers; for shady crevices. 6in (15cm)

♈ *Saxifraga fortunei* Five-pointed, white autumn flowers. 15in (38cm)

♈ *Smilacina racemosa* Clusters of white flowers; glossy leaves. 3ft (90cm)

♈ *Tricyrtis hirta* Curious white flowers, speckled purple. 3ft (90cm)

♈ *Trillium grandiflorum* Bold, three-petalled white flowers. 15in (38cm)

♈ *Uvularia grandiflora* Pendulous yellow flowers in spring. 18in (45cm)

---

†   This can be difficult to find in garden centres; see *The Plantfinder*.

GROUND COVER PLANTS

Many woodland perennials will carpet the ground well when thriving but the following are especially good weed-suppressors.

♀ *Anemone blanda 'White Splendour'* White; spring; vigorous. 9in (23cm)
  Dicentra 'Snowflakes' White flowers for months; blue leaves. 1ft (30cm)
  Euonymus fortunei Many yellow and silver variegated forms. 1ft (30cm)
♀ *Gaultheria procumbens* Bright red berries in winter; creeps. 6in (15cm)
♀ *Hosta 'Shade Fanfare'* All hostas are suitable, this is superb. 18in (45cm)
  Hypericum calycinum Big yellow summer flowers; carpeter. 1ft (30cm)
* *Pulmonaria* Red, blue, pink or white flowers; spotted leaves. 1ft (30cm)
  Sasa veitchii Tough dwarf bamboo; parchment-edged leaves. 3ft (90cm)
  Symphytum 'Hidcote Pink' Pink comfrey; very vigorous. 18in (45cm)
  Viburnum davidii Spreading evergreen; turquoise berries. 3ft (90cm)

BULBS

Many woodland bulbs thrive in damp shade and spread well, although a few, such as bluebells, can become very invasive.

♀ *Anemone nemorosa* Wood anemone; many colours and forms. 9in (23cm)
♀ *Convallaria majalis* Lily of the valley; slow to settle down. 9in (23cm)
♀ *Cyclamen coum* Hardy cyclamen in magenta, pink or white. 4in (10cm)
♀ *Eranthis hyemalis* Winter aconite; yellow flowers; self sows. 4in (10cm)
♀ *Erythronium dens-canis* Recurved pink or white flowers. 1ft (30cm)
  Fritillaria pontica Easy fritillary; green and brown flowers. 2ft (60cm)
* *Galanthus* Snowdrops in many singles and doubles. 6–12in (15–30cm)†
  Lilium martagon Pink, spotted, turk's cap flowers; prepare well. 4ft (1.2m)
  Narcissus Most daffodils should thrive; plant a selection. 6–18in (15-45cm)
  Polygonatum hybridum 'Striatum' Variegated Solomon's seal. 2ft (60cm)

---

† Dry bulbs from garden centres grow poorly, buy from a specialist.

ANNUALS AND BEDDING PLANTS

Annuals are almost always sun-lovers and none will thrive in dry shade. Only a small range of varieties will succeed in damp shade.

    Begonia semperflorens Fibrous begonia; many varieties. 9in (23cm)

    Borago pygmaea Small blue flowers; can be a thug. 9in (23cm)

♀ *Impatiens Super Elfin Series* Eighteen different colours. 6in–1ft (15–30cm)

    Lunaria annua Honesty; purple flowers; pretty flat seed pods. 2ft (60cm)

    Lunaria annua 'Alba Variegata' White flowers; variegated. 2ft (60cm)

    Nemophila maculata White flowers with five purple spots. 9in (23cm)

    Nemophila menziesii Sky blue flowers; self sows when happy. 9in (23cm)

    Smyrnium olusatrum Green flowered biennial for wild spots. 3ft (90cm)

    Viola 'Johnny Jump Up' Small purple and yellow pansy. 6in (15cm)

♀* *Viola Ultima Series* Twenty-six colours, plain and blotched. 9in (23cm)†

Windy sites

Plants set out in unusually windy positions are best protected or supported until well established and able to support themselves.

TREES

Trees for windy sites should be able to tolerate the ferocity of gales and at the same time provide some protection for smaller plants.

♀ *Acer platanoides* Norway maple; tough and quick growing. 30ft (9m)

    Alnus glutinosa Not for dry soils; 'Imperialis' has cut leaves. 30ft (9m)

♀ *Betula utilis var. jacquemontii* White bark; autumn colour. 30ft (9m)

♀ *Carpinus betulus* Hornbeam; tough; makes a good hedge. 25ft (7.5m)

♀ *Crataegus laevigata* 'Paul's Scarlet' Double red flowers. 20ft (6m)

♀ *Fagus sylvatica* Beech; stately tree also good as a hedge. 25ft (7.5m)

♀ *Pinus nigra ssp. laricio* Good in bleak spots and by the sea. 12ft (3.6m)

    Populus alba Quick and tough; do not plant near buildings. 30ft (9m)

*   *Sorbus aucuparia* Mountain ash; berries in different colours. 15ft (4.5m)

♀ *Thuya plicata* 'Atrovirens' Rich green; good as tall hedge. 10ft (3m)

---

†   By far the best pansy for winter and spring flowering in all sites.

SHRUBS

The best wind-tolerant shrubs are either unusually tough and resistant, are good at filtering the wind, or are simply low growing.

℣ *Berberis × ottawensis 'Superba'* Purple leaf; yellow flowers. 6ft (1.8m)

Colutea arborescens Yellow pea flowers; inflated seed pods. 7ft (2.1m)

Euonymus 'Emerald Cushion' Domed evergreen; deep green. 1ft (30cm)

℣ *Ilex aquifolium* Tough, good in most soils; many variegated. 4–8ft (1.2–2.4m)

Ligustrum ovalifolium Privet; tough and quick; white flowers. 7ft (2.1m)

Pinus mugo 'Gnom' Attractive dwarf pine; slow but tough. 2ft (60cm)

Potentilla fruticosa Yellow, white or pink flowers; twiggy. 2–4ft (60cm–1.2m)

℣ *Pseudosasa japonica* Tough bamboo; tall arching growth. 8ft (2.4m)

Ruscus aculeatus Evergreen for any spot; red autumn berries. 2ft (60cm)

* *Sambucus nigra* Purple and green-leaved forms best. 8–10ft (2.4m–3m)

PERENNIALS†

Perennials for windy places should have the ability to sway in the storm, be self-supporting or keep low and neat to escape buffeting.

℣ *Achillea 'Coronation Gold'* Flat yellow flowerheads. 3ft (90cm)

Ajuga reptans Creeping growth; many coloured foliage forms. 9in (23cm)

Anemone × hybrida White or pink flowers in autumn. 2–4ft (60cm–1.2m)

Centaurea montana Spidery purple flowers let wind through. 18in (45cm)

℣ *Crocosmia 'Lucifer'* Scarlet flowers; elegant flat leaves. 3–4ft (90cm–1.2m)

Festuca glauca Neat, tufted grass with steely blue leaves. 9in (23cm)

* *Miscanthus sinensis 'Silberfeder'* Swaying flowering grass. 6ft (1.8m)

Nepeta × faassenii Catmint; clip promptly after flowering. 18in (45cm)

℣ *Phalaris arundinacea 'Picta'* Variegated grass; invasive. 3ft (90cm)

℣ *Stipa gigantea* Elegant weed suppressing grass; not invasive. 6ft (1.8m)

---

† Planting perennials on the leeward side of a shrub is helpful.

GROUND COVER PLANTS

Many ground cover plants are good in windy sites, the low habit and dense growth of many allowing the wind to sweep over them.

♀ *Berberis wilsoniae* Pink berries; fiery autumn foliage; spiny. 3ft (90cm)

* *Calluna vulgaris* Many varieties, all suitable; acid soil only. 18in (45cm)

♀ *Campanula portenschlagiana* Lilac bells; can be invasive. 9in (23cm)

♀ *Cotoneaster dammeri* Prostrate evergreen; roots as it runs. 9in (23cm)

Erica cinerea Bell heather in red, pink or white; acid soil only. 1ft (30cm)

♀ *Gaultheria mucronata* Fruits in purples, reds, pinks and white. 3ft (90cm)

Juniperus sabina 'Tamariscifolia' Wide, flat, greyish mats. 15in (38cm)

Leptinella potentillina Frilly foliage on low rooting stems. 3in (7.5cm)

Lonicera pileata Neat glossy evergreen; flat branching growth. 2ft (60cm)

Rhododendron Yakushimanum Hybrids Neat, leafy domes. 3ft (90cm)

ALPINES

Alpines grow naturally in open, exposed sites high in the mountains, so a great number are suited to windy sites in gardens.

Acaena 'Kupferteppich' Flat coppery carpet; roots as it goes. 9in (23cm)

♀ *Armeria maritima 'Vindictive'* Hummocky; dark pink flowers. 1ft (30cm)

Campanula poscharskyana Blue bells; neat green foliage. 9in (23cm)

Geranium sanguineum 'Cedric Morris' Bright pink flowers. 1ft (30cm)

♀ *Hebe pinguifolia 'Pagei'* Flat shoots with small silver leaves. 9in (23cm)

* *Phlox subulata* Red, pink, blue, lilac and white; flat growth. 9in (23cm)

♀ *Pulsatilla vulgaris* Yellow-eyed purple flowers; silky seeds. 1ft (30cm)

♀ *Saxifraga 'Gregor Mendel'* Tight mat; yellow spring flowers. 3in (7.5cm)

Sempervivum Houseleek; good range of foliage colours. 6–12in (15–30cm)†

Thymus serpyllum Flowers in pinks or white; aromatic leaves. 6in (15cm)

---

† Houseleeks even grow on exposed dry walls and on roofs.

BULBS

Strong winds can ruin bulbs, so they must either be determinedly
self-supporting or sufficiently dwarf to escape the battering.

♀ *Allium oreophilum 'Zwanenburg'* Bold carmine flowers. 6in (15cm)
♀ *Chionodoxa luciliae* Dainty blue and white flowers in spring. 4in (10cm)
   Crocus Dutch Hybrids Bold flowers; yellow, blue or white. 5in (13cm)†
♀ *Eranthis hyemalis* Winter aconite; glistening yellow bowls. 3in (7.5cm)
♀ *Iris reticulata* Dwarf irises in purple, blue or white; love sun. 6in (15cm)
♀ *Muscari azureum* Tight heads of bright blue flowers. 5in (13cm)
   Narcissus 'Little Gem' Pretty dwarf trumpet daffodil. 6in (15cm)
   Ornithogalum umbellatum Flat heads, shining white flowers. 8in (20cm)
   Scilla siberica 'Spring Beauty' Deep blue flowers; dark leaves. 4in (10cm)
* *Tulipa kauffmanniana* Vivid colours; mottled leaves. 5–10in (13-25cm)

ANNUALS AND BEDDING PLANTS

Many half-hardy summer bedding plants are slow to establish in exposed
gardens or are easily damaged by buffeting from the wind.

   Atriplex hortensis var. rubra Purple leaves; self-supporting. 3ft (90cm)
   Briza maxima Annual quaking grass; fluttering paper heads. 18in (45cm)
♀ *Calendula 'Fiesta Gitana'* Very compact mixture of colours. 1ft (30cm)
   Centaurea 'Baby Blue' Unusually dwarf blue cornflower. 10in (25cm)
   Crepis rubra Annual with pink or white dandelion flowers. 1ft (30cm)
   Eschscholtzia 'Sundew' Neat California poppy; lemon yellow. 6in (15cm)
♀ *Ionopsidium acaule* Tiny hardy annual; pale violet flowers. 3in (7.5cm)
♀ *Limnanthes douglasii* Bright, yellow-eyed, white annual. 9in (23cm)
* *Lobularia maritima 'Easter Bonnet'* The best alyssum mix. 6in (15cm)
   Verbascum 'Silver Lining' Broad, silver-felted rosette; biennial. 4ft (1.2m)

---

† Try forms of *Crocus chrysanthus* too, they come in softer colours.

Seaside gardens

Gardens by the sea often benefit from a milder climate than other areas, but many plants cannot withstand the salt in the sea winds.

TREES

Trees for seaside gardens must not only tolerate heavy deposits from salt laden winds, but should also give shelter to the garden.

Acer pseudoplatanus Sycamore; tough but with hungry roots. 30ft (9m)
℣ *Arbutus unedo* Strawberry tree; white flowers, red fruits. 10ft (3m)
℣ *Castanea sativa* Sweet chestnut; may not produce nut crop. 30ft (9m)
    × *Cupressocyparis leylandii* The quickest growing conifer. 35ft (10.5m)
* *Cupressus macrocarpa* Fine seaside tree; shelter belt or hedge. 20ft (6m)
℣ *Fraxinus excelsior* Ash; elegant specimen or windbreak. 30ft (9m)
℣ *Ilex aquifolium 'J.C. van Tol'* Tree-sized spineless holly. 15ft (4.5m)
℣ *Pinus nigra var. laricio* Fine conifer for seaside shelter. 12ft (3.6m)
    Populus alba Vigorous, tough; roots may damage buildings. 30ft (9m)
℣ *Quercus ilex* Evergreen oak; slow but eventually impressive. 20ft (6m)

SHRUBS

The soft, delicate new growth of deciduous shrubs is especially vulnerable to salt, so evergreens are generally more successful.

Escallonia 'Slieve Donard' Appleblossom flowers; good hedge. 6ft (1.8m)†
℣ *Fuchsia 'Riccartonii'* Scarlet and violet flowers; good hedge. 4ft (1.2m)†
    Griselinia littoralis 'Variegata' Best seaside variegated shrub. 8ft (2.4m)
℣ *Hippophaë rhamnoides* Orange fruits; plant both sexes. 12ft (3.6m)
    Olearia × haastii Fragrant white daisies in summer; evergreen. 6ft (1.8m)
    Pinus mugo 'Gnom' Slow, characterful, mound forming pine. 2ft (60cm)
* *Rosa pimpinellifolia* Many flower colours; black fruits; spiny. 4ft (1.2m)
    Rosmarinus 'Benenden Blue' Bright blue; lower than many. 3ft (90cm)
    Tamarix ramosissima Brown stems; grey leaves; pink plumes. 8ft (2.4m)
    Ulex europaeus Gorse; excellent on banks facing the sea. 5ft (1.5m)

---

†   All escallonias and many fuchsias are good seaside plants.

CLIMBERS AND WALL SHRUBS

Choosing the right site for climbers and wall shrubs is especially vital in coastal areas, where wall protection can ensure survival.

♀ *Buddleia globosa* Spherical orange flower heads in summer. 10ft (3m)

♀ *Choisya ternata* Scented white flowers; rounded evergreen. 6ft (1.8m)

♀ *Fallopia baldschuanica* Rampageous climber; white flowers. 40ft (12m)

  Garrya 'Pat Ballard' Very long, red-tinted catkins; evergreen. 12ft (3.6m)

♀ *Laurus nobilis* Bay tree; aromatic; appreciates wall protection. 10ft (3m)

♀ *Lonicera periclymenum* 'Serotina' Red and white twiner. 12ft (3.6m)

  Pyracantha 'Mohave' Prolific orange fruits; very salt resistant. 12ft (3.6m)

  Ribes sanguineum 'King Edward VII' Deep red flowers. 8ft (2.4m)

♀ *Spartium junceum* Tall, waving; yellow summer flowers. 10ft (3m)

* *Teucrium fruticans* Grey foliage; blue flowers all summer. 7ft (2.1m)

PERENNIALS AND BULBS

Relatively few perennials and bulbs will take full exposure to salty winds, but shelter from shrubby evergreens will help enormously.

  Amaryllis bella-donna Hardy pink relative of indoor amaryllis. 2ft (60cm)

  Catananche caerulea Dark-eyed, lavender daisies; grey leaves. 2ft (60cm)

  Crambe maritima Clouds of small white flowers; bold leaves. 2ft (60cm)

  Dierama pulcherrima Arching stems with dangly pink flowers. 4ft (1.2m)

  Eryngium maritimum Spiny, blue-grey leaves; bluish flowers. 1ft (30cm)

♀ *Euphorbia characias* Brown-eyed, green flowers; good leaves. 4ft (1.2m)†

* *Kniphofia 'Atlanta'* Masses of orange-red pokers in May. 4ft (1.2m)

  Limonium platyphyllum Leathery leaves and lavender flowers. 1ft (30cm)

♀ *Persicaria bistorta* 'Superba' Bright pink spikes; vigorous. 3ft (90cm)

  Phormium tenax Clumps of narrow leaves in many colours. 2–8ft (60cm–2.4m)

♀ *Salvia* × *superba* Purple flowers which keep their colour well. 3ft (90cm)

---

†   Look out for 'Blue Hills', 'Lambrook Gold' and 'Humpty Dumpty'.

GROUND COVER PLANTS

Ground cover for the seaside includes low growers which can keep down out of the wind, and the toughest of taller plants.

♀ *Brachyglottis 'Sunshine'* Grey leaves; bright yellow daisies. 3ft (90cm)

   Calluna vulgaris Ling; many good foliage and flower forms. 18in (45cm)

♀ *Cotoneaster microphyllus* Flat, evergreen shrub with red fruits. 1ft (30cm)

   Erica vagans Cornish heath; red, pink or white flowers. 1–2ft
     (30cm–60cm)

   Euonymus 'Dart's Silver Blanket' Low, silvered evergreen. 1ft (30cm)

   Hebe 'Youngii' Dark evergreen hummock; violet flowers. 1ft (30cm)

   Hypericum calycinum Bright yellow flowers; steady spreader. 1ft (30cm)

♀ *Juniperus virginiana 'Grey Owl'* Low, evergreen, grey mat. 1ft (30cm)

   Leymus arenarius Lovely but rampageous silver foliage grass. 4ft (1.2m)

* *Rosa rugosa forms* Good flowers and red hips; suckering. 4–6ft (1.2-1.8m)

ALPINES AND DWARF BULBS

These low plants are invaluable by the sea and often seem to grow more vigorously, yet more compact, than when grown inland.

♀ *Aethionema 'Warley Rose'* Neat, twiggy shrublet; pink heads. 9in (23cm)

   Agapanthus 'Headbourne Hybrids' Bold heads in many blues. 2ft (60cm)

♀ *Anemone blanda* Bright flowers in many colours; creeping. 4in (10cm)

   Anemone × fulgens Brilliant Mediterranean red; sunny place. 1ft (30cm)

   Armeria maritima Tight green tussocks; reds, pinks and white. 9in
     (23cm)†

♀ *Campanula portenschlagiana* Blue bells; floppy stems, runs. 1ft (30cm)

   Iris Dwarf Bearded Early flowering; vast range of colours. 1ft (30cm)

* *Phlox subulata* Tight mossy mats; covered in soft colours. 4in (10cm)

   Scilla siberica 'Spring Beauty' Deep blue stars; dark foliage. 6in (15cm)

♀ *Silene schafta* Prolific clumps of magenta or pink summer stars. 6in
   (15cm)

---

†   Thrift, a British native growing naturally by the sea.

ANNUALS AND BEDDING PLANTS

A number of annuals and bedders are naturally seaside plants and others will grow there happily; a little shelter helps them all greatly.

♀ *Dahlia 'Rigoletto'* Dwarf, semi-double mix in bright colours. 18in (45cm)

Dimorphotheca 'Salmon Queen' Unusual soft salmon daisies. 2ft (60cm)

Erysimum 'Tom Thumb' Dwarf, compact, bushy mixture. 9in (23cm)

Gazania 'Talent' Silver foliage; brilliant daisies open in sun. 15in (38cm)

Glaucium flavum Silvery leaves; bright yellow poppy flowers. 2ft (60cm)

♀ *Lavatera 'Silver Cup'* Pretty, silky pink, dark veined flowers. 3ft (90cm)

Lobularia 'Snow Crystals' Best white alyssum; large flowers. 6in (15cm)

* *Mesembryanthemum 'Harlequin'* Many colours; prolific. 6in (15cm)

Papaver 'Mother of Pearl' Delicate pinks and lavenders. 18in (45cm)

Petunia 'Carpet Mixed' Spreading growth, clear rich colours. 15in (38cm)

——————————— **Cold gardens** ———————————

Some plants are just not tough enough for the coldest places while late frosts may damage the new shoots of otherwise hardy plants.

SHRUBS

In cold gardens always leave spring pruning until the plants start into growth as the weather warms, or new shoots may be frosted.

Aronia arbutifolia Bright red berries and fiery autumn colour. 6ft (1.8m)

Buddleia davidii Purple, blue, pink or white pikes; prune hard. 6ft (1.8m)

Clethra alnifolia Slender spikes of white flowers; hates lime. 4ft (1.2m)

Elaeagnus commutata Silvery foliage; tiny fragrant flowers. 6ft (1.8m)

♀* *Euonymus alatus* Truly spectacular red autumn colour; slow. 5ft (1.5m)

♀ *Gaultheria mucronata* Berries like coloured marbles; acid soil. 3ft (90cm)†

Juniperus scopulorum 'Skyrocket' Slender blue column. 5ft (1.5m)

♀ *Prunus × cistena* Red leaves; pink flowers; black berries. 4ft (1.2m)

♀ *Spiraea thunbergii* White spring flowers; yellow autumn leaf. 5ft (1.5m)

Viburnum rhytidophyllum Impressive; branching evergreen. 10ft (3m)

————————————————————————————

†   This is the plant known until recently as *Pernettya mucronata*.

CLIMBERS AND WALL SHRUBS

Walls usually provide valuable extra warmth and shelter in cold areas, although lap fences may provide poor protection for plants.

♀ *Actinidia kolomikta* Unique pink, white and green foliage. 10ft (3m)

Celastrus orbiculatus Red and yellow autumn fruits; twines. 15ft (4.5m)

Clematis × *jouiniana* Scrambler with blue-tinted yellow flowers. 10ft (3m)

Clematis viticella Small flowers in red, purple, pink or white. 10ft (3m)

Hydrangea anomala ssp. petiolaris White lacecap flowers. 15ft (4.5m)

* *Lonicera periclymenum* Honeysuckle; early and late forms. 10ft (3m)

♀ *Parthenocissus quinquefolia* Red and orange autumn foliage. 15ft (4.5m)

♀ *Rosa 'New Dawn'* Pale pink, shapely, scented, long flowering. 15ft (4.5m)

♀ *Vitis 'Brant'* Coppery orange autumn leaves; edible grapes. 15ft (4.5m)

Wisteria floribunda Supremely elegant; best pruned regularly. 15ft (4.5m)

PERENNIALS

In dry areas or well-drained conditions many perennials can stand lower temperatures than in wet areas and in waterlogged soil.

Achillea millefolium Divided leaves; red, pink, yellow flowers. 3ft (90cm)

Cimicifuga simplex Elegant arching spikes of creamy flowers. 4ft (1.2m)

Coreopsis verticillata 'Zagreb' Bright yellow summer daisies. 2ft (60cm)

♀ *Echinops ritro* Spiky, steely blue balls on stout stems; prickly. 4ft (1.2m)

* *Iris sibirica* Stately small-flowered iris in blues and white. 4ft (1.2m)

Malva moschata Pretty pink or white mallow with cut leaves. 3ft (90cm)

♀ *Osmunda regalis* Superb fern; first rusty then bold and green. 4ft (1.2m)

Phlox maculata Fewer colours but hardier than other tall phlox.
    3ft (90cm)†

Primula vulgaris The wild yellow primrose is very tough. 6in (15cm)

♀ *Tiarella wherryi* Delicate fluffy white spikes; best in shade. 1ft (30cm)

---

† Look out for 'Alpha' (pink) and 'Omega' (lilac-eyed white).

GROUND COVER PLANTS

Low growing plants may suffer from cold air drifting into frost pockets, so the exact garden location may influence their hardiness.

     Bergenia 'Autumn Red' Good autumn foliage; late flowers. 1ft (30cm)

♀ *Brunnera macrophylla* Forget-me-not flowers; bold leaves. 18in (45cm)

     Calluna vulgaris Many flower and leaf colours; hates lime. 18in (45cm)

     Dicentra formosa Blue-grey foliage; pink or white flowers. 15in (38cm)

     Erica tetralix Grey leaves; pink or white flowers all summer. 18in (45cm)

♀ *Geranium endressii* Slow but steady spreader; pink flowers. 15in (38cm)

♀ *Juniperus procumbens 'Nana'* Flat growth; blue green leaves. 1ft (30cm)

     Lamium maculatum Silvered foliage; pink or white flowers. 9in (23cm)

♀ *Pachysandra terminalis* Neat, dense evergreen; white flowers. 1ft (30cm)

♀* *Pulmonaria saccharata* Silvered leaves; blue or white flowers. 1ft (30cm)

ALPINES

Originating high in the mountains, most alpines tolerate cold well but they usually dislike cold combined with waterlogged soil.

     Ajuga reptans Many coloured leaf forms; blue or pink flowers. 9in (23cm)

♀* *Campanula carpatica* Large blue or white bells on neat plants. 9in (23cm)

♀ *Dryas octopetala* Dense spreading hummocks; white flowers. 9in (23cm)

♀ *Epimedium grandiflorum* Delicate spidery flowers; for shade. 9in (23cm)†

♀ *Gentiana acaulis* Classic blue-flowered gentian; unpredictable. 9in (23cm)

     Geranium sanguineum Fast spreading mounds; pink flowers. 1ft (30cm)

     Iberis saxatilis Rich green hummocks of leaves; white flowers. 9in (23cm)

♀ *Persicaria affinis 'Superba'* Short pink spikes over dense mat. 1ft (30cm)

     Phlox subulata Pink, lilac, blue or white flowers; flat growth. 6in (15cm)

     Saxifraga paniculata Silvered rosettes; clouds of white flowers. 1ft (30cm)

---

†   Comes in a variety of forms from deep red to white.

BULBS

Bulbs are best chosen carefully, as many familiar varieties originate in the Mediterranean and may not be hardy in cold gardens here.

    Allium narcissiflorum Pretty dark pink flowers in spring. 10in (25cm)

    Camassia quamash Tall summer spikes in blue, white or violet. 3ft (90cm)

♛ *Chionodoxa luciliae* Sparkling blue and white spring flowers. 4in (10cm)†

♛ *Eranthis hyemalis* Winter aconite; neat, bright yellow flowers. 3in (7.5cm)†

♛ *Fritillaria meleagaris* White or purple chequered flowers. 18in (45cm)†

♛* *Galanthus elwesii* Bold, broad-leaved snowdrop; spreads well. 9in (23cm)

♛ *Lilium regale* Large, white, fragrant trumpets in summer. 4ft (1.2m)

♛ *Muscari armeniacum* Neat clumps of blue spring flowers. 6in (15cm)†

    Narcissus Cyclamineus Hybrids Tough, but very dainty. 9–18in (23cm–45cm)

    Scilla sibirica 'Spring Beauty' Deep blue flowers; dark leaves. 4in (10cm)

ANNUALS AND BEDDING PLANTS†

These hardy annuals and biennials are tough enough to sow direct into the soil outside in colder areas and still give a good display.

    Adonis annua Small scarlet flowers over pretty ferny leaves. 15in (38cm)

    Agrostemma 'Milas' Tall, swaying stems of lilac-pink flowers. 2ft (60cm)

♛ *Centaurea 'Blue Diadem'* Traditional bright blue cornflowers. 3ft (90cm)

* *Chrysanthemum segetum* Butter yellow corn marigold. 18in (45cm)

    Clarkia 'Love Affair' Good mixture of reds, pinks and white. 2ft (60cm)

    Echium 'Dwarf Mixed' Blue, pink and white summer flowers. 1ft (30cm)

    Godetia 'Sybil Sherwood' Pretty in lavender-pink and white. 1ft (30cm)

    Hesperis matronalis Fragrant biennial in lavender or white. 18in (45cm)

♛ *Nigella 'Miss Jekyll'* Sky blue flowers over feathery leaves. 18in (45cm)

♛ *Papaver rhoeas 'Shirley Mixed'* Excellent annual poppy mix. 2ft (60cm)

---

†   Spreads by self-sown seedlings when happy.

———————————— **Hot dry sites†** ————————————

Many of the best plants for hot, dry conditions come from the
Mediterranean area or similar climates in other parts of the world.

TREES

Even trees which enjoy hot, dry conditions when mature appreciate thorough
soil preparation and attention to watering after planting.

♀ *Acer campestre* Adaptable native maple; good autumn colour. 15ft (4.5m)
♀ *Calocedrus decurrens* Incense cedar; tall slender conifer. 20ft (6m)
   Cupressus sempervirens Lombardy cypress; very elegant. 15ft (4.5m)
♀* *Eucalyptus gunnii* Silver foliage good for cutting; vigorous. 30ft (9m)
♀ *Genista aetnensis* Fragrant yellow pea flowers; open habit. 10ft (3m)
   Gleditsia triacanthos Attractive leaves; showy fruits; spiny. 20ft (6m)
♀ *Laurus nobilis* Bay tree; dense, aromatic evergreen foliage. 10ft (3m)
♀ *Robinia pseudacacia* Attractive shape; white flowers; spiny. 30ft (9m)
♀ *Juniperus communis 'Hibernica'* Tiny, tree-like conifer. 2ft (60cm)
   Thuya plicata 'Atrovirens' Bold evergreen; shelter or hedge. 15ft (4.5m)

SHRUBS

Shrubs which thrive in hot conditions often have grey foliage, which helps
reduce the amount of water lost through the leaves.

♀ *Cistus* × *hybridus* Pink buds then white flowers; evergreen. 3ft (90cm)
♀ *Convolvulus cneorum* Silky, silver leaves; white flowers. 2ft (60cm)
♀ *Helichrysum italicum* Narrow grey leaves; yellow flowers. 18in (45cm)
   Olearia × *scillonensis* Grey leaves smothered in white daisies. 3ft (90cm)
♀ *Perovskia atriplicifolia* Blue summer spikes; aromatic leaves. 3ft (90cm)
♀* *Phlomis fruticosa* Greyish foliage; yellow flowers; spreading. 2ft (60cm)
♀ *Rosmarinus 'Miss Jessup's Upright'* Blue flowers; aromatic. 5ft (1.5m)
♀ *Ruta graveolens 'Jackman's Blue'* Blue leaf; may blister skin. 2ft (60cm)
♀ *Spartium junceum* Big, yellow, fragrant flowers on bare stems. 8ft (2.4m)
♀ *Yucca filamentosa* Bold, spiky rosette; dramatic cream spikes. 3ft (90cm)

———

† You may find Plants for Dry Gardens by Jane Taylor helpful.

CLIMBERS AND WALL SHRUBS

Many Mediterranean-type plants are too tender to be grown in the open garden but will thrive, if only in the south, on a sunny wall.

♀* *Ceanothus 'Puget Blue'* Clouds of blue in spring; evergreen. 10ft (3m)

Coronilla valentina Yellow flowers all year; bushy evergreen. 4ft (1.2m)†

♀ *Cytisus battandieri* Fragrant yellow flowers; grey leaves. 10ft (3m)

Lathyrus nervosus Rare blue climbing pea; clings by tendrils. 6ft (1.8m)

Mutisia ilicifolia Yellow and pink daisies; climbs by tendrils. 6ft (1.8m)

♀ *Myrtus communis* Myrtle; highly fragrant, white evergreen. 5ft (1.5m)

♀ *Olea europaea* Olive; grey-leaved evergreen, rarely fruits. 5ft (1.5m)

♀ *Robinia hispida* Pink pea flowers; spiny but attractive. 10ft (3m)

Rosmarinus lavandulaceus Low rosemary; trails *down* walls. 1ft (30cm)

Teucrium fruticans Grey foliage; blue flowers all summer. 8ft (2.4m)

PERENNIALS

Even these perennials need a little attention, early planting and watering especially, before they can cope with the hottest weather.

♀ *Achillea 'Coronation Gold'* Flat yellow summer flowerheads. 3ft (90cm)

♀ *Alstroemeria 'Ligtu Hybrids'* Orange and pink; running roots. 3ft (90cm)

♀ *Anthemis punctata ssp. cupaniana* Silver leaf; white daisies. 15in (38cm)

♀ *Cynara cardunculus* Cardoon; bold silver leaf; purple heads. 6ft (1.8m)

♀ *Eryngium × tripartitum* Small blue thistle-like flowers; spiny. 2ft (60cm)

♀* *Euphorbia characias* Heads of dark-eyed, green flowers. 3ft (90cm)

Malvea alcea var. fastigiata Pink flowers; finely cut leaves. 4ft (1.2m)

♀ *Sedum 'Ruby Glow'* Dark purplish leaves; deep red flowers. 6in (15cm)

Sempervivum Houseleeks; rosettes in red, green and silver. 6in (15cm)

♀ *Zauschneria californica 'Dublin'* Brilliant autumn scarlet. 18in (45cm)

---

† Available in a variegated form, and two different shades of yellow.

GROUND COVER PLANTS

When choosing ground cover for hot sites where shrubs are also grown, choose varieties whose roots are not too thirsty.

   Achillea ptarmica 'The Pearl' Small white poms; running root. 2ft (60cm)

   Armeria maritima Green hummocks; pink or white flowers. 1ft (30cm)

   Berberis 'Dart's Red Lady' Dense purple foliage; spreading. 2ft (60cm)

*   *Cistus 'Silver Pink'* Greyish leaves; silvery pink flowers. 2–3ft (60–90cm)

♀   *Cytisus × kewensis* Creamy white flowers; spreading habit. 1ft (30cm)

♀   *Gypsophila repens* Tiny pink flowers; ground hugging. 3in (7.5cm)

   Helianthemum Rock rose; single and double; many colours. 1ft (30cm)†

♀   *Iberis sempervirens* Tight green hummocks; white flowers. 1ft (30cm)

   Raoulia hookeri Pale green mats; tiny yellow flowers. 2in (5cm)

♀   *Salvia officinalis 'Purpurascens'* Velvety purple leaves. 2ft (60cm)

BULBS

Many bulbs grow naturally in hot climates so are well adapted to hot places in the garden; excess damp may be the biggest problem.

♀   *Allium karataviense* Blue-grey leaves; balls of purple flowers. 8in (20cm)

   Amaryllis belladonna Outdoor relative of indoor amaryllis. 2ft (60cm)

   Galtonia candicans White summer bells on tall, elegant stems. 4ft (1.2m)

   Hermodactylus tuberosus Unusual green and black flowers. 15in (38cm)

   Iris bucharica Fan of lush foliage; bright yellow flowers. 18in (45cm)

♀   *Iris reticulata* Dwarf purple or blue spring iris; unpredictable. 6in (15cm)

♀*   *Nerine bowdenii* Pink heads of autumn flowers before leaves. 2ft (60cm)

   Sternbergia lutea Flowers like yellow crocuses; hates wet. 6in (15cm)

♀   *Tulipa tarda* Pretty, starry white flowers with yellow eye. 4in (10cm)

   Zephyranthes candida Like a white autumn-flowering crocus. 6in (15cm)

---

†   Clip over after flowering to encourage a second crop of flowers.

ANNUALS AND BEDDING PLANTS

Many annuals thrive in hot conditions but may flower in one dramatic burst; dead-heading and watering will prolong the display.

    Calandrinia grandiflora Large, silky, pinky-purple flowers. 2ft (60cm)

♀ *Eschscholtzia 'Dalii'* Fluted red flowers with yellow eyes. 1ft (30cm)

♀ *Gazania 'Talent'* Silvery foliage; daisies in brilliant colours. 15in (38cm)

    Hunnemanniana fumariifolia 'Sunlite' Bright yellow poppies. 2ft (60cm)

    Linaria 'Fairy Lights' Tiny, multicoloured snapdragons. 1ft (30cm)

    Lupinus luteus Bold bright yellow spikes; likes rich soil. 2ft (60cm)

    Mesembryanthemum 'Harlequin' Sparkling colours; spreads. 6in (15cm)

* *Osteospermum 'Glistening White'* White, blue-eyed daisies. 1ft (30cm)

    Portulaca grandiflora Brilliant carpet of colour; poor in shade. 6in (15cm)

    Zinnia 'Persian Carpet' Neat double flowers; spreading habit. 15in (38cm)

Specific problems

Most gardens have at least one rather individual problem which demands particular plants to provide an attractive solution.

Ground cover plants for slopes

For slopes choose plants which bind the soil either by rooting as they spread or as they increase by underground runners.

    Aegopodium podagraria 'Variegata' Pretty cream variegation. 1ft (30cm)†

    Ajuga reptans 'Silver Shadow' White flowers; vigorous. 9in (23cm)

    Convolvulus altheoides Silvery leaves; pink flowers; rampant. 1ft (30cm)

♀ *Cotoneaster dammeri* Prostrate evergreen; red fruits in autumn. 6in (15cm)

    Geranium macrorrhizum Good for shade; pink or white. 1ft (30cm)

* *Hedera helix* Many variegated varieties root as they run. 6in (15cm)

    Leymus arenarius Grey-blue leaved grass which binds dunes. 4ft (1.2m)

    Omphalodes verna Pretty blue or white stars; good in shade. 6in (15cm)

    Vinca major Blue flowers; some forms have variegated leaves. 15in (38cm)

    Vinca minor Blue, purple or white flowers; some variegated. 1ft (30cm)

---

†   Variegated ground elder! Cut off flowers, seedlings come green.

Covering manholes

Plants to cover manholes must spread out widely but be tall enough and flexible enough to give easy access when necessary.

    Buxus sempervirens 'Prostrata' Widely spreading box; rare. 4ft (1.2m)

    Calluna vulgaris Good low, evergreen screen; hates lime. 18in (45cm)

♲ *Ceanothus thyrsiflorus var. repens* Clouds of blue; evergreen. 3ft (90cm)

♲ *Cotoneaster atropurpureus* 'Variegatus' Red fruit; variegated. 2ft (60cm)

    Euonymus fortunei 'Variegatus' White-edged evergreen. 18in (45cm)

*   *Juniperus sabina var. tamariscifolia* Broad and flat conifer. 18in (45cm)

    Rubus 'Betty Ashburner' Prostrate evergreen; rusty stems. 6in (15cm)

♲ *Taxus baccata* 'Repandens' Low and spreading; sun or shade. 2ft (60cm)

♲ *Viburnum davidii* Low and spreading; blue berries on females. 3ft (90cm)

    Vinca major Blue flowers, some forms variegated; tough. 15in (38cm)

Windbreaks

Many gardens, both small and large, benefit from wind protection but fences may create more swirling currents than shelter.

TREES

Trees are the mainstay of wind protection for larger gardens but shelter is enhanced by planting shrubs on both sides of the trees.

    Acer pseudoplatanus Tough and reliable; hungry roots. 25ft (7.5m)

♲ *Carpinus betulus* Good on wet soil; makes a good tall hedge. 20ft (6m)

    Crataegus monogyna Thick, tangled and spiny growth. 15ft (4.5m)

♲ *Fraxinus excelsior* Good on most soils; elegant when mature. 25ft (7.5m)

    Picea sitchensis Sitka spruce; superb in cool wet areas. 30ft (9m)

♲ *Pinus nigra ssp. laricio* Corsican pine; good by the sea. 14ft (4.2m)

♲ *Pinus sylvestris* Scots pine; tough and adaptable native tree. 14ft (4.2m)

    Populus alba Suckers soon increase the density of planting. 30ft (9m)†

    Populus nigra var. italica Good shelterbelt; beware roots. 40ft (12m)†

*   *Sorbus aucuparia* Tough tree for cold areas and most soils. 18ft (5.4m)

---

†   The roots of poplars can undermine foundations and block drains.

SHRUBS

Shrubs are vital features of shelter planting, they provide low cover under trees in large shelterbelts and do the whole job for small plots.

    Berberis julianae Dense spiny evergreen; yellow flowers. 6ft (1.8m)

♀* *Buxus sempervirens* Indispensable evergreen; clip to any size.

    Corylus avellana Thinnings provide the best of all pea sticks. 10ft (3m)

    Eleagnus × ebbingei Mature plants have scented flowers. 10ft (3m)

♀ *Hippophaë rhamnoides* Plant males and females for berries. 10ft (3m)

♀ *Ilex × altaclerensis 'Golden King'* Gold edged leaves; female! 6ft (1.8m)

    Ligustrum vulgare White flowers in summer; black berries. 5ft (1.5m)

    Sambucus nigra Cut-leaved forms are the least effective. 8–10ft (2.4–3m)†

♀ *Taxus baccata* Slow, but eventually makes a superb barrier. 6ft (1.8m)

    Viburnum tinus White winter flowers are a great bonus. 8ft (2.4m)

Noise filtration

For the best possible noise reduction choose plants with dense growth, large leaves, or rounded leaves with rolled edges.

TREES

Trees are needed for long-distance noise reduction, and while evergreens are ideal, long-season deciduous trees are also good.

♀ *Acer platanoides* Large-leaved, quick-growing; elegant crown. 25ft (7.5m)

♀ *Carpinus betulus 'Fastigiata'* Dense growth; attractive shape. 20ft (6m)

    × Cupressocyparis leylandii Dense, evergreen and very quick. 30ft (9m)

    Fagus grandifolia Larger leaves, but a smaller tree than beech. 10ft (3m)

♀ *Pinus radiata* Dense, speedy growth; best in milder areas. 12ft (3.6m)

♀ *Platanus × hispanica* Imposing tree with very large leaves. 35ft (10.5m)

♀ *Pterocarya fraxinifolia* Impressive spreading tree; big leaves. 30ft (9m)

♀* *Quercus ilex* Evergreen oak, but slow; can be clipped. 15ft (4.5m)

♀ *Thuya plicata 'Atrovirens'* Dense, dark green; good hedge. 10ft (3m)

    Tilia americana Enormous pale green leaves on stately tree. 30ft (9m)

---

†   Although elders can be pruned, for shelter they are best left unpruned.

SHRUBS

A mixture of small-and large-leaved shrubs gives the best protection against the widest range of noise frequencies.

    Cornus alba Vigorous but deciduous; can be clipped to size. 8ft (2.4m)

    Corylus avellana Rounded ribbed leaves in flat sprays. 10ft (3m)

♀ *Ilex × altaclerensis 'Wilsonii'* Tight growth; very large leaves. 8ft (2.4m)

♀ *Juniperus × media 'Pfitzeriana'* Upwards sweeping branches. 5ft (1.5m)

    Lonicera maackii Large-leaved honeysuckle; shrub; red fruits. 6ft (1.8m)

    Prunus laurocerasus 'Latifolia' Huge glossy foliage. 15ft (4.5m)

    Rhododendron Hardy Hybrids Choose your flower colour. 6–10ft (1.8–3m)

    Sambucus nigra Mix narrow-leaved and broad-leaved forms. 15ft (4.5m)

    Syringa vulgaris Heavy, dull green leaves; many forms. Up to 10ft (3m)

* *Viburnum rhytidophyllum* Long-veined evergreen leaves. 10ft (3m)

Animal problems

Deer and rabbits can be very destructive but fencing against them is often impossibly expensive. Resistant plants can be a solution.

DEER-RESISTANT PLANTS†

It is probably true that most plants will occasionally be eaten, but research has shown that varieties of the following plants are usually ignored. Young plants are the most likely to suffer.

Agapanthus	*Helleborus*	*Narcissus*
Aquilegia	*Hydrangea*	*Philadelphus*
Bamboo	*Jasminum*	*Potentilla fruticosa*
Buddleia davidii	*Kerria*	*Ribes*
Buxus	*Kniphofia*	*Romneya coulteri*
Cistus	*Lavandula*	*Rosa pimpinellifolia*
Clematis	*Lonicera*	*Rosa rugosa*
Daphne	*Lupinus*	*Vinca*
Delphinium	*Magnolia*	*Weigela*
Digitalis	*Mahonia*	*Yucca*
Forsythia		

---

†   It is especially important to protect young trees using tree guards.

RABBIT-PROOF PLANTS

Rabbits are a serious problem in many rural gardens and in some urban ones as well. Humane traps are available but gardeners have reported that the following plants do show some resistance, especially when mature. †

Acanthus	*Convallaria*	*Lavatera*
Aconitum	*Cotoneaster*	*Liriope*
Agapanthus	*Crocosmia*	*Lonicera*
Alchemilla	*Cyclamen*	*Lupinus*
Alnus	*Dahlia*	*Narcissus*
Anaphalis	*Daphne*	*Papaver*
Aquilegia	*Delphinium*	*Philadelphus*
Aster	*Digitalis*	*Rhododendron*
Astilbe	*Eranthis*	*Ribes*
Araucaria	*Eucalyptus*	*Rosmarinus*
Aucuba	*Euphorbia*	*Ruscus*
Berberis	*Fuchsia*	*Ruta*
Bergenia	*Galanthus*	*Sambucus*
Brunnera	*Helleborus*	*Syringa*
Buddleia	*Hemerocallis*	*Tagetes*
Ceanothus	*Hydrangea*	*Trillium*
Choisya	*Impatiens*	*Tulipa*
Cistus	*Iris*	*Verbena*
Clematis	*Kniphofia*	*Vinca*
Colchicum	*Laburnum*	*Yucca*

† Rabbits will often try new young shoots of these plants, and may also sample any new plants they come across rather than leaving them alone.

PART TWO

USING PLANTS

PLANTS FOR PURPOSES

PLANTS FOR THEIR HABIT

PLANTS FOR PURPOSES

Walls †

Walls are an invaluable asset, but remember that the soil at the base of any wall may be drier than the soil in the borders alongside.

NORTH-FACING

North walls may get little winter sun, but they provide valuable protection especially if sheltered from icy winds by near-by shrubs.

Aristolochia durior Big leaves, strange flowers; twines. 15ft (4.5m)

Camellia × williamsii Flamboyant evergreens; prefers acid soil. 10ft (3m)

* *Chaenomeles 'Fire Dance'* Scarlet flowers; spreading growth. 5ft (1.5m)

♀ *Cotoneaster horizontalis* Herring bone structure; red berries. 5ft (1.5m)

♀ *Hedera helix 'Glacier'* Grey and white foliage; self-clinging. 10ft (3m)

♀ *Hydrangea anomala ssp. petiolaris* White lacecap flowers; 10ft (3m)

♀ *Itea ilicifolia* Long green catkins in summer; holly-like leaves. 10ft (3m)

♀ *Jasminum nudiflorum* Invaluable yellow winter flowers. 12ft (3.6m)

♀ *Osmanthus delavayi* Fragrant white spring flowers; slow at first. 3ft (90cm)

♀ *Rosa 'Mme Alfred Carrière'* White and scented; superb. 8ft (2.4m)

EAST-FACING

Plants on east-facing walls can suffer from the early morning sun burning frosted flowers, so must be tough enough to cope.

Akebia quinata Attractive leaves; big brown fruits; twines. 20ft (6m)

♀ *Azara microphylla* Vanilla-scented yellow flowers in spring. 8ft (2.4m)

Celastrus orbiculatus Yellow autumn colour; colourful fruits. 20ft (6m)

Ercilla volubilis Spring pink flowers; self-clinging. Rare. 8ft (2.4m)

♀ *Euonymus fortunei 'Silver Queen'* Variegated evergreen. 6ft (1.8m)

♀ *Lathyrus latifolius* Perennial pea in red, pink or white. 8ft (2.4m)

♀ *Parthenocissus tricuspidata* Spectacular autumn colour. 20ft (6m)

* *Pyracantha 'Mohave'* White flowers, orange berries; superb. 10ft (3m)

---

† It pays to fix wires or trellis to walls as support for the plants.

Schisandra grandiflora Unusual twiner, small red flowers. 10ft (3m)
Tropaeolum peregrinum Canary creeper; pretty yellow annual. 6ft (1.8m)

SOUTH-FACING

South-facing walls are usually hot and dry, and while many plants will scorch, shrivel and die in such conditions others will thrive.

Abeliophyllum distichum Fragrant white flowers in winter. 5ft (1.5m)

Abutilon × suntense Spectacular mauve saucers; grey leaves. 15ft (4.5m)

♀ *Acacia dealbata* Lacy silver foliage; yellow winter flowers. 15ft (4.5m)

♀ *Campsis 'Madame Galen'* Soft red trumpets; self-clinging. 20ft (6m)

♀ *Carpenteria californica* Bushy evergreen; white flowers. 6ft (1.8m)

♀ *Ceanothus 'Puget Blue'* Dark leaves; clouds of summer blue. 10ft (3m)

♀ *Clianthus puniceus* Red 'lobster-claw' flowers; needs moisture. 8ft (2.4m)

♀ *Cytisus battandieri* Pineapple-scented yellow flowers. 10ft (3m)

♀* *Fremontodendron 'California Glory'* Big yellow saucers. 15ft (4.5m)

♀ *Ipomoea 'Heavenly Blue'* Exquisite annual; blue trumpets. 8ft (2.4m)

♀ *Passiflora caerulea* Unique flowers; orange fruits; vigorous. 15ft (4.5m)

WEST-FACING

West-facing walls are warm, not too dry and not too hot, although they do receive afternoon sun. They suit many plants very well.

Aloysia triphylla Strongly lemon-scented leaf; prune annually. 5ft (1.5m)

♀ *Choisya ternata* Rounded evergreen; fragrant white flowers. 6ft (1.8m)

Clematis Valuable for west walls. See lists p. 263. 6–10ft (1.8–3m)

♀ *Cobaea scandens* Purple or white bells; half-hardy annual. 10ft (3m)

♀ *Eccremocarpus scaber* Orange flowers; self-sows; tendrils. 6ft (1.8m)

♀ *Escallonia 'Iveyi'* Dark evergreen leaves; white flowers. 10ft (3m)

Lonicera 'Dropmore Scarlet' Bright scarlet flowers; twines. 15ft (4.5m)

♀* *Solanum crispum 'Glasnevin'* Blue and yellow 'potato' flowers. 8ft (2.4m)

Thunbergia alata Black-eyed Susan; orange half-hardy annual. 6ft (1.8m)

♀ *Wisteria sinensis* Many lovely new colours; expensive to buy. 25ft (7.5m)†

---

† Wisterias are best pruned in summer and autumn to flower well.

——————————— **Quick-growing plants** ———————————

In new gardens quick-growing plants create a mature effect in a short time; but of course they may soon grow uncomfortably large.

TREES

Think carefully before planting fast-growing trees; their thirsty roots may undermine foundations or they may cast too much shade.

    Acer pseudoplatanus Sycamore; vigorous; stately but hungry. 30ft (9m)

♀ *Alnus cordata* Narrow shape; winter catkins; good in wet soil. 40ft (12m)

    × *Cupressocyparis leylandii* Leyland cypress; fastest conifer. 35ft (10.5m)

♀ *Eucalyptus gunnii* Hardiest eucalyptus; pretty blue-grey leaves. 35ft (10.5m)

♀ *Metasequoia glyptostroboides* Deciduous conifer; slender. 18ft (5.4m)

* *Nothofagus obliqua* Like a very fast beech; good in autumn. 30ft (9m)

    Populus balsamifera Balsam-scented foliage; invasive roots. 35ft (10.5m)

♀ *Salix* 'Chrysocoma' Weeping willow; only for huge gardens. 30ft (9m)

♀ *Taxodium distichum* Slender deciduous conifer; good in wet. 18ft (5.4m)

♀ *Thuya plicata* 'Atrovirens' Dark foliage; good in drought. 20ft (6m)

SHRUBS

Fast-growing shrubs quickly give a garden maturity but some are short-lived while others may soon need removing to make space.

* *Buddleia davidii* Butterfly bush, many types; prune to size. 6–10ft
    (1.8–3m)†

♀ *Ceanothus* 'Autumnal Blue' Blue clouds; best on warm wall. 10ft (3m)

    Cornus alba Winter stems in various colours; prune to size. 3–8ft
    (90cm–2.4m)

♀ *Corylus maxima* 'Purpurea' Rich purple foliage and catkins. 8ft (2.4m)

    Elaeagnus × *ebbingei* 'Limelight' Yellow variegated evergreen. 8ft (2.4m)

♀ *Lavatera* 'Barnsley' Dark-eyed, blushed flowers; prune hard. 10ft (3m)†

♀ *Philadelphus* 'Virginal' Sweet-scented white spring flowers. 9ft (2.7m)

    Salix exigua Wispy branches, narrow silver foliage; suckers. 10ft (3m)

    Sambucus nigra Purple and variegated forms; all are good. 12ft (3.6m)

♀ *Viburnum opulus* 'Notcutt's Variety' Large white lacecaps. 10ft (3m)

———————————————————————————————————

†   Prune hard each spring to encourage plenty of flowers.

CLIMBERS AND WALL SHRUBS†

Like other fast plants, quick climbers are a mixed blessing. They cover rickety sheds in no time but may pull down whole trees.

    Celastrus orbiculatus Clusters of red and orange fruits. 20ft (6m)

♀ *Clematis 'Bill MacKenzie'* Orange flowers; fluffy seed heads. 20ft (6m)

♀ *Fallopia baldshuanica* Rampageous but spectacular in flower. 40ft (12m)

♀ *Hedera colchica* Enormous dark green leaves; self-clings. 15ft (4.5m)

♀ *Jasminum officinale* Fragrant white summer jasmine. 20ft (6m)

♀ *Lonicera 'Graham Thomas'* Cream flowers, very long season. 12ft (3.6m)

    Parthenocissus Virginia creeper; all have good autumn colour. 15ft (4.5m)

♀ *Passiflora caerulea* Unique scented flowers; clings by tendrils. 15ft (4.5m)

♀* *Vitis coignetiae* Red and purple in autumn; clings by tendrils. 20ft (6m)

♀ *Wisteria sinensis* Stunning in flower; needs regular pruning. 35ft (10.5m)

PERENNIALS

The dividing line between vigorous perennial and pernicious weed is a fine one, and all these may need controlling at some time.

    Achillea ptarmica 'The Pearl' Neat white buttons in summer. 2ft (60cm)

    Aegopodium podagraria 'Variegata' Variegated ground elder! 1ft (30cm)

    Ajuga reptans 'Silver Shadow' White-flowered bugle; runs. 9in (23cm)

♀ *Alchemilla mollis* Limy flowers; self seeds all too generously. 18in (45cm)

♀* *Anaphalis margaritacea ssp. yedoensis* Silver foliage. 2ft (60cm)

    Geranium × oxonianum 'Claridge Druce' Magenta-pink. 2ft (60cm)

♀ *Hosta 'Royal Standard'* Bright green leaves; white flowers. 3ft (90cm)

    Lamium maculatum White-splashed leaves; pink or white. 1ft (30cm)

♀ *Persicaria bistorta 'Superba'* Bright summer pink; likes damp. 3ft (90cm)

    Tanacetum vulgare 'Crispum' Curly tansy; poor flowers. 3ft (90cm)

---

†   Given guidance at first, all these climbers will soon support themselves.

GROUND COVER PLANTS

Quick-growing ground cover plants can do a wonderful job suppressing weeds but may cause trouble by spreading too much.

    Convolvulus altheoides Finely cut silver leaves; pink flowers. 1ft (30cm)

    Dicentra 'Snowflakes' Pretty blue-green leaves; white flowers. 1ft (30cm)†

*   *Geranium 'Ann Folkard'* Gold-green leaves; magenta flowers. 1ft (30cm)

♀ *Hedera hibernica* Best green ivy for ground cover; bold leaves. 9in
     (23cm)†

    Lamium galeobdolon 'Florentinum' White-splashed leaves. 15in (38cm)†

♀ *Lupinus arboreus* Self-seeding, yellow flowered, tree lupin. 4ft (1.2m)

    Pleioblastus pumilis Vigorous bamboo for sun or shade. 4ft (1.2m)

    Rosa rugosa All varieties good; many make a dense thicket. 5ft (1.5m)

    Rubus 'Betty Ashburner' Dense, ground-hugging evergreen. 9in (23cm)†

♀ *Vinca major 'Variegata'* White-splashed leaves; blue flowers. 15in (38cm)†

ALPINES

Many alpines are very compact, so it pays to grow them separately from these more vigorous spreaders. All are best in full sun.

♀ *Acaena microphylla* Bronzed mats of leaves with red burrs. 3in (7.5cm)

    Aubrieta hybrids Don't let familiarity breed contempt. 6in (15cm)

♀ *Campanula portenschlagiana* Tufted but vigorous; blue stars. 9in (23cm)

    Campanula poscharskyana Wandering stems; lavender-blue. 9in (23cm)

    Centaurea pulchra Purple thistle-heads in late summer. 1ft (30cm)

    Coronilla minima Broad spreader with golden pea flowers. 4in (10cm)

*   *Phlox subulata* Dependable carpeter; blue, pink or white. 6in (15cm)

    Persicaria affinis Pink summer spikes; rusty leaves in winter. 1ft (30cm)

    Pratia angulata Relentless spreader for damper spots; white. 2in (5cm)

    Waldsteinia ternata Yellow flowers then strawberry-like fruit. 6in (15cm)†

---

†   These varieties will all do well in shady places which are not dry.

———————————— Specimen plants ————————————

Some plants are not at their best in crowded borders, they show their
character better when grown in isolation as single specimens.

TREES†

Some of the most attractive of trees are best set apart where they can be seen
from a distance and their elegant habit admired.

   Acer platanoides 'Royal Red' Rich red foliage; very shapely. 25ft (7.5m)

♀ *Betula pendula 'Tristis'* Weeping birch; slender habit. 18ft (5.4m)

♀ *Fagus sylvatica 'Pendula'* Weeping beech; spectacular shape. 18ft (5.4m)

♀ *Fraxinus excelsior 'Pendula'* Strange, contorted weeping ash. 30ft (9m)

   Liquidambar styraciflua Spectacular in autumn; symmetrical. 15ft (4.5m)

♀ *Morus nigra* Looks elderly before its time; scrumptious fruits. 12ft (3.6m)

♀ *Parrotia persica* Broadly spreading habit; stunning in autumn. 15ft (4.5m)

♀ *Prunus* × *yedoensis* Wide, arching growth; white flowers. 15ft (4.5m)

♀ *Salix* × *sepulcralis 'Chrysocoma'* Weeping willow; vigorous. 45ft (13.5m)

♀* *Tilia 'Petiolaris'* Weeping silver lime; elegant but bad for bees. 30ft (9m)

SHRUBS

As a focal point in a border or at the end of path, as a lawn feature, or in a
corner in full view these shrubs with character are ideal.

♀ *Acer palmatum 'Sango-kaku'* Red twigs; yellow autumn leaf. 6ft (1.8m)

♀ *Aralia elata 'Variegata'* White-edged leaves; like a small tree. 8ft (2.4m)

♀* *Cornus controversa 'Variegata'* White-variegated; expensive. 8ft (2.4m)

♀ *Cotinus 'Flame'* Pink smoky flowers; good autumn colour. 10ft (3m)

♀ *Magnolia 'Lennei Alba'* White goblets on spreading plant. 8ft (2.4m)

♀ *Mahonia* × *media 'Charity'* Bold leaf; yellow winter flowers. 10ft (3m)

   Rhododendron All larger hardy hybrids are good; hate lime. 6ft (1.8m)

♀ *Rosa xanthina 'Canary Bird'* Yellow flowers; arching habit. 8ft (2.4m)

   Sambucus nigra Left unpruned, elders soon make big shrubs. 12ft (3.6m)

   Viburnum plicatum 'Lanarth' White flowers; tiered branches. 6ft (1.8m)

---

†   For conifers to grow as specimens, see page 268.

PERENNIALS

The choice of hardy perennials with sufficient presence to make specimen plants is rather small, but the best are very good indeed.

℗ *Aruncus dioicus* Cream feathery plumes in summer; adaptable. 6ft (1.8m)

Cortaderia selloana 'Rendatleri' Huge pink pampas grass. 9ft (2.7m)

℗ *Crambe cordifolia* Vast clouds of tiny white summer flowers. 8ft (2.4m)

Delphinium 'Southern Noblemen' Many shades; needs support. 6ft (1.8m)

Eremurus robustus 4ft of pink flowers on tall straight spikes. 8ft (2.4m)

℗ *Gunnera manicata* Like a vast rhubarb; best at water's edge. 6ft (1.8m)

Helianthus salicifolius Tall perennial sunflower; good foliage. 7ft (2.1m)

℗ *Hosta 'Krossa Regal'* Imposing mound; large grey-blue leaves. 4ft (1.2m)†

* *Kniphofia 'Prince Igor'* Tall, vigorous poker in bright orange. 6ft (1.8m)

℗ *Macleaya cordata* Coral pink plumes over blue-tinted leaves. 6ft (1.8m)

ALPINES

The concept of a specimen alpine implies a mature individual plant with particular appeal, even if it's only a few inches across.

Aciphylla scott-thompsonii Rare, spiny, yellow-edged rosettes. 3ft (90cm)

Anemonella thalictroides Clumps of fragile pink buttercups. 6in (15cm)†

℗ *Clematis marmoraria* Rare dwarf shrubby clematis; white. 9in (23cm)

* *Daphne cneorum 'Eximia'* Broad mat; sweet pink flowers. 6in (15cm)

℗ *Hepatica nobilis* Blue, pink or white; slow, eventually superb. 6in (15cm)†

℗ *Juniperus communis 'Compressa'* Pencil juniper for troughs. 1ft (30cm)

℗ *Pulsatilla vulgaris* Dense clump of gold-centred purple bells. 15in (38cm)

℗ *Salix 'Boydii'* Tiny gnarled shrub; grey leaves, silver catkins. 9in (23cm)

℗ *Saxifraga 'Tumbling Waters'* Silver rosette; white sprays. 15in (38cm)

℗ *Trillium grandiflorum* Stunning woodlander when mature. 18in (45cm)†

---

† All these varieties will do well in shady places.

ANNUALS, BEDDING PLANTS AND BIENNIALS

New bedding plant varieties are becoming ever smaller, but there are still some which make substantial plants in one season.

    Antirrhinum 'Giant Forerunner' Tallest mix; best in a group. 4ft (1.2m)†

♀ *Argyanthemum foeniculaceum* Bluish leaves, white daisies. 3ft (90cm)

    Canna 'Roi Humbert' Tropical purple leaves; orange flowers. 6ft (1.8m)

    Dahlia Large cactus and large decorative types are spectacular. 4ft (1.2m)

    Datura sanguinea Pendulous orange bells on a spreading plant. 4ft (1.2m)

    Onopordum acanthium Silver rosettes; branched silver stems. 6ft (1.8m)†

    Petunia Surfinia Series Spectacular, vigorous, trailing. 3–4ft (90cm–1.2m)

*   *Ricinus 'Impala'* Like huge sycamore leaves in glossy purple. 4ft (1.2m)†

    Solanum laciniatum Big fingered leaves; purple flowers, fruits. 6ft (1.8m)†

    Verbascum 'Silver Lining' Big woolly rosettes; yellow spikes. 5ft (1.5m)†

Native plants

When planting with the intention of attracting wildlife, or in unspoilt rural areas, native plants are often the most effective.

TREES

Planting native trees in rural gardens helps create a seamless join with the landscape and attracts the most birds and other wildlife.

♀ *Ash (Fraxinus excelsior)* Striking tree with 'keys' in autumn. 30ft (9m)

♀ *Beech (Fagus sylvatica)* Magnificent tree; hates waterlogging. 25ft (7.5m)

♀ *Birch (Betula pendula)* Gentle weeping habit; casts light shade. 30ft (9m)

♀* *Field maple (Acer campestre)* Red and gold autumn colour. 18ft (5.4m)

    Hawthorn (Crataegus) White flowers; red haws; sharp thorns. 15ft (4.5m)

♀ *Oak (Quercus robur)* Attracts more insects than other trees. 25ft (7.5m)

♀ *Pine (Pinus sylvestris)* Tough and adaptable conifer. 13ft (3.6m)

    Rowan (Sorbus aucuparia) White flowers; orange berries. 18ft (5.4m)

    White willow (Salix alba) Grey leaves, white catkins; quick. 25ft (7.5m)

♀ *Yew (Taxus baccata)* Dense, dark-leaved conifer; red berries. 6ft (1.8m)

---

†   These are grown from seed, the others in the list from plants.

SHRUBS AND CLIMBERS

As nest sites, cover for wildlife, sources of food or refuges for a wide variety of species, these are invaluable in the wildlife garden.

℣ Box (*Buxus sempervirens*) Slow evergreen; good as low hedge. 6ft (1.8m)

  Buckthorn (*Rhamnus frangula*) Black fruits; best in wet soil. 15ft (4.5m)

  Dogwood (*Cornus sanguinea*) Red stems; good autumn colour. 8ft (2.4m)

  Elder (*Sambucus nigra*) Grows well in poor soil; black fruits. 12ft (3.6m)

* *Guelder rose* (*Viburnum opulus*) White lacecaps; adaptable. 10ft (3m)

℣ *Holly* (*Ilex aquifolium*) Male and female needed for berries. 12ft (3.6m)

  Juniper (*Juniperus communis*) Spiky conifer; good on chalk. 8ft (2.4m)

  Old man's beard (*Clematis vitalba*) Pretty silvery seed heads. 20ft (6m)

℣ *Sea buckthorn* (*Hippophaë rhamnoides*) Silver leaf; suckers. 12ft (3.6m)

℣ *Strawberry tree* (*Arbutus unedo*) Slow evergreen; red fruits. 6ft (1.8m)

PERENNIALS

This is a selection of the more colourful British wild perennials to add colour to natural plantings; many also have especially ornamental forms.

  Chives (*Allium schoenoprasum*) Pink, globular flowers. 18in (45cm)

℣* *Cowslip* (*Primula veris*) Neat yellow flowers; best in the open. 9in (23cm)

  Cranesbill (*Geranium pratense*) Blue flowers, rather variable. 2ft (60cm)†

  Giant bellflower (*Campanula latifolia*) Blue bells; self sows. 4ft (1.2m)†

  Gladdon (*Iris foetidissima*) Lilac flowers; red fruits in winter. 18in (45cm)

℣ *Kingcup* (*Caltha palustris*) Yellow flowers; hates drought. 1ft (30cm)

  Primrose (*Primula vulgaris*) Likes some shade and heavy soil. 6in (15cm)

  Red campion (*Silene dioica*) Prolific pink flowers in spring. 2ft (60cm)†

  Stinking hellebore (*Helleborus foetidus*) Green winter flowers. 2ft (60cm)

℣ *Wood anemone* (*Anemone nemorosa*) Pretty white woodlander. 6in (15cm)

---

†   These plants can spread rather too quickly if not dead-headed.

ALPINES

Britain also has relatively few alpine plants, and while some are very colourful, to appreciate others requires closer inspection.

    Birch (Betula nana) Neat and compact birch with tiny leaves. 2ft (60cm)

♀ *Boyd's willow (Salix 'Boydii')* Tight shrublet, good in a trough. 1ft (30cm)

    Moss campion (Silene acaulis) Bright cushions; pink flowers. 3in (7.5cm)

    Mountain pansy (Viola lutea) Tufted pansy; bright yellow. 6in (15cm)

♀ *Pasque flower (Pulsatilla vulgaris)* Purple flowers, silver seeds. 1ft (30cm)

♀ *Reticulate willow (Salix reticulata)* Veined leaves; prostrate. 6in (15cm)

    Rock rose (Helianthemum nummularium) Yellow; spring. 6in (15cm)

    Saxifrage (Saxifraga oppositifolia) Purple flowers in spring. 4in (10cm)

    Thrift (Armeria maritima) Tight heads of pink flowers. 9in (23cm)

* *Creeping thyme (Thymus serpyllum)* Pinkish purple; aromatic. 3in (7.5cm)

BULBS

Britain has relatively few bulbs and bulb-like plants, but those we have inspire great affection; fortunately they are easy to grow.

    Bath asparagus (Ornithogalum pyrenaicum) White spikes. 2ft (60cm)

    Bluebell (Hyacinthoides non-scripta) Self-sows when settled. 18in (45cm)†

    Celandine (Ranunculus ficaria) Cheerful winter buttercups. 4in (10cm)†

* *Daffodil (Narcissus pseudonarcissus)* Modest but lovely. 1ft (30cm)

♀ *Fritillary (Fritillaria meleagris)* Chequered purple flowers. 18in (45cm)

♀ *Lily-of-the-valley (Convallaria majalis)* Fragrant white bells. 1ft (30cm)

    Meadow saffron (Colchicum autumnale) Mauve, autumn. 8in (20cm)

♀ *Snowdrop (Galanthus nivalis)* First sign that winter is over. 6in (15cm)

    Snowflake (Leucojum aestivum) White bells; loves damp. 15in (38cm)

    Squill (Scilla verna) Small blue flowers; for dry spots. 6in (15cm)

---

† This can be an irritating weed in many wilder gardens.

ANNUALS AND BIENNIALS

The elegance and natural habit of British annuals and biennials makes a
pleasant change from highly bred marigolds and salvias.

    Alyssum (Lobularia maritima) Sweetly scented white flowers. 1ft (30cm)

    Corn cockle (Agrostemma githago) Purple flowers; slender. 3ft (90cm)

    Corn marigold (Chrysanthemum segetum) Yellow daisies. 2ft (60cm)

    Corn poppy (Papaver rhoeas) The bright red field poppy. 2ft (60cm)

    Cornflower (Centaurea cyanus) Blue flowers on slender stems. 3ft (90cm)

* *Foxglove (Digitalis purpurea)* Biennial, self-sows once grown. 5ft (1.5m)

    Pheasant's eye (Adonis annua) Small, bright red flowers. 1ft (30cm)

    Quaking grass (Briza minor) Small-flowered 'everlasting' grass. 1ft (30cm)

    Spreading bellflower (Campanula patula) Blue bells; biennial. 1ft (30cm)

    Wallflower (Erysimum cheiri) Dwarf shrub grown as biennial. 18in (45cm)

Butterfly plants

Gardeners find more pleasure in planting flowers to attract adult butterflies
to the garden rather than food plants for caterpillars.

SHRUBS

A bold shrub covered in adult butterflies feeding on its nectar is a wonderful
sight; and there are more to choose than just buddleias.

* *Buddleja* The classic butterfly plant, most varieties are suitable.

    Calluna vulgaris Avoid the double forms like 'Joan Sparkes'.

    Caryopteris × *clandonensis* All varieties are blue; prune in spring.

    Erica Plant a range of different species for year round attraction.†

    Escallonia Not for coldest areas; leave unpruned for most flowers.

    Hebe Superb for summer and autumn; many tender in cold areas.

    Lavandula For hot, dry sites nothing can beat them; many forms.

    Mahonia Valuable early food for hibernating types as they emerge.

    Rubus Favourites with many types; includes cultivated blackberry.

    Syringa Some less common types have a longer season than most.

---

†   Most types, except *E. carnea*, require an acid soil to thrive.

PERENNIALS

Again there is one perennial, sedum, which always comes to mind in this context, but there are many others which are equally good.

* *Aster amellus* Butterflies look wonderful on purple or blue daisies.
  Centranthus Red, pink or white; good, but can be invasive.
  Dahlia Species, and varieties with single flowers, are the best.
  Echinops Silvery blue thistles in summer and autumn; spiny.
  Hyssopus Blue, pink or white aromatic herb; twiggy and bushy.
  Mentha Many gardeners don't let their mint flower; they should.
  Nepeta Butterflies, as well as cats, appreciate catmint.
  Scabiosa As good for butterflies in gardens as it is in the wild.
  Sedum All varieties are good; 'Meteor' and 'Brilliant' seem best.†
  Solidago Choose modern, semi-dwarf forms like 'Goldenmosa'.

ALPINES

Spring-flowering alpines are especially valuable for hibernating species, providing a first feed of nectar after the long winter.

  Ajuga Huge variety of leaf colour and blue, pink or white flowers.
  Arabis Single forms, in pink or white, are better than the doubles.
  Armeria Thrift; in pinks and white, above tight green cushions.
  Aubrieta A yellow brimstone feeding on aubrieta is a lovely sight.
  Aurinia saxalitis This alpine alyssum is easy in well drained soil.
  Erigeron Creeping alpine types; herbaceous perennials good too.
  Iberis sempervirens Makes a green cushion in sun; white heads.
* *Saponaria ocymoides* Rock hugging habit; small pink flowers.
  Sedum Small species for warm sunny places; pink, yellow, white.
  Thymus Creeping thyme on paving or scree is a great attractor.

---

† 'Herbstfreude' ('Autumn Joy') is the most popular but least useful.

ANNUALS, BIENNIALS AND BEDDING PLANTS

It is with annuals and other rapidly maturing plants that the quickest results can be had, while shrubs and perennials mature.

Ageratum Edgers and taller types in blue plus pink and white.
Calendula Medium and tall types like 'Touch of Red' last longest.
Callistephus Aster; medium and tall types last best; singles only.
Cheiranthus Bedding wallflowers are good for hibernators.
Heliotropium Vanilla-scented purple, lilac or white flowers.
* *Hesperis* Sweet rocket; sweet-scented biennal in mauve or white.
Iberis Candytuft; modern mixes like 'Flash' are the most colourful.
Lobularia Annual alyssum; traditional white is the most vigorous.
Lunaria Honesty; purple or white biennial; also variegated forms.
Zinnia Single-flowered varieties with their spreading habit are best.

LARVAL FOOD PLANTS

While adults can feed from many flowers, caterpillars will only feed on a specific plant and this is usually a particular wild flower.†

Alder buckthorn (Frangula alnus) Likes a damp, not too limy spot.
Birdsfoot trefoil (Lotus corniculatus) Often a weed in poor lawns.
Cabbages (Brassica) White butterflies love them – and nasturtiums.
Docks (Rumex) Cut off the flowers to ensure plants never seed.
Garlic mustard (Alliaria petiolata) Happy in a dry hedgerow.
Grasses Many useful; cut in spring then not again until autumn.
Lady's smock (Cardamine pratensis) Prefers damp conditions.
* *Nettle (Urtica dioica)* Best in a sunny spot; cut in midsummer.
Sorrel (Rumex) Sometimes found in neglected, damp, acid lawns.
Thistles (Carduus and Cirsium) These weeds are rather a gamble!

---

†   Check on the wild flowers growing near by – and grow others.

Bee plants

Many different species of bees, not just the familiar honeybees, visit flowers to collect both pollen for protein and nectar for sugar.

TREES

Trees are often rather variable in their attractiveness to bees and in some years may not produce enough nectar to be worth visiting.

℞ *Aesculus hippocastanum* Horse chestnut; usually reliable, but tall.

℞ *Castanea sativa* Sweet chestnut; an elegant tree but very tall.

℞ *Catalpa bignonoides* Pretty two-lipped flowers, long pods; slow.

℞ *Crataegus persimilis 'Prunifolia'* White flowers, red fruits.

℞ *Kolreuteria paniculata* Yellow summer flowers then fat pods.

Malus Crab, eating and culinary apples are all good for bees.

Mespilus germanica Medlar; traditional garden fruit, rarely seen.

℞* *Prunus padus 'Watereri'* Longest strings of white flowers.

℞ *Robinia pseudacacia* White summer flowers; many good forms.

Tilia Most good, but *T. cordata, T. petiolaris. T. tomentosa* toxic.

SHRUBS

In most gardens planting trees specifically for bees is a low priority, but with shrubs, which are more manageable, it is more realistic.

℞ *Aesculus parviflora* Shrubby horse chestnut; good autumn colour.

℞ *Buddleja globosa* Small spherical clusters of orange flowers.

℞ *Buxus sempervirens* Box; small creamy flowers among leaves.

Daphne mezereum Valuable early shrub; purple or white flowers.

* *Eleagnus* Small-flowers often go unnoticed except for their scent.

Erica carnea Many foliage and flower colours; tolerates lime.†

℞ *Perovskia atriplicifolia* Slender blue spikes; aromatic leaves.

Ribes sanguineum Colourful early shrub; red, pink or white.

Spiraea Great variety of habits and flower forms, all useful.

Viburnum opulus Many forms, white flowers and good berries.

---

† These lime-tolerant winter heathers are vital for early foragers.

CLIMBERS AND WALL SHRUBS

Bees are often reluctant to visit flowers in open, windy conditions, so it's helpful to plant some good bee plants in the shelter of walls.

*   *Ceanothus* Evergreen and deciduous types; spring to autumn.
   Chaenomeles speciosa Useful early shrub, for cold walls.
   Clematis vitalba Vigorous scrambler for old trees and walls.
♀ *Forsythia suspensa* Attractive arching habit; good on cold walls.
   Lonicera Honeysuckles of all types are useful, on walls or trellis.
   Parthenocissus Virginia creeper; small flowers; good in autumn.
   Pyracantha White heads in early summer; berries in autumn.
♀ *Ribes speciosum* Dainty, fuchsia-like flowers on spiny plant.
   Rosa All roses, even the fully double varieties, are good for bees.
   Rubus fruticosus Cultivated blackberry; vigorous but tough.

PERENNIALS

A vast range of perennials is visited by bees, especially those in the daisy and mint families, so this selection is very personal.

   Anemone The autumn anemones have masses of yellow pollen.
   Asclepias Vigorous but unpredictable plants; good for moths too.†
   Centaurea From 1–5ft (30cm–1.5m), the knapweeds are great bee
     favourites.
   Galega Lilac, white or occasionally white pea flower in clouds.
   Helleborus Valuable suppliers of winter nectar, even at Christmas.
   Hyssopus Noisy buzzing from the blue, pink or white flowers.
   Inula Bold yellow daisies on plants 2ft–6ft (60cm–1.8m); some invasive.
*   *Origanum* The marjorams are good for both butterflies and bees.
   Salvia Hundreds of varieties, some tender, some usefully autumnal.
   Sedum Sometimes bees and butterflies have to fight for space.

---

†   These are also unusual yet very long-lasting cut flowers.

ALPINES

Few gardeners would consider planting alpines specifically for bees, but to beekeepers and fruit growers they are important.

Antirrhinum The alpine species may be subtle or spectacular.

Arabis White or purple flowers; some are variegated; best in sun.

Armeria Thrift; good in sun, good in dry soil, good by the sea.

Aubrieta Avoid double varieties; variegated ones flower feebly.

♀ *Aurinia saxatilis* The shrubby alysum in yellow or ochre.

Campanula Spring bells in blue or white; creeping or tufted.

Geranium Many varieties, tufted and spreading; all easy to grow.

Helianthemum Rock rose; many colours, some silver-leaved.

♀ *Iberis sempervirens* Dense dark green hummocks; white heads.

* *Thymus* Shrubby and creeping types, some variegated; all good.

BULBS

Bulbs are not the first plants we consider when planning to attract bees to the garden and provide them with food, but they are useful.

* *Allium* All good, especially spherical species like *A. christophii.*

Alstroemeria Choose modern hybrids which flower for months.†

Camassia Elegant blue or cream spikes in summer; naturalizes.

Colchicum Valuable in autumn, avoid the double 'Water Lily'.

Crocus Choose varieties carefully to flower from autumn to spring.

Dahlia Single-flowered varieties are more useful than doubles.

Eranthis Winter aconite; invaluable for the first bees of the season.

Galanthus Avoid doubles, the common singles are more valuable.

Galtonia Elegant towers of white or green summer bells.

Hyacinthus Again, avoid doubles like 'Hollyhock', others all good.

---

† There's been a revolution in alstroemerias, look for Princess lilies.

ANNUALS AND BEDDING PLANTS

Bees are less likely to visit clumps of annuals if they are dotted about in ones and twos than if planted in substantial groups.

Antirrhinum The open throated and snap types are equally useful.

Borago Blue borage, and the rare white, will self-sow if happy.

Callistephus Aster; 'Andrella' and other singles better than doubles.

Centaurea Cornflower; choose either wild and cultivated varieties.

Cosmos Neat 'Sonata' and tall 'Sensation' and 'Sea Shells' all good.

*   *Echium* Viper's bugloss; mixes now include blues, pink and red.

Eschscholzia California poppy; wonderful range of colours.

Phacelia A must; *P. tanacetifolia* best but one of the less colourful.

Reseda Mignonette; good sown in patio pots as well as the border.

Zinnia Easy singles like 'Orange Star' better than tight doubles.

Birds and wildlife†

Wild creatures are used to depending on familiar plants, so British natives are the most useful; many garden plants are also valuable.

TREES

Trees provide nest and roost sites, food for caterpillars, beetles and other insects; it pays to leave a few logs to rot in an odd corner.

♀   *Betula pendula* Birds eat catkins; moth caterpillars eat leaves.

    Crataegus Hawthorns; good tangled cover for nests; plus berries.

♀   *Fraxinus excelsior* Birds eat seeds; a good host for insects.

*   *Malus* Crab apple; birds enjoy fruits; dense crown good for nests.

    Prunus spinosa Blackthorn; flowers for butterflies; fruits for birds.

♀   *Quercus petraea* Oaks support the most insects; mainly acid soil.

♀   *Quercus robur* Grows better on limy soil; has more garden forms.

    Sorbus aria Whitebeam; flowers for bees, berries for many birds.

    Sorbus aucuparia Rowan; berries feed a wide variety of birds.

♀   *Taxus baccata* Excellent nest cover; berries eaten by birds.

---

†   See *The Wildlife Garden Month-by-Month* by Jackie Bennett.

SHRUBS AND CLIMBERS†

Shrubs and climbers help a great many species by providing food, shelter, roosting and hibernation sites, nest sites and nest material.

♀ *Choisya ternata* Dense evergreen shrub; excellent cover for nests.
Clematis vitalba Flowers for butterflies, bark and seeds for nests.
Hedera helix Good nest cover; attracts hoverflies and butterflies.
♀ *Ilex aquifolium* Cat-proof nest cover; birds appreciate berries.
Lonicera Scented flowers of climbers attract insects; berries too.
* *Pyracantha* Wall-grown plants widely used for nesting; berries too.
Salix caprea Early pollen for bees, leaves for insects, sites for nests.
Sambucus nigra Wild and garden forms good for birds and insects.
Viburnum lanata Wayfaring tree; flowers for insects, plus berries.
Viburnum opulus Guelder rose; flowers, fruit; avoid sterile forms.

PERENNIALS†

Many perennials help wildlife by providing food for butterflies or bees, some also provide food for other insects and seeds for birds.

Achillea Butterflies and hoverflies use flowers; birds like seeds.
Bupleurum falcatum Greeny flowers for insects; seeds for birds.
♀* *Cynara cardunculus* Seed heads attract goldfinches in autumn.
Echinops Finches pull the spherical heads to pieces to eat seeds.
Foeniculum vulgare Good attractor for aphid-eating hoverflies.
Grasses Many are good caterpillar food plants; birds eat seeds.
Lamium maculatum Good evergreen cover for small mammals.
Rudbeckia Bees and butterflies like flowers; birds eat seeds.
Verbascum Host for the spectacular mullein moth – which eats it.
Vinca minor Good cover for ground insects and small mammals.

---

† Cover and shelter is as vital as food for both animals and birds.

ANNUALS

Many annuals are good for bees and butterflies but some are also great attractors of other beneficial insects and also garden birds.

 Ammi majus Pretty white lacy flowers good for many insects.
 Angelica archangelica Biennial; good for hoverflies† and moths.
 Calendula Tall, single forms best for insects and seed-eating birds.
 Convolvulus minor Good hoverfly food, now in many colours.†
 Dipsacus fullonum Flowers for butterflies, seed heads for finches.
* *Fagopyron esculentum* Buckwheat; the finest hoverfly attractor.†
 Helianthus Flowers for insects, seeds for birds; singles only.
 Limnanthes douglasii Yellow and white flowers for many insects.
 Matthiola bicornis Night scent attracts a new range of insects.
 Papaver Annual poppy; flowers for bees, seeds for finches.

Plants for troughs and sinks

In troughs and sinks, where root room is limited, there is often risk of drought. Vigorous plants must be banished to protect the others.

SHRUBS

Dwarf and slow-growing shrubs give structure and often provide colour and interest in winter when most other plants are invisible.

 ♀ *Berberis 'Corallina Compacta'* Coral buds, yellow flowers. 1ft (30cm)
 ♀ *Cassiope 'Muirhead'* Tufted evergreen; white bells; hates lime. 6in (15cm)
 Chamaecyparis obtusa 'Minima' Tiny, rich green conifer. 1ft (30cm)
 ♀* *Daphne petraea 'Grandiflora'* Pink, sweetly scented flowers. 4in (10cm)
 Hedera helix 'Marginata' White-edged leaf; tight and twisted. 1ft (30cm)
 Jasminum parkeri Tangled mound; yellow summer flowers. 1ft (30cm)
 ♀ *Juniperus communis 'Compressa'* Slim and very slow conifer. 1ft (30cm)
 ♀ *Polygola chamaebuxus 'Grandiflora'* Carmine and yellow. 6in (15cm)
 ♀ *Salix reticulata* Netted leaves; catkins in summer; flat growth. 4in (10cm)
 Sorbus poteriifolia Gnarled stems; white flowers; white fruits. 6in (15cm)

---

† Hoverflies are among the best predators of aphids in the garden.

ALPINES†

Troughs are intended for small, slow-growing alpines but many are quite difficult to grow well; these are less tricky than many.

    Draba rigida var. bryoides Dense cushions; yellow flowers. 2in (5cm)

♀ *Erodium glandulosum* Pale mauve flowers; scented foliage. 4in (10cm)

* *Gentiana verna ssp. balcanica* Brilliant blue; hates drought. 3in (7.5cm)

♀ *Geranium cinereum ssp. subcaulescens* Silver leaves; pink. 4in (10cm)

    Paraquilegia anemonoides Grey leaves; lavender flowers. 6in (15cm)

    Phlox nana ssp. ensifolia White-eyed pale pink; hates lime. 8in (20cm)

    Primula × *forsteri 'Bilekii'* White-eyed pink; hates full sun. 2in (5cm)

♀ *Ramonda myconi* Like a hardy African violet; best in shade. 4in (10cm)

    Saxifraga oppositifolia Tufted dark green mat; purple flowers. 2in (5cm)

    Soldanella alpina Delicate frilled flowers; can be temperamental. 4in
      (10cm)

BULBS

Bulbs for troughs must be chosen carefully; some are too large, some need lots of root space while others are too invasive.

♀ *Cyclamen coum* Silver or green leaves; pink or white flowers. 3in (7.5cm)

♀ *Fritillaria pallidiflora* Large primrose flowers on neat plants. 8in (20cm)

* *Iris 'Katherine Hodgkin'* Exquisite blue and yellow dwarf iris. 6in (15cm)

    Iris winogradowii Bright yellow iris; best out of full sun. 3in (7.5cm)

♀ *Muscari azureum* Dense spikes of sky blue flowers; prolific. 4in (10cm)

    Narcissus asturiensis Tiny trumpet daffodil; dainty and easy. 4in (10cm)

    Narcissus rupicola Deep yellow jonquil; fragrant flowers. 6in (15cm)

♀ *Oxalis adenophylla* Bluish leaves, pink flowers; demands sun. 3in (7.5cm)

♀ *Rhodohypoxis baurii* Red, pink or white flowers; hates lime. 3in (7.5cm)

    Scilla autumnalis Small lilac or purple flowers in autumn; 4in (10cm)

---

†   Many alpines grow naturally in crevices so are happy in troughs.

Container plants

Containers provide a way of growing plants unsuited to the natural garden soil and tender plants which can be moved inside for winter.

Permanent plants

A large container is required for most permanent plants and as they fill the pots with roots watering may become a daily requirement.

SHRUBS

Try to select varieties which will not outgrow their pots quickly and feed and water regularly once the plants become established.

ϒ *Acer palmatum var. dissectum* Pretty, dissected leafy mound. 4ft (1.2m)

ϒ *Buxus sempervirens* Box; ideal for topiary in pots and tubs. 2–6ft (60cm–1.8m)

  Camellia All superb but must never, *ever* dry out; hate lime. 5ft (1.5m)

ϒ *Convolvulus cneorum* Shining silver foliage; white flowers. 2ft (60cm)

  Daphne odora 'Aureo-Marginata' Variegated and scented. 4ft (1.2m)

ϒ *Myrtus communis* Myrtle; fragrant white summer flowers. 6ft (1.8m)

  Nerium oleander Exotic look; move to conservatory in winter. 4ft (1.2m)

* *Pieris japonica* 'Débutante' White flowers, bushy; hates lime. 3ft (90cm)

  Rhododendron On limy soil, grow in large tubs of acid soil. 1–6ft (30cm–1.8m)

ϒ *Rosa* 'Mountbatten' Stunning dwarf yellow scented floribunda. 3ft (90cm)

CLIMBERS

Some climbers are very vigorous and unsuited to containers but these are either slow-growing or can be kept to size by pruning.

ϒ *Actinidia kolomikta* Green leaves splashed pink and cream. 8ft (2.4m)

  Araujia sericifera Fragrant creamy flowers; sun and shelter. 6ft (1.8m)

  Bougainvillaea Mediterranean climbers in pinks and purples. 8ft (2.4m)

  Clematis Late-flowering hybrids are cut back hard each spring. 8ft (2.4m)

* *Clematis viticella* Small-flowers but prolific; prune in spring. 8ft (2.4m)

♀ *Eccremocarpus scaber* Orange flowers for months; needs sun. 8ft (2.4m)
♀ *Hedera helix 'Glacier'* Grey-variegated; lights up dark spots. 10ft (3m)
  Lonicera japonica 'Aureoreticulata' Yellow-veined leaves. 8ft (2.4m)
♀ *Rosa 'Handel'* Climber; red-edged white flowers; spring prune. 8ft (2.4m)†
♀ *Solanum jasminoides 'Album'* White flowers; spring prune. 8ft (2.4m)

PERENNIALS

Perennials are either used as feature plants in their own right or to provide
colour and interest at the base of climbers and shrubs.

   Acaena 'Blue Haze' Pretty blue grey leaves; spreads and trails. 6in (15cm)
   Aegopodium podagraria 'Variegata' Yellow variegated. 15in (38cm)
   Agapanthus Blues and white; best protected from winter frost. 2ft (60cm)
* *Dianthus* Modern pinks are colourful and scented; best in sun. 15in (38cm)
   Diascia 'Salmon Supreme' Salmon clouds for under shrubs. 1ft (30cm)
   Hakenochloa macra 'Aureola' Yellow fountain of leaves. 15in (38cm)
   Hosta All are super in shade, improving as they mature. 1–3ft (30–90cm)
   Lamium maculatum White-splashed foliage; excellent filler. 1ft (30cm)
♀ *Melianthus major* Big, blue-grey leaves; impressive specimen. 4ft (1.2m)
♀ *Penstemon 'Beech Park'* Long flowering, pink and white. 2ft (60cm)

Temporary summer plants ††

Containers allow you to create a bold and colourful planting which can then
be repeated, adapted or changed entirely the next year.

FLOWERING BEDDING PLANTS FROM SEED

Many seed-raised bedders are good in containers and the variety of colours is
enormous, but they need regular feeding and watering.
♀ *Begonia 'Chanson'* Large-flowered, double mix; trailing habit. 1ft (30cm)
♀ *Dahlia 'Rigoletto'* Dwarf mix in bright colours; easy to grow. 15in (38cm)
♀ *Impatiens Super Elfin Series* Twenty colours and mixtures. 9in (23cm)
♀ *Ipomoea 'Heavenly Blue'* Sky blue trumpets; climbs and trails. 5ft (1.5m)

---

† For more shorter-growing climbing roses, see page 259.
†† *The Terracotta Gardener* by Jim Keeling has lots of planting ideas.

*   *Lobelia Fountain Series* Five colours plus mix; compact trailer. 9in (23cm)

     Mimulus Magic Series Twelve colours and mix; hates drought. 9in (23cm)

     Pelargonium Multibloom Series Eight colours and mix. 15in (38cm)

     Petunia Supercascade Series Eight colours plus mix; stunning. 9in (23cm)

     Thunbergia alata Black-eyed yellow flowers; twines and trails. 3ft (90cm)

     Viola 'Imperial Silver Princess' White, red blotch; impressive. 9in (23cm)

FLOWERING BEDDING PLANTS FROM CUTTINGS

These summer bedders raised from cuttings tend to make bigger and bushier plants than seed-raised sorts; dead-head regularly.

♀ *Argyanthemum foeniculaceum* Bluish leaves; white daisies. 2ft (60cm)

     Begonia 'Remco' Double red, dark-leaved, fibrous begonia. 1ft (30cm)

♀ *Fuchsia 'Swingtime'* Red and white double flowers; trails. 9in (23cm)†

     Heliotropum 'Princess Marina' Dark purple, vanilla scent. 18in (45cm)

     Impatiens 'Peach Ice' Double pink flowers; variegated leaves. 1ft (30cm)

     Lobelia 'Richardii' Large pale blue flowers on trailing plants. 9in (23cm)†

     Pelargonium Cascade Types Prolific trailers in many shades. 9in (23cm)†

*   *Petunia Surfinia Series* Spectacular trailers, rich colours. 3–4ft
     (90cm–1.2m)†

♀ *Tropaeolum 'Hermine Grashof'* Vigorous, double red trailer. 1ft (30cm)†

     Verbena 'Pink Parfait' Pretty, scented red and white trailer. 9in (23cm)†

FOLIAGE BEDDING PLANTS

All summer containers need foliage as well as flowering plants to make an effective colour balance and the range is increasing fast.

     Beta 'Bulls Blood' Shining red-leaved beet; for looks not roots. 1ft (30cm)

     Brassica 'Christmas Bouquet' Frilly pink and white heads. 1ft (30cm)

     Centaurea 'Silverdust' Silver foliage, ideal with pastels. 1ft (30cm)

     Coleus 'Wizard Scarlet' Yellow-edged red leaves; unique. 1ft (30cm)

     Heliotropum 'Mini-Marine' Neat, deep blue-green leaves. 1ft (30cm)

♀ *Lotus berthelotii* Finely cut silver foliage; vigorous trailer. 2ft (60cm)†

     Plectranthus hirtus 'Variegatus' White-edged leaves; trails. 18in (45cm)†

     Tanacetum ptarmiciflorum Flat sprays of pewtery foliage. 15in (38cm)

---

†   Figures for trailing varieties are the lengths they trail *down*.

Tanacetum 'Golden Moss' Neat, bright yellow hummocks. 6in (15cm)

* Tropaeolum 'Alaska' Bushy plants; white mottled foliage, 18in (45cm)

BULBS

Many bulbs are best used to grow up through the middle of other plants where their less than elegant foliage is hidden by flowers.

Begonia 'Giant Double Fringed' Large frilly flowers. 15in (38cm)

♀ Crocosmia 'Lucifer' Brilliant scarlet flowers, pleated foliage. 3ft (90cm)

* Dahlia Dahlietta Series Neat, rounded plants; bright colours. 15in (38cm)

Eucomis bicolor Fat spikes in purple and green; tender. 18in (45cm)

Galtonia candicans Open heads of fat white bells; rather late. 3ft (90cm)

Gladiolus Many colours, choose to match colour scheme. 2–4ft
    (60cm–1.2m)†

♀ Gladiolus callianthus 'Mureliae' Elegant, white and scented. 2ft (60cm)

♀ Lilium regale Spectacular white, highly scented trumpets. 3ft (90cm)

Mirabilis jalapa Fragrant evening flowers; bushy and leafy. 2ft (60cm)

Ranunculus 'Giant Strain' Brilliant colours and bicolours. 18in (45cm)

Spring plants

Spring plants in containers often flower earlier than those in beds, but they need well-drained compost to prevent rotting in winter.

BEDDING PLANTS

Spring bedding plants for containers are usually raised from seed sown the previous summer, or perennial plants are split in autumn.

Aubrieta Purple or blue alpine; easy from seed but hates wet. 6in (15cm)

Bellis 'Bright Carpet' Neat double daisies; red, pink or white. 6in (15cm)

Digitalis 'Foxy' Dwarf foxglove in mixed colours for big tub. 3ft (90cm)

Doronicum caucasicum 'Magnificum' Bright yellow daisies. 18in (45cm)

Erysimum Bedder Series Dwarf wallflowers; bright colours. 1ft (30cm)

Matthiola Brompton type Pretty, pastel, scented stocks. 18in (45cm)

♀ Myosotis 'Ultramarine' Deep blue, dwarf forget-me-not. 6in (15cm)

---

† Smaller-flowered varieties often look better than blowsier ones.

Primula 'Rainbow' Tough polyanthus in eight bright shades. 9in (23cm)
Silene dioica 'Minikin' Dwarf campion; split in autumn. 1ft (30cm)
* *Viola Ultima Series* Twenty plain and blotched colours. 9in (23cm)

BULBS

Bulbs are an essential part of the spring display and associate well with other container plants, but it's important to match heights well.

♀ *Chionodoxa luciliae* Blue and white flowers; easy and prolific. 6in (15cm)
♀ *Crocus chrysanthus* Prettily patterned and shaded; many forms. 4in (10cm)
  Hyacinthus Bedding types with bold spikes and that scent. . . 1ft (30cm)
♀ *Iris reticulata* Dainty window-box irises in many colours. 6in (15cm)
  Muscari armeniacum 'Blue Spike' Fat, long-lasting spikes. 9in (23cm)
  Narcissus 'Fortune' Big trumpet daffodil for larger tubs. 18in (45cm)
  Narcissus 'Hawera' Delicate lemony flowers in threes. 8in (20cm)
  Scilla siberica 'Spring Beauty' Large, dark blue flowers. 8in (20cm)
  Tulipa Griegii Hybrids Purple striped leaves, wind-resistant. 9in (23cm)
* *Tulipa Lily-flowering Hybrids* Pointed petals; many colours. 2ft (60cm)

Food in containers

There's nothing like fresh food from the garden but we don't all have the space for a vegetable plot – so we must use containers.

VEGETABLES

More gardeners are now growing vegetables in containers; shorter, compact varieties are best chosen specially for the purpose.

  Aubergine 'Bambino' Tiny black fruits on 1ft (30cm) plant; good grilled.
♀ *Carrot 'Parmex'* Quick growing, short variety with good flavour.
  Chili pepper 'Apache' 3in (7.5cm) hot peppers on an attractive 18in (45cm) plant.
  Cucumber 'Bush Champion' Good growing bag variety, 9in (23cm) fruit.
♀ *Lettuce 'Little Gem'* The smallest and tastiest of all lettuces.
  Lettuce 'Red Salad Bowl' Red, oak-leaved type; pick leaf by leaf.

Strawberry 'Temptation' Dark tasty fruits and with no runners.†
Sweet pepper 'Redskin' Use green or red, attractive 18in (45cm) plant.
Tomato 'Totem' Naturally dwarf and bushy variety reaching 18in (45cm).
Tomato 'Tumbler' Compact, trailing variety for hanging baskets.

HERBS††

Herbs will succeed in containers in the smallest of spaces and will look
especially good if you choose their ornamental forms.

Apple mint (Mentha × suaveolens 'Variegata') Spectacular, white
  variegated leaves. Cut out any white or green shoots. 18in (45cm)
Basil (Ocimum 'Dark Opal') Purple-leaved variety; loves sun. 15in (38cm)
♀ *Bay (Laurus nobilis)* Looks good trained as cone or lollipop. 2–6ft
  (60cm–1.8m)
Chives (Allium schoenoprasum 'Forescate') Neat and prolific. 15in (38cm)
Ginger mint (Mentha × gentilis 'Variegata') Yellow-veined green leaves
  on small, and less rampagous mint than many. 15in (38cm)
♀ *Lavender (Lavandula* 'Hidcote') Deep violet; less straggly than most. 2ft
  (60cm) Look out also for 'Alba' (white) and 'Loddon Pink'. 3ft
  (90cm)
Lemon balm (Melissa officinalis 'Allgold') Yellow-leaved. 2ft (60cm)
Lemon thyme (Thymus × citriodorus 'Silver Queen') Lemony scented
  thyme with white edges to the small leaves; twiggy. 1ft (30cm)
* *Parsley (Petroselinum crispum* 'Curlina') Deep green, tightly curled leaves;
  looks lovely with flowering summer bedding. 1ft (30cm)
♀ *Rosemary (Rosmarinus* 'Severn Sea') Neater and more spreading than
  most. 2ft (60cm) 'Prostratus' is low and trails over pots prettily.
♀ *Sage (Salvia officinalis* 'Purpurascens') Soft, velvety purple leaves; blue
  flowers. 'Icterina' is mottled green and yellow. 2ft (60cm)
Thyme (Thymus vulgaris 'Silver Posie') Pink tipped, white variegated
  foliage; usual fragrance; bushy and twiggy. 1ft (30cm)

---

† An unusual strawberry grown from seed, fruiting in its first year.
†† For more ornamental herbs see page 247.

PLANTS FOR THEIR HABIT

Flowers may be colourful but a plant's growth habit is an enduring feature which becomes increasingly striking as plants mature.

———————————— Upright habit ————————————

Slender plants shaped like pencils or with a narrow, upright habit of growth can provide important accents on a large or small scale.

TREES†

Narrow, columnar trees not only make excellent focal points but allow a taller than usual specimen to be grown in a confined space.

    Acer platanoides 'Crimson Sentry' Bold, red-leaved column. 20ft (6m)

♀ *Alnus cordata* Fast alder for most soils; shining foliage. 35ft (10.5m)

    Betula pendula 'Fastigiata' Stiff habit, eventually spreads. 15ft (4.5m)

♀ *Corylus colurna* First a column, later a pyramid; catkins. 30ft (9m)

♀* *Fagus sylvatica 'Dawyck'* Fine column; good autumn colour. 18ft (5.4m)

♀ *Liriodendron tulipifera 'Fastigiatum'* Superb autumn colour. 30ft (9m)

♀ *Prunus 'Amanogawa'* Very tight growth; pale pink flowers. 15ft (4.5m)

♀ *Prunus 'Spire'* Conical rather than columnar; pink flowers. 20ft (6m)

    Pyrus communis 'Beech Hill' White flowers; good in autumn. 15ft (4.5m)

♀ *Sorbus aucuparia 'Sheerwater Seedling'* Orange-red fruits. 18ft (5.4m)

CONIFERS†

Tall slender conifers need careful placing as, being mostly evergreen, their presence can dominate the garden relentlessly.

♀ *Calocedrus decurrens* Dark leaves; eventually a large tree; 8ft (2.4m)

    Cephalotaxus harringtoniana 'Fastigiata' Very dark leaves. 8ft (2.4m)

♀ *Chamaecyparis lawsoniana 'Kilmacurragh'* Slender; tough. 10ft (3m)

    Cupressus sempervirens Italian cypress; slender but tender. 15ft (4.5m)

    Juniperus scopulorum 'Skyrocket' Exceptionally narrow. 6ft (1.8m)

    Juniperus scopulorum 'Springbank' Silvery grey foliage. 10ft (3m)

---

†   Trees and conifers with upswept shoots may be damaged by snow.

♀ *Metasequoia glyptostroboides* Broadly conical; deciduous. 15ft (4.5m)

♀* *Picea omorika* Narrow; short upward-curving branches. 10ft (3m)

♀ *Taxodium distichum* Pretty; deciduous, rusty in autumn. 15ft (4.5m)

Taxus baccata 'Fastigiata Aurea' Golden Irish yew; slow. 4ft (1.2m)

SHRUBS

Narrow, upright shrubs are as useful as slender trees but there are far fewer good varieties with this valuable distinctive habit.

Berberis thunbergii 'Erecta' Very tight habit; autumn colour. 4ft (1.2m)

* *Berberis thunbergii 'Helmund Pillar'* Very tight; purple leaf. 4ft (1.2m)

♀ *Buxus sempervirens* Box; can be clipped into tight columns. 6ft (1.8m)

♀ *Camellia 'Donation'* The most upright camellia; pink flowers. 6ft (1.8m)

Ilex aquifolium 'Green Pillar' Dark green, spiny; red berries. 8ft (2.4m)

♀ *Lavandula stoechas ssp. pedunculata* Long slim stems. 18in (45cm)

♀ *Mahonia × media 'Charity'* Upright branches, wider with age. 10ft (3m)

♀ *Perovskia atriplicifolia* Grey leaves, blue spikes; spring prune. 2ft (60cm)

Rhododendron 'Blue Diamond' Best dwarf blue; thrives in sun. 3ft (90cm)

♀ *Salix 'Boydii'* Slow, dwarf shrub, but looks mature; grey leaves. 1ft (30cm)

PERENNIALS AND BULBS

These are not the first plants to spring to mind when considering a vertical accent, but on a border scale they are very suitable.

Allium giganteum Purple balls in July topping stiff stems. 4ft (1.2m)

♀ *Crocosmia 'Lucifer'* Bold, vertical, pleated leaves; red flowers. 4ft (1.2m)

Galtonia candicans Tall, fat stems with large white bells. 3ft (90cm)

Helianthus salicifolius Very tall sunflower; unbranched stems. 10ft (3m)

Iris Tall Bearded Stiff, upright leaf; flowers in all shades. 3ft (90cm)

Kniphofia 'Prince Igor' Tall and fiery spikes; foliage slim. 6ft (1.8m)†

Macleaya cordata Greyish vertical shoots; spreading clump. 6ft (1.8m)

Tulipa Lily-flowered Even flowers have a vertical accent. 2ft (60cm)

* *Verbena bonariensis* Sparse but striking stems; purple flowers. 5ft (1.5m)

Miscanthus varieties Wide range of bold, vertical grasses. 3–8ft (90cm–2.4m)

---

† All kniphofias, even dwarf ones, have the same vertical boldness.

--------- **Weeping habit** ---------

Plants with a weeping habit look very restful and elegant and make superb features but they spread more than non-weeping types.

TREES

The eventual height of many of these trees depends on the main shoot being trained and supported to prevent it weeping itself.†

♀* *Betula pendula* 'Tristis' Tall, elegant; good autumn colour. 18ft (5.4m)

♀ *Betula pendula* 'Youngii' Smaller and tighter; needs support. 10ft (3m)

♀ *Fagus sylvatica* 'Pendula' The most grand weeping tree of all. 15ft (4.5m)

♀ *Fraxinus excelsior* 'Pendula' Bold, elegant; striking in winter. 20ft (6m)

   Ilex aquifolium '*Argentea Marginata Pendula*' Variegated. 10ft (3m)

♀ *Prunus pendula* 'Pendula Rubra' Train main shoot up. 12ft (3.6m)

♀ *Pyrus salicifolia* 'Pendula' Silver leaves, white flowers; train. 12ft (3.6m)

♀ *Salix caprea* 'Kilmarnock' Vertical branches; silver catkins. 10ft (3m)

♀ *Salix* × *sepulcralis* 'Chrysosoma' *The* weeping willow; huge. 40ft (12m)

♀ *Tilia* 'Petiolaris' Narrow crown, weeping branches; beautiful. 25ft (7.5m)

CONIFERS

The broad weeping crowns of some of these evergreens may hang very low and so restrict the range of planting options underneath.

   Cedrus atlantica 'Glauca Pendula' Silvery blue foliage. 10ft (3m)

♀ *Chamaecyparis nootkanensis* 'Pendula' Extremely elegant. 8ft (2.4m)

   Ginkgo biloba 'Pendula' Deciduous; yellow autumn colour. 10ft (3m)

   Larix kaempferi 'Pendula' Bluish leaves, yellow in autumn. 12ft (3.6m)

♀* *Picea breweriana* Branchlets hang down like curtains. 5ft (1.5m)

♀ *Picea omorika* 'Pendula' Narrow habit, weeping branches. 8ft (2.4m)

   Picea pungens 'Glauca' Silvery foliage; leader needs support. 8ft (2.4m)

   Pseudotsuga menziesii 'Pendula' Greyish leaves; hates chalk. 8ft (2.4m)

   Sequioadendron giganteum 'Pendulum' Not beautiful, weird. 8ft (2.4m)

♀ *Taxus baccata* 'Dovastoniana' Branchlets hang in curtains. 6ft (1.8m)

---

†   Train the main stem to the rough height you wish the tree to be.

SHRUBS

Weeping shrubs make good focal points in small gardens and their distinctive habit ensures interest even when they are not flowering.

    Buxus sempervirens 'Pendula' Open habit, pendulous shoots. 5ft (1.5m)

    Caragana arborescens 'Pendula' Yellow pea flowers; fat pods. 8ft (2.4m)

    Corylus avellana 'Pendula' Uncommon but attractive hazel. 6ft (1.8m)

*   *Cotoneaster salicifolius 'Pendulus'* Wide habit; red berries. 5ft (1.5m)

♀   *Exochorda 'The Bride'* Naturally weeping; white flowers. 5ft (1.5m)

♀   *Forsythia suspensa* Small, pale flowers; naturally weeping. 10ft (3m)†

    Holodiscus discolor Arching habit; creamy summer plumes. 10ft (3m)

♀   *Jasminum nudiflorum* Winter jasmine; best trained on wall. 6ft (1.8m)

    Rosa Weeping standards are especially pretty; prune carefully. 6ft (1.8m)

    Stephanandra tankae Upright, weeping tips; red winter stems. 6ft (1.8m)

───────────────── **Horizontal habit** ─────────────────

This selection includes plants which grow out flat across the ground as well as taller plants with an attractive tiered habit.

SHRUBS AND CONIFERS

Although shrubs and conifers are really the only plants which grow in this way there is still a limited but varied selection of both types.

♀   *Cornus controversa 'Variegata'* Truly elegant, but expensive. 8ft (2.4m)

♀   *Cotoneaster atropurpureus 'Variegata'* Flat sprays; creamy. 2ft (60cm)

    Euonymus 'Dart's Blanket' Evergreen, bronzed in winter. 1ft (30cm)

    Juniperus sabina 'Tamariscifolia' 'Tabletop'; bright green. 1ft (30cm)

♀   *Juniperus virginiana 'Grey Owl'* Nearly horizontal; grey leaf. 18in (45cm)

    Lonicera pileata Low, spreading evergreen; good in poor soil. 2ft (60cm)

    Prunus laurocerasus 'Zabeliana' Broadly spreading, not flat. 3ft (90cm)

    Rosa County Series For ground cover; flat or mounded. 1–2ft (30–60cm)

    Symphoricarpus × *chenaultii 'Hancock'* Widely spreading. 2ft (60cm)

♀* *Viburnum plicatum 'Mariesii'* Spectacular white tiers. 6ft (1.8m)

───

†   Makes an especially attractive feature when trained on a wall.

Rounded habit

The rounded habit of these plants is attractive in itself, but the smaller varieties are also especially valuable in formal situations.

CONIFERS

Rounded conifers vary from the slowest, neatest of buns for alpine gardens to more vigorous varieties which make bold specimens.

Chamaecyparis lawsoniana 'Green Globe' Bright green. 1ft (30cm)

♀ *Chamaecyparis lawsoniana* 'Pygmaea Argentea' Creamy. 15in (38cm)

Chamaecyparis pisifera 'Squarrosa Sulphurea' Creamy. 3ft (90cm)

♀ *Cryptomeria japonica* 'Vilmoriana' Green, bronze in winter. 15in (38cm)

♀ *Picea pungens* 'Globosa' Spiky blue mound; best in spring. 18in (45cm)

♀ *Pinus heldriechii* 'Schmidtii' Tight green cushion; rare. 1ft (30cm)

Pinus mugo 'Humpy' Tight, slightly irregular; wider than high. 1ft (30cm)

♀ *Thuya occidentalis* 'Rheingold' Summer, gold; winter, copper. 3ft (90cm)

♀ *Thuya orientalis* 'Aurea Nana' Vertical gold-green sprays. 2ft (60cm)

Thuya orientalis 'Rosedalis' Cream, then green, then brown. 18in (45cm)

SHRUBS

The lower shrubs with rounded habit are good on the corners of paths, the taller varieties fill corners at the back of the border.

♀ *Acer palmatum var. dissectum* Fine green leaves; wide dome. 2ft (60cm)

♀ *Berberis thunbergii* 'Bagatelle' Neat balls of purple foliage. 1ft (30cm)

♀ *Cornus mas* Large shrub, yellow flowers in winter; red fruits. 12ft (3.6m)

♀ *Magnolia stellata* Slow and compact; wonderful white spring stars. 5ft (1.5m)

Potentilla fruticosa Flowers red, pink, orange, yellow or white. 4ft (1.2m)†

Rhododendron Yakushimanum Hybrids Neat dome; no lime. 3ft (90cm)

* *Rosa* 'Wife of Bath' Dwarf English rose; pink cupped flowers. 2ft (60cm)

Salix purpurea 'Nana' Purplish silver catkins in early spring. 3ft (90cm)

♀ *Skimmia × confusa* 'Kew Green' Cream, scented; evergreen. 3ft (90cm)

Viburnum plicatum 'Nanum Semperflorens' Long-flowering. 8ft (2.4m)

---

†   Pink- and red-flowered forms tend to fade in hot, all day sun.

PART THREE

CHOOSING PLANTS

TREES

SHRUBS

EVERGREEN

DECIDUOUS

CLIMBERS AND WALL SHRUBS

HARDY PERENNIALS

ALPINES AND ROCK PLANTS

HABIT

FLOWERING ALPINES

FOLIAGE

GROUND COVER PLANTS

FLOWERS

FOLIAGE

HARDY ANNUALS

HALF-HARDY ANNUALS AND BEDDING PLANTS

BIENNIALS

TENDER PERENNIALS

BULBS

ORNAMENTAL HERBS

ROSES

BUSH ROSES

RAMBLING AND CLIMBING ROSES

OTHER ROSES

CLEMATIS

CONIFERS

AND FINALLY . . .

TREES†

Trees may start small and not reach full maturity for decades but some can make surprisingly effective specimens in a short time.

Flowering

In smaller gardens flowering trees can create gasps of joy when at their peak and still have great presence for the rest of the year.

SPRING FLOWERS

The freshness of spring flowers against new unfolding foliage is always a very special attraction early in the year if frost holds off.

♀ *Aesculus flava* Pale yellow flowers in late spring; good leaves. 30ft (9m)
♀ *Caragana arborescens 'Lorbergii'* Yellow flowers; spiny. 12ft (3.6m)
♀ *Crataegus 'Paul's Scarlet'* Double red flowers; few fruits. 20ft (6m)
♀ *Davidia involucrata* Fluttering white bracts; slow to flower. 20ft (6m)
* *Magnolia kobus* Fragrant white flowers; slow and spreading. 20ft (6m)
Malus 'Royalty' Wine red flowers amongst purple leaves. 20ft (6m)
♀ *Paulownia tomentosa* Blue foxglove flowers on older trees. 20ft (6m)
Prunus pendula 'Pendula Rubra' Dark pink; weeping habit. 12ft (3.6m)
♀ *Pyrus salicifolia 'Pendula'* White flowers, silver leaves. 10ft (3m)
Sorbus commixta The best mountain ash for its white flowers. 15ft (4.5m)

SUMMER FLOWERS

Some summer-flowering trees give the most spectacular of shows and deserve a site where their full splendour can be appreciated.

♀ *Aesculus indica* Stately chestnut with blushed white candles. 25ft (7.5m)
♀ *Catalpa bignonioides* White flowers, black pods, good leaves. 25ft (7.5m)
♀ *Cladrastis lutea* Scented white pea-flowers; hates lime. 15ft (4.5m)
Embothrium coccineum Stunning scarlet flowers; hates lime. 12ft (3.6m)
♀ *Kolreuteria paniculata* Yellow spikes; best in sun; bushy. 25ft (7.5m)
♀* *Laburnum 'Vossii'* Fewer poisonous seeds than other forms. 20ft (6m)

---

† See also *Trees for Small Gardens* by Keith Rushforth.

♉ *Ligustrum lucidum* White feathery plumes, needs staking. 12ft (3.6m)
♉ *Liriodendron tulipifera* Cream and green tulips on old trees. 20ft (6m)
   Magnolia grandiflora Huge white flowers; mild areas only. 12ft (3.6m)
♉ *Stewartia pseudocamellia* White, camellia flowers; acid soil. 12ft (3.6m)

AUTUMN AND WINTER FLOWERS

Autumn- and especially winter-flowering trees bring invaluable colour at a height where it is not usually seen at this season.

♉ *Acacia dealbata* Silvery foliage, yellow fluffy flowers; tender. 20ft (6m)
♉ *Eucryphia 'Nymansay'* White rose-like flowers; hates lime. 12ft (3.6m)
   Magnolia campbellii Stunning pink 'tulips'; tender, hates lime. 12ft (3.6m)
   Oxydendrum arboreum White flowers; good autumn colour. 10ft (3m)
♉ *Populus tremula* Long winter catkins; leaves silvery below. 12ft (3.6m)
   Prunus mume Pink winter flowers on multi-stemmed tree. 12ft (3.6m)
♉ *Prunus* × *subhirtella 'Autumnalis'* White flowers when mild. 15ft (4.5m)
   Rhododendron arboreum 'Album' White; hardier than most. 10ft (3m)
*   *Salix aegyptiaca* Yellow winter catkins on broad-headed tree. 25ft (7.5m)
   Sorbus megalocarpa Clouds of white foam in late winter; bushy. 8ft (2.4m)

SCENTED FLOWERS

Trees produce so many flowers that you might think the garden would be overpowered by scent but some dissipates on the breeze.

♉ *Eucryphia* × *intermedia 'Rostrevor'* Prefers shelter; acid soil. 12ft (3.6m)
♉ *Fraxinus ornus* Clouds of creamy flowers; good leaves. 30ft (9m)
   Laburnum alpinum Yellow pea flowers; seeds poisonous. 12ft (3.6m)
♉* *Luma apiculata* White myrtle for mild areas; edible fruits. 6ft (1.8m)
♉ *Magnolia salicifolia* White flowers in spring; best in acid soil. 20ft (6m)
♉ *Malus hupehensis* Pink buds, opening white; upright habit. 15ft (4.5m)
   Pittosporum eugenioides Small, honey-scented flowers; tender. 9ft (2.7m)
♉ *Prunus padus 'Watereri'* Prolific early summer white spikes. 25ft (7.5m)
♉ *Styrax japonicus* Trails of small white flowers; hates lime. 10ft (3m)
♉ *Tilia* × *euchlora* Yellow and white flowers; no honeydew. 18ft (5.4m)†

---

†   Most limes attract aphids which exude messy, sticky honeydew.

———————————— **Ornamental foliage** ————————————

Flowers, however colourful, are fleeting and for summer- or year-long
interest foliage in its many attractive variations is needed.

VARIEGATED LEAVES†

Variegated foliage is often the most effective; the two colours are clearly
visible close up but from a distance give a hazier look.

    Acer negundo 'Elegans' Leaves have bright yellow edges. 15ft (4.5m)

♀ *Acer platanoides 'Drummondii'* Greyish leaves edged cream. 20ft (6m)

    Castanea sativa 'Albomarginata' Stark, white-edged leaves. 40ft (12m)

♀ *Cornus controversa 'Variegata'* Superb, but very slow. 10ft (3m)

♀ *Ilex × altaclerensis 'Belgica Aurea'* Grey-green, cream edges. 18ft (5.4m)

♀ *Ligustrum 'Excelsum Superbum'* Edged greenish yellow. 8ft (2.4m)

    Liquidambar styraciflua 'Golden Treasure' Yellow-edged. 15ft (4.5m)

♀* *Liriodendron tulipifera 'Aureomarginatum'* Yellow-edged. 14ft (4.2m)

    Platanus × hispanica 'Suttneri' Splashed creamy white. 25ft (7.5m)

    Quercus cerris 'Argenteovariegata' White-edged, slow. 8ft (2.4m)

GOLD AND YELLOW LEAVES

Most trees whose foliage starts out gold or yellow in spring fades to green
later; those which burn badly in full sun are excluded.

♀* *Acer cappadocicum 'Aureum'* Red, then yellow then green. 30ft (9m)

    Alnus incana 'Aurea' Fades in summer; must have wet soil. 20ft (6m)

♀ *Catalpa bignonioides 'Aurea'* Bright, bold but slightly tender. 10ft (3m)

♀ *Fagus sylvatica 'Dawyck Gold'* Fades to pale green; slender. 15ft (4.5m)

♀ *Gleditsia triacanthos 'Sunburst'* Yellow, spring and autumn. 16ft (4.8m)

♀ *Laurus nobilis 'Aurea'* Gold all year, good in winter; slow. 6ft (1.8m)

    Liquidambar styraciflua 'Moonbeam' Pale yellow; slow. 15ft (4.5m)

    Populus alba 'Richardii' Yellow above, white below; superb. 20ft (6m)

♀ *Robinia pseudacacia 'Frisia'* Yellow, spring to autumn. 20ft (6m)

    Sorbus aria 'Chrysophylla' Pale at first, richer in autumn. 20ft (6m)

———————————————————————————

†   Prune out any all green shoots, otherwise they will take over.

SILVER AND GREY LEAVES

Grey foliage tends to bring a slightly Mediterranean look and many grey leaved trees can cope with drier than usual conditions.

♀ *Buddleja alternifolia* Small weeping tree; lilac flowers. 12ft (3.6m)

♀ *Eucalyptus gunnii* The hardiest of all eucalyptus; very fast. 35ft (10.5m)

♀ *Eucalyptus pauciflora ssp. niphophila* Attractive trunk. 25ft (7.5m)

Populus × *canescens* Superb on chalky soils; red catkins. 30ft (9m)

Pyrus nivalis Almost white leaves, white flowers; bushy habit. 15ft (4.5m)

♀* *Pyrus salicifolia 'Pendula'* Lovely small weeping tree. 15ft (4.5m)

Salix exigua Foams of long, slender silver leaves; may sucker. 10ft (3m)

♀ *Sorbus aria 'Lutescens'* Almost white leaves; orange berries. 20ft (6m)

♀ *Sorbus thibetica 'John Mitchell'* Green above, white below. 12ft (3.6m)

♀ *Tilia 'Petiolaris'* Superb large specimen, neat weeping habit. 25ft (7.5m)

PURPLE AND BRONZE LEAVES

Trees with dark leaves need using in moderation and must be placed very carefully to avoid creating a dour and deadening effect.†

♀ *Acer platanoides 'Crimson King'* Purple, then red in autumn. 20ft (6m)

Betula pendula 'Purpurea' Purple fading to dark green. 20ft (6m)

Carpinus betulus 'Purpurea' Purple tint soon turns green. 25ft (7.5m)

♀ *Cercis canadensis 'Forest Pansy'* Purple then scarlet; bushy. 8ft (2.4m)

♀ *Fagus sylvatica 'Dawyck Purple'* An elegant purple pillar. 9ft (2.7m)

* *Gleditsia triacanthos 'Rubylace'* New leaves red then green. 9ft (2.7m)

Malus 'Royalty' Dense, twiggy growth good for nesting birds. 20ft (6m)

Pittosporum tenuifolium 'Purpureum' Green turning purple. 7ft (2.1m)

♀ *Prunus cerasifera 'Nigra'* Single pink flowers before leaves. 20ft (6m)

Quercus robur 'Atropurpurea' Wine-purple then greyish; 10ft (3m)

---

† It's also important to avoid colour clashes with yellow foliage.

MULTICOLOURED LEAVES†

Few trees are truly multicoloured and those which are tend to be rather less
easy to grow well than other trees; but what colours.

♀ *Acer negundo 'Flamingo'* New leaves pink, old variegated. 15ft (4.5m)

♀ *Acer pseudoplatanus 'Brilliantissimum'* Pink then green. 12ft (3.6m)

♀ *Acer pseudoplatanus 'Leopoldii'* Pinky yellow, then greener. 20ft (6m)

Acer pseudoplatanus 'Prinz Handjery' Pink, purple below. 12ft (3.6m)

Acer pseudoplatanus 'Simon-Louis Frères' Pink, then green. 25ft (7.5m)

Crataegus laevigata 'Gireoudii' New shoots pink and white. 14ft (4.2m)

* *Fagus sylvatica 'Roseomarginata'* Purple, edged pinky white. 18ft (5.4m)

Fagus sylvatica 'Tricolor' Purple, edged pale pink; variable. 18ft (5.4m)

Ligustrum lucidum 'Tricolor' Leaves edged in pink; rare. 9ft (2.7m)

Populus 'Aurora' New leaves splashed pink and white. 30ft (9m)

AUTUMN-COLOURING LEAVES

Autumn colour makes a spectacular conclusion to the year but can be
unpredictable, depending on temperature and soil conditions.

♀ *Acer campestre* Yellow sometimes tinged red; British native. 15ft (4.5m)

♀ *Amelanchier lamarckii* Orangey red; with black berries. 20ft (6m)

♀ *Betula 'Jermyns'* Yellow in autumn; superb white bark. 30ft (9m)

♀ *Cercidiphyllum japonicum* Red and yellow; rich, acid soil. 25ft (7.5m)

♀ *Ginkgo biloba* Buttercup yellow; superb specimen tree. 10ft (3m)

♀ *Liquidambar styraciflua 'Worplesdon'* Orange and purple. 25ft (7.5m)

♀ *Metasequoia glyptostroboides* Bronzed green, then gold. 15ft (4.5m)

♀ *Nyssa sylvatica* Red and yellow; hates lime and drought. 12ft (3.6m)

Oxydendrum arboreum Red and orange; hates any lime. 10ft (3m)

♀* *Prunus sargentii* Best cherry for autumn colour; broad crown. 20ft (6m)

♀ *Sorbus commixta 'Embley'* Wine red, orange and yellow. 15ft (4.5m)

---

† Prune out any all green shoots, otherwise they will take over.

Ornamental fruits†

Berries and other fruits are not only an attractive autumn feature in themselves, but also provide food for birds and other wildlife.

RED AND PURPLE FRUITS

There are many theories as to which colour berries last the longest, but some red fruits are quickly eaten while others last for months.

℘ *Amelanchier lamarckii* Wine red, then black; white flowers. 20ft (6m)

℘ *Arbutus unedo* Red 'strawberries' after white bells; acid soil. 6ft (1.8m)

℘ *Cornus 'Norman Hadden'* Prolific fruits like red strawberries. 8ft (2.4m)

℘ *Cotoneaster 'Cornubia'* Clusters of small glistening berries. 12ft (3.6m)

℘ *Crataegus persimilis 'Prunifolia'* Scarlet fruit; purplish leaf. 14ft (4.2m)

  Magnolia tripetala Scarlet conical fruits; white flowers. 15ft (4.5m)

℘* *Malus* × *robusta 'Red Siberian'* Red crabs well into winter. 20ft (6m)

℘ *Morus nigra* Mulberry; dark red then black; scrumptious. 15ft (4.5m)

℘ *Sorbus aria 'Lutescens'* Crimson berries, colouring leaves; 20ft (6m)

  Sorbus aucuparia 'Edulis' Big bright red berries; edible! 15ft (4.5m)

ORANGE AND YELLOW FRUITS

Orange and especially yellow fruits are more clearly visible in the autumn garden than red or black, especially from a distance.

  Crataegus × *lavallei* Persistent orange berries; autumn colour. 14ft (4.2m)

  Diospyrus kaki Edible fruits like tomatoes; autumn colour. 12ft (3.6m)

  Malus 'Golden Gem' Large numbers of small yellow fruits. 15ft (4.5m)

℘ *Malus 'Golden Hornet'* Big creamy yellow fruits; lasts well. 20ft (6m)

* *Malus 'Wintergold'* Unusually long lasting yellow crabs. 12ft (3.6m)

  Poncirus trifoliata Like miniature yellow oranges; very spiny. 6ft (1.8m)

℘ *Sorbus aucuparia 'Sheerwater Seedling'* Orange; upright. 18ft (5.4m)

  Sorbus aucuparia 'Xanthocarpa' The best yellow-berried form. 18ft (5.4m)

℘ *Sorbus commixta 'Embley'* Bulging clusters of orange fruits. 15ft (4.5m)

  Sorbus 'Leonard Springer' Large orange fruits; last well. 18ft (5.4m)

---

†   Most of these fruits are distasteful at the very least.

OTHER ORNAMENTAL FRUITS

There's more to fruits than just red or orange berries; there are berries in a variety of other shades and other interesting types.

♈ *Aesculus* × *carnea* 'Briotii' Small horse-chestnut; pink spikes. 12ft (3.6m)

♈ *Ailanthus altissima* Large reddish-green keys, females only. 45ft (13.5m)

♈ *Catalpa bignonioides* Slim, 12in (30cm) pods; green then black. 20ft (6m)

♈ *Cercis siliquastrum* Grey-green pods lasting well into winter. 10ft (3m)

♈ *Fraxinus ornus* Prolific 'keys' last into winter; white flowers. 20ft (6m)

♈ *Kolreuteria paniculata* Bronzy-yellow inflated fruits. 25ft (7.5m)

♈ *Pterocarya fraxinifolia* Long strings of 1in (2.5cm) green fruits. 25ft (7.5m)

♈* *Sorbus cashmiriana* Dwarf mountain ash with white berries. 10ft (3m)

Sorbus hupehensis 'Pink Pagoda' Small pink berries. 15ft (4.5m)

♈ *Sorbus vilmorinii* Mauve berries, purplish-grey leaves. 15ft (4.5m)

─────────────── **Ornamental bark** ───────────────

It is particularly in winter that trees with attractive bark come into their own; plant them near paths, where they can be appreciated.

Acer davidii Vertically striped green and white bark. 13ft (3.6m)

♈ *Acer griseum* Brown bark peels to show cinnamon below. 12ft (3.6m)

♈ *Arbutus* × *andrachnoides* Slightly flaky cinnamon branches. 6ft (1.8m)

♈* *Betula* 'Jermyns' Stunning pure white trunk and branches. 35ft (10.5m)†

♈ *Corylus colurna* Unusual, flaking, slightly corky bark. 25ft (7.5m)

♈ *Eucalyptus pauciflora ssp. niphophila* Green and white. 30ft (9m)

Pinus bungeana Grey, cream, purple and brown in patches. 12ft (3.6m)

Prunus maackii Golden brown peeling bark; white flowers. 18ft (5.4m)

♈ *Prunus serrula* Smooth mahogany bark; polishes well. 15ft (4.5m)

♈ *Tilia platyphyllos* 'Rubra' Bright red twigs shine in winter. 27ft (8.1m)

---

† This is quite an uncommon variety, so look too for *Betula utilis*.

SHRUBS

Shrubs are the backbone of most gardens. In flower they can be spectacular, many have other features like fruits or autumn colour.

EVERGREEN

Evergreen shrubs have that valuable ability to bring a presence to the garden even when their period of flowering or fruiting is over.

Spring-flowering

When the freshness and optimism of spring flowers is past, these evergreens all have good foliage to provide a foil for later flowers.

Tall   These shrubs should all reach about 6ft (1.8m) in height after ten years, or sooner if planted in sheltered positions and looked after carefully.

♈* *Berberis darwinii* Small, holly-like leaves; drips in orange blooms.

♈ *Camellia 'Donation'* Perfect double pink flowers from winter on.

♈ *Crinodendron hookerianum* Red lanterns; no lime; a little tender.

♈ *Leptospermum scoparium 'Nichollsii'* Carmine; no lime; tender.

♈ *Mahonia 'Buckland'* Strings of yellow winter flowers for weeks.

   Osmanthus decorus Highly scented white flowers; black fruits.

♈ *Pittosporum tenuifolium* Honey-scented flowers; many forms.

   Prunus laurocerasus 'Latifolia' Huge bold leaves; white spikes.

♈ *Rhododendron 'Alice'* Rose-pink flowers; erect habit; acid soil.

   Viburnum rhtyidophyllum White flowers; imposing; likes chalk.

Medium   These shrubs should all reach between 2ft (60cm) and 6ft (1.8m) in height after ten years depending on the variety and how they are grown.

  Berberis gagnepainii Clusters of small yellow flowers; very spiny.

  Choisya ternata White scented spring flowers; rounded habit.

  Daphne × *burkwoodii 'Somerset'* Palest pink, dreamily fragrant.

♀ *Erica arborea 'Albert's Gold'* White flowers, yellow leaves.

  Leucothoë fontanesiana 'Rainbow' Creamy pink leaves; no lime.†

♀ *Mahonia aquifolium 'Apollo'* Bronzed in winter; yellow flowers.

♀ *Osmanthus delavayi* Dark green foliage; fragrant white flowers.

♀ *Pieris japonica 'Debutante'* Smaller than most pieris; no lime.†

♀* *Rhododendron 'Yellowhammer'* Bright yellow; rather upright.†

♀ *Rosmarinus 'Miss Jessup's Upright'* Tall and narrow rosemary.

Small   These shrubs should all reach no more than 2ft (60cm) in height after about ten years except perhaps in mild gardens on rich soil.

  Arctostaphyllos uva-ursi Blushed white flowers, red fruits; creeps.

  Berberis buxifolia 'Nana' Dense rounded hummock; few flowers.

♀ *Ceanothus thyrsiflorus var. repens* Clouds of blue; broad mound.

  Daphne cneorum Fragrant pink flowers; may be slow to start.

♀* *Erica carnea 'Springwood White'* Pure white, but all are good.††

  Gaultheria shallon Tasty purple fruits; dense growth; slow at first.

♀ *Hebe pimelioides 'Quicksilver'* Silver-blue leaves; lilac flowers.

♀ *Pieris japonica 'Little Heath'* Dwarf, variegated; hates lime.

  Rhododendron 'Grumpy' Pale pink, orange spots; good leaves.

♀ *Skimmia* × *confusa 'Kew Green'* Highly fragrant creamy flowers.

---

†   These acid-loving plants can be grown in tubs if the garden soil is limy.

††   Clip over with shears immediately after flowering.

--------------------- **Summer-flowering** ---------------------

The choice of summer-flowering shrubs is enormous so these have been chosen to represent a wide variety of valuable features.

Tall   These shrubs should all reach about 6ft (1.8m) in height after ten years, or sooner if planted in sheltered positions and looked after carefully.

♀* *Ceanothus 'Puget Blue'* Stunning clouds of blue; sunny wall.

♀   *Cistus laurifolius* Yellow-eyed white flowers; hardiest and tallest.

♀   *Cotoneaster lacteus* Small, long-lasting red berries in big clusters.

♀   *Cotoneaster sternianus* Pink flowers; large, orange-red berries.

   Escallonia 'C. F. Ball' Crimson flowers; large leaves; good by sea.

♀   *Eucryphia 'Nymansay'* White flowers like single roses; vigorous.

♀   *Ligustrum lucidum* Bold heads of cream flowers; almost a tree.

♀   *Magnolia grandiflora 'Exmouth'* Huge, heady, cream flowers.

♀   *Myrtus communis* White flowers, black berries; aromatic leaves.

♀   *Pyracantha 'Orange Glow'* Branches droop with orange berries.

Medium   These shrubs should all reach between 2ft (60cm) and 6ft (1.8m) in height after ten years, depending on the variety and how they are grown.

♀   *Brachyglottis 'Sunshine'* Bright yellow daisies; silvery leaves.

♀   *Carpenteria californica 'Ladham's Variety'* White flowers; sun.†

   Cistus 'Silver Pink' Pink flowers; one of the toughest of all cistus.

♀   *Convolvulus cneorum* Silvery foliage, white flowers; full sun.

♀   *Desfontainea spinosa* Yellow-throated scarlet flowers; hates lime.

♀   *Hebe 'La Séduisante'* Crimson spikes into autumn; glossy leaves.

♀   *Hypericum 'Rowallane'* Stunning yellow flowers; needs shelter.

♀   *Itea ilicifolia* Like a friendly holly with greeny-white catkins.

♀   *Kalmia latifolia* Bright pink flowers; many other forms; hates lime.

   Lotus hirsutus Neat woolly leaves, white flowers, red pods; sun.

---

†   This large-flowered form is scarce, the ordinary form is also good.

Small   These shrubs should all reach no more than 2ft (60cm) in height after about ten years except perhaps in mild gardens on rich soil.

Berberis candidula Yellow; dark green leaves, silver below.

Calluna vulgaris Fine range of flower and foliage forms; no lime.

Daboecia cantabrica 'Atropurpurea' Purple bell flowers; no lime.

Erica cinerea 'C. D. Eason' Deep pink flowers; hates lime.

♀ *Erica tetralix 'Con Underwood'* Red bells, grey leaves; no lime.

♀ *Erica vagans 'Lyonesse'* Long spikes of white flowers; no lime.

♀ *Hebe pinguifolia 'Pagei'* White flowers; silver leaves; loves lime.

* *Lavandula 'Munstead '* Bluer than most lavenders; compact; sun.

♀ *Santolina chamaecyparissus* Neat yellow pompoms; silver leaves.

♀ *Vaccinium vitis-idea 'Koralle'* White bells, red berries; no lime.

--------------------------------- **Autumn-flowering** ---------------------------------

In the autumn the choice of flowering evergreens again becomes rather smaller, although there is still a surprisingly wide range.

Tall   These shrubs should all reach about 6ft (1.8m) in height after ten years, or sooner if planted in sheltered positions and looked after carefully.

♀ *Arbutus unedo* Small, lily-of-the-valley flowers; red fruits.

♀ *Ceanothus 'Autumnal Blue'* One of the hardiest of ceanothus.

Elaeagnus macrophylla Small, fragrant flowers; silvery leaves.

Elaeagnus × *ebbingei* Bold leaves, scented flowers, orange berries.

♀ *Escallonia 'Iveyi'* Impressive heads of white flowers; south wall.

♀ *Fatsia japonica* Big open heads of creamy flowers; very dramatic.

♀* *Fremontodendron 'California Glory'* Bright yellow; short-lived.†

♀ *Mahonia 'Lionel Fortescue'* The earliest mahonia; vigorous.

Osmanthus armatus White, good scent; spiny; very adaptable.

Osmanthus heterophyllus All forms sweetly scented; rather slow.

---

†   Given a warm wall this spectacular shrub will flower for months.

Medium   These shrubs should all reach between 2ft (60cm) and 6ft (1.8m) in height after ten years depending on the variety and how they are grown.

♀ *Abelia × grandiflora* Scented, blushed white flowers; arched habit.

♀ *Camellia sasanqua 'Crimson King'* Single, red; for a south wall,

Cistus 'Sunset' Brilliant magenta; greyish leaves; unusually late.

Colletia paradoxa White scented flowers; no leaves, lots of spines.

♀ *Colquhounia coccinea* Brilliant orange-scarlet flowers; warm site.

♀ *Grevillea juniperina 'Sulphurea'* Yellow spidery flowers; tender.

♀* *Hebe 'Great Orme'* Pale pink flowers; many others also good.

♀ *Hebe 'Midsummer Beauty'* Lilac spikes for a very long season;

♀ *Hypericum 'Hidcote'* Big bright yellow saucers; very long season.

♀ *Viburnum tinus 'Eve Price'* Pink buds, blushed flowers; compact.

Small   These shrubs should all reach no more than 2ft (60cm) in height after about ten years except perhaps in mild gardens on rich soil.

* *Calluna vulgaris 'H. E. Beale'* Long spikes, bright pink; no lime.

♀ *Erica terminalis* Rose-pink flowers fade to brown; good on chalk.

Erica terminalis 'Thelma Woolner' Good deep pink flowers.

Hebe 'Amanda Cook' Variegated version of 'Autumn Glory'.

♀ *Hebe 'Blue Clouds'* Blue flowers; foliage purplish in winter.

♀ *Hebe pinguifolia 'Pagei'* White flowers on flat silver mats.

Medicago arborea Yellow pea flowers; best in sun and shelter.

♀ *Mimulus aurantiacus* Orange tubular flowers; best in warm place.

Salvia greggii Cerisey-red flowers; new colours now appearing.†

Salvia microphylla var. neurepia Brilliant scarlet flowers.†

---

† This plant needs a warm and sheltered situation to thrive heartily.

----------------------------- **Winter-flowering** -----------------------------

Winter-flowering shrubs are especially welcome as they bring light and joy to
dark winter months. Most appreciate a little shelter.

Tall   These shrubs should all reach about 6ft (1.8m) in height after ten
years, or sooner if planted in sheltered positions and looked after carefully.

♀ *Camellia 'Cornish Snow'* Clouds of small white flowers; no lime.
  Camellia 'Salutation' Semi-double, pale rose-pink; no lime.
♀ *Cytisus 'Porlock'* Bright yellow, scented flowers; quick but tender.
♀ *Garrya elliptica 'James Roof'* Unusually long grey-green catkins.
♀ *Leptospermum scoparium 'Red Damask'* Tight double, dark red.
  Lonicera fragrantissima Creamy fragrant flowers; red berries.
♀ *Mahonia japonica* Yellow spikes; best scented of larger mahonias.
  Rhododendron 'Nobleanum' Pink, spotted with dark red; no lime.
  Sycopsis sinensis Small fluffy, red flowers line the branches.
♀* *Viburnum tinus 'Gwenllian'* White heads and blue fruits together.

Medium   These shrubs should all reach between 2ft (60cm) and 6ft (1.8m)
in height after ten years depending on the variety and how they are grown.

♀ *Camellia sasanqua 'Crimson King'* Dark red; warm wall, no lime.
♀ *Coronilla valentina ssp. glauca* Yellow pea flowers; rounded.
♀ *Correa backhouseana* Slender, tubular cream flowers; warm wall.
  Daphne odora Sweetly scented purple flowers; shelter from east.
♀ *Daphne pontica* Greeny-yellow; adaptable, spreading habit.
  Erica erigena 'Superba' Pink; tall and vigorous; stands some lime.
♀ *Erica lusitanica* Pink buds, scented white flowers; no lime.
  Rhododendron 'Ima-shojo' Pink buds, white flowers; no lime.
♀* *Sarcococca confusa* Fragrant creamy white flowers; black berries.
♀ *Skimmia japonica 'Rubella'* Red buds all winter, white flowers.

Small   These shrubs should all reach no more than 2ft (60cm) in height after about ten years except perhaps in mild gardens on rich soil.

Daphne blagayana Creamy and scented; flat growth; rather fussy.

Daphne jezoensis Yellow and fragrant; loses leaves in summer.

Daphne laureola 'Margaret Mathew' Creamy green; neat growth.

♀ *Erica carnea 'Springwood White'* Superb, tight white heather.†

Erica carnea 'Winter Beauty' Bright pink, flowers all winter.†

Erica × darleyensis 'Darley Dale' Spectacular taller pink heather.†

Erica × darleyensis 'Silberschmelze' Fine taller white heather.†

Hebe 'Autumn Glory' Long series of violet spikes; warm place.

♀ *Pachysandra terminalis* White; low ground cover, good in shade.

Sarcococca hookeriana var. humilis Pinkish, scented; black fruits.

---

†   Unlike most heathers these varieties are all tolerant of limy soil.

───────── **Attractive flowers†** ─────────

Most gardeners grow shrubs for their flowers, even evergreen ones which obviously have other attractions. In general, apart from the huge numbers of camellias, heathers and rhododendrons, the choice is relatively modest.

WHITE FLOWERS

White flowers are more easily damaged by frost and rain than other colours so give the plants shelter to protect the flowers if possible.

Camellia 'Alba Plena' Double; old and reliable; no lime. sp

Camellia 'Devonia' Single; weather resistant; no lime. sp

♀ *Carpenteria californica* Single; floppy growth; sunny spot. su

♀* *Choisya ternata* Scented flowers for many months. sp, su, au

♀ *Cistus laurifolius* Single, pure white; one of the hardiest cistus. su

♀ *Convolvulus cneorum* Single; silvery foliage; hot, dry place. su

Erica × darleyensis 'Silberschmeltze' Superb winter heather. wi

♀ *Escallonia 'Iveyi'* Unusual bold variety; best on warm wall. su

♀ *Eucryphia 'Nymansay'* Like a white dog rose; no lime. su, au

♀ *Fatsia japonica* Big open creamy heads; bold foliage. su, au

♀ *Hebe albicans* Spikes of small flowers; silvered foliage. sun; su

♀ *Ligustrum lucidum* Like a huge flamboyant privet; warm spot. au

♀ *Magnolia grandiflora 'Exmouth'* Gigantic, cream flowers. su, au

Olearia × haastii Heads of fragrant daisies; pretty leaves. su

♀ *Pieris japonica 'Grayswood'* Best pieris for flower; no lime. sp

♀ *Pyracantha 'Watereri'* Flat heads, then red berries; spiny. su

♀ *Rhododendron 'Ptarmigan'* Superb dwarf variety; broad habit. sp

♀ *Rhododendron 'Sappho'* White with crimson speckles; acid soil. sp

♀ *Skimmia × confusa 'Kew Green'* Best for flower and scent. wi

♀ *Viburnum tinus 'Gwenllian'* Flowers and blue berries together. wi

───────────────────────

† In this section sp = spring, su = summer, au = autumn, wi = winter.

PINK FLOWERS

Pink covers such a range of shades from slightly blushed white to deep salmon and rich rose, that this list is rather a mix of colours.

Calluna vulgaris 'H. E. Beale' Long pink spikes; no lime; su

♀ *Camellia* 'Donation' Best pink camellia; upright habit; no lime. sp

Camellia 'Otome' Superb single; early flowering; no lime. wi, sp

Cistus 'Silver Pink' Lovely silvered pink; very hardy; full sun. su†

Erica carnea 'Springwood Pink' Best pink winter heather. wi

♀ *Erica cinerea* 'C. D. Eason' Deep pink bells; no lime. su

Erica × *darleyensis* 'Darley Dale' Tall elegant pink heather. wi

♀ *Erica terminalis* Fades to brown for winter; stands some lime. au

♀ *Erica tetralix* 'Pink Star' Lilacish, greyish leaves; no lime. su, au

Erica vagans 'St Keverne' Bright rose, flared bells; no lime. su

Escallonia 'Slieve Donard' Appleblossom pink, arching habit. su

♀ *Hebe* 'Great Orme' Fades to white; neat; hardier than many. su

♀* *Helianthemum* 'Rhodanthe Carneum' Single, silver foliage. su

Kalmia latifolia 'Olympic Fire' Deep red buds; no lime. su

Lavandula 'Loddon Pink' Silvery leaves; compact growth. su.

♀ *Leptospermum scoparium* 'Kiwi' Dwarf; sunny wall; no lime. sp

♀ *Pieris japonica* 'Pink Delight' Flowers white at base; no lime. sp

Rhaphiolepis × *delacourii* Spikes of cherry-like flowers; sun. su

♀ *Rhododendron* 'Doc' Rose, dark rim, fades to white; no lime. sp

♀ *Rhododendron* 'Tessa Roza' Best early deep pink; no lime. wi, sp

---

† This cistus does well in both heavy clay soils and sandy soil.

RED FLOWERS

Here varieties have been chosen whose flowers in various shades of red show up well against the leafy richness of many evergreens.

    Berberis linearifolia 'Jewel' Scarlet buds opening rich orange. sp

♆ *Camellia japonica 'Adolphe Audusson'* Semi-double crimson. sp

♆ *Camellia sasanqua 'Crimson King'* Bright red, warm wall. wi

    Correa 'Dusky Bells' Clear red, pendulous, tubular flowers. wi†

♆ *Crinodendron hookerianum* Spectacular red lanterns. no lime; sp

♆ *Daboecia* × *scotica 'Jack Drake'* Large ruby bells; no lime. su

♆ *Desfontanea spinosa* Scarlet, yellow-throated tubes; no lime. su

♆ *Erica carnea 'Vivellii'* Dark red flowers; bronze winter leaves. wi

♆ *Erica* × *darleyensis 'Arthur Johnson'* Magenta; OK on lime. wi

♆ *Erica tetralix 'Con Underwood'* Crimson; greyish-green leaves. su

    Escallonia 'Red Elf' Deep red; vigorous, compact; glossy leaves. su

    Garrya × *issaquahensis 'Pat Ballard'* Long red-tinted catkins. wi

    Grevillea rosmarinifolia Spidery crimson flowers; mild areas. su

♆* *Hebe 'Simon Delaux'* Deep crimson spikes; glossy foliage. su, au†

♆ *Helianthemum 'Mrs C. W. Earle'* Double scarlet; likes sun. su

♆ *Leptospermum scoparium 'Red Damask'* Double cherry red. su

♆ *Pieris japonica 'Valley Valentine'* Crimson bells; no lime. sp

♆ *Rhododendron 'Dopey'* Bright orange red; neat habit; no lime. sp

    Rhododendron 'Lady Chamberlain' Elegant; bluish leaves. sp

♆ *Skimmia japonica 'Rubella'* Deep red winter buds, then white. wi

---

†   In most areas this plant thrives best if sheltered by a warm wall.

YELLOW AND GREEN FLOWERS

This list covers a range of colours, from brilliant buttercup yellow through softer primrose and paling to creams plus greeny shades.

♆ *Acacia dealbata* Yellow, scented; silver leaves; tender. wi
Berberis buxifolia 'Nana' Neat, relatively thorn free mound. sp
Berberis × stenophylla 'Lemon Queen' Cream, dark leaves. sp
♆ *Brachyglottis 'Sunshine'* Bright yellow daisies; floppy habit. su
Camellia × williamsii 'Jury's Yellow' Not yellow, more cream. sp†
Corokia cotoneaster Tiny yellow flowers; unique twiggy habit. su
♆ *Coronilla valentina 'Citrina'* Peach-scented lemon flowers. wi-sp
Daphne jezoensis Buttercup yellow, scented; dwarf but tricky. wi
♆ *Daphne pontica* Yellow-green, scented; spreading growth. wi, sp
♆ *Garrya elliptica 'James Roof'* Very long greyish-green catkins. wi
Grevillea juniperina 'Sulphurea' Bright yellow; hardiest form. su
Halimium lasianthum Bright yellow, maroon marks; spreading. su
Helianthemum 'Boughton Double Primrose' Very dark leaves. su
♆ *Itea ilicifolia* Long pale green, scented catkins; holly-like leaves. su
♆ *Mahonia 'Charity'* Deep yellow; bold foliage, bold plant. wi
♆ *Mahonia lomariifolia* Deep yellow; superb foliage; shelter. wi
Rhododendron 'Chikor' Prolific yellow; compact but tough. sp
♆* *Rhododendron 'Yellow Hammer'* Bright yellow; erect; tough. sp
♆ *Santolina chamaecyparissus* Lemon pompoms; silver foliage. su
Ulex europaeus 'Flore Pleno' Bright, double, long lasting; sp-su

---

† The truly yellow camellia has still not yet been developed.

BLUE FLOWERS

The choice of evergreen shrubs with blue flowers is a more restricted one and unfortunately many of them are rather tender.

♉* *Ceanothus 'Autumnal Blue'* The hardiest variety; vigorous. su-au
♉ *Ceanothus thyrsiflorus var. repens* Low, creeping mound. su
♉ *Hebe hulkeana* Long spikes, open habit; warm, sunny place. su†
  Hebe 'Marjorie' Lavender blue fading to white; very tough. su
  Rhododendron 'Blue Diamond' Compact habit; no lime. sp
♉ *Rhododendron 'Blue Peter'* Rich blue, white throat; vigorous. sp
♉ *Rosmarinus officinalis 'Severn Sea'* Dwarf and spreading. sp-au
  Salvia guaranitica 'Blue Enigma' Spikes in strong blue; full sun. su-au†
  Salvia lavandulifolia Lavender-tinted; grey leaves; full sun. su†
  Teucrium fruticans Pale flowers, grey leaves; sunny place. su

PURPLE FLOWERS

Here too the choice is small and spread among all too few different types. Choose neighbouring colours carefully to avoid clashes.

♉ *Calluna vulgaris 'Robert Chapman'* Leaves orange; no lime. su
  Daboecia cantabrica 'Atropurpurea' Darkest purple; no lime. su
  Erica cinerea 'Velvet Night' Almost black, tinged red; no lime. su
♉ *Hebe 'Alicia Amherst'* Long deep purple spikes; likes shelter. su
  Hebe 'Autumn Glory' Short spikes, long season; quite tough. su-au
♉ *Lavandula 'Hidcote'* Dense violet spikes; grey foliage; sun. su
* *Lavandula stoechas 'James Compton'* Superb butterfly type. su
♉ *Rhododendron 'Purple Splendour'* Rich purple, black spots. sp
  Rhododendron 'Songbird' Some late flowers; compact habit. sp
♉ *Salvia officinalis 'Purpurascens'* Bluish tint; purple leaves. su

---

†   This plant may die back to a woody base in winter then regrow

SCENTED FLOWERS

Scent is a very personal characteristic and is also notoriously difficult to describe. It always pays to sniff before you buy.

Azara petiolaris Small yellow winter puffs; vanilla scented. 12ft (3.6m)†

♀ *Choisya ternata* White and sweet scented; aromatic foliage. 6ft (1.8m)†

♀ *Coronilla valentina ssp. glauca* Yellow peas; peachy scent. 6ft (1.8m)†

* *Daphne odora* Reddish-purple; heavy and sweet; likes shelter. 2ft (60cm)

♀ *Daphne pontica* Greeny-yellow in late winter; sweet; spreading. 2ft (60cm)

Elaeagnus × *ebbingei* Tiny silver autumn flowers; strong scent. 6ft (1.8m)

Eucryphia milliganii White and sweet; slower than other types. 6ft (1.8m)

Lomatia myricoides Small, sweet and white flowers; no lime. 10ft (3m)

♀ *Lupinus arboreus* Tree lupin; sweet yellow spikes; vigorous. 4ft (1.2m)

Magnolia grandiflora Huge exotic white flowers; rich scent. 10ft (3m)†

♀ *Mahonia 'Lionel Fortescue'* Yellow winter spikes; striking. 10ft (3m)

♀ *Myrtus communis* Small white flowers; dark aromatic leaves. 6ft (1.8m)

♀ *Olearia* × *macrodonta* White daisies; greyish, holly-like leaves. 6ft (1.8m)

♀ *Osmanthus delavayi* White winter flowers; deep green leaves. 5ft (1.5m)†

Pimelea prostrata White flowers and fruits; hates clay; sun. 1ft (30cm)

♀ *Pittosporum tenuifolium* All foliage forms honey-scented. 8ft (2.4m)

Rhododendron 'Albatross' Wonderful heavy scent; cream. 10ft (3m)

♀ *Sarcococca confusa* Tiny white winter flowers; very sweet. 3ft (90cm)

♀ *Skimmia japonica 'Fragrans'* Lily-of-the-valley scent; prolific. 2ft (60cm)

♀ *Viburnum* × *burkwoodii 'Fulbrook'* Pink buds opening white. 6ft (1.8m)

---

† This plant will grow well against a wall or fence.

Attractive foliage†

The main feature of evergreen shrubs is of course their foliage and those
which are variegated or coloured provide interest all year.

VARIEGATED LEAVES – EDGED

This selection of evergreens is confined to varieties whose leaves are green
but which are edged with gold, yellow, cream or white.

℗ *Buxus sempervirens 'Elegantissima'* Cream; good low hedge. 3ft (90cm)
   Coronilla valentina 'Variegata' Pale cream; yellow flowers. 4ft (1.2m)
   Daphne odora 'Aureomarginata' Yellow fading to cream. 2ft (60cm)
℗* *Euonymus 'Emerald 'n' Gold'* Gold, then pinkish in winter. 2ft (60cm)
℗ *Euonymus japonicus 'Latifolius Albomarginatus'* White. 6ft (1.8m)
   Griselinia littoralis 'Variegata' White-edged; best by sea. 6ft (1.8m)
   Hebe × andersonii 'Variegata' Creamy-white; lavender spikes. 3ft (90cm)
℗ *Ilex × altaclerensis 'Golden King'* Yellow, few spines; fruits. 10ft (3m)
   Osmanthus heterophyllus 'Aureomarginatus' Yellow; scent. 6ft (1.8m)
℗ *Pieris 'Flaming Silver'* Pink margin fading to white; no lime. 3ft (90cm)

VARIEGATED LEAVES – SPLASHED

Evergreens whose foliage is boldly marked in the centre are often the most
dramatic varieties, speckled varieties are more subtle.

   Abutilon megapotanicum 'Variegatum' Yellow-mottled. 6ft (1.8m)
   Aucuba japonica 'Gold Dust' Gold-speckled; red berries. 5ft (1.5m)
* *Eleagnus × ebbingei 'Limelight'* Bright yellow central stripe. 6ft (1.8m)
   Euonymus fortunei 'Sunspot' Yellow stripe; pinkish in winter. 3ft (90cm)
   Euonymus japonicus 'Aureus' Deep green, bold gold centre. 6ft (1.8m)
   Griselinia littoralis 'Dixon's Cream' Cream splashes; tender. 8ft (2.4m)
℗ *Ilex aquifolium 'Golden Milkboy'* Gold stripe; purple stems. 8ft (2.4m)
℗ *Pittosporum tenuifolium 'Irene Paterson'* Marbled white. 4ft (1.2m)
   Prunus laurocerasus 'Castlewellan' Marbled white; slow. 3ft (90cm)
   Rosmarinus officinalis 'Aureus' Tipped or splashed in gold. 3ft (90cm)

---

†   Most coloured-leaved evergreens are useful for flower-arranging.

GOLD AND YELLOW LEAVES

Plants with yellow- or gold-flushed leaves need careful positioning so they fit in well with other colours. Some must also be sited so that they avoid scorch or to ensure they develop their best colour.

♈* *Calluna vulgaris 'Gold Haze'* Very bright; acid soil, sun. 2ft (60cm)

Cassinia leptophylla ssp. fulvida Crowded yellow shoots. 4ft (1.2m)

♈ *Choisya ternata 'Sundance'* Bright yellow; slightly tender. 4ft (1.2m)

♈ *Erica carnea 'Foxhollow'* Green tint in summer, red in winter. 9in (23cm)

Erica × darleyensis 'Jack H. Brummage' Red tinted in winter. 2ft (60cm)

♈ *Erica vagans 'Valerie Proudley'* Very bright all year; no lime. 2ft (60cm)

Ilex aquifolium 'Flavescens' Primrose and gold; red berries. 10ft (3m)

♈ *Ilex crenata 'Golden Gem'* Colour fades during season. 18in (45cm)

♈ *Laurus nobilis 'Aurea'* Slower and less hardy than green bay. 6ft (1.8m)

Ligustrum lucidum 'Aureum' Yellow in spring, slowly fades. 9ft (2.7m)†

♈ *Ligustrum ovalifolium 'Aureum'* Golden privet; invaluable. 8ft (2.4m)†

Ligustrum 'Vicaryi' Gold, bronzed in winter; semi-evergreen. 5ft (1.5m)†

♈ *Lonicera nitida 'Baggesen's Gold'* Yellow, greenish in winter. 3ft (90cm)

Olearia solandri Overall yellow haze; appreciates shelter. 6ft (1.8m)

♈ *Phlomis chrysophylla* Golden tinted in summer; loves heat. 3ft (90cm)

Pieris 'Bert Chandler' Creamy all winter if planted in sun. 4ft (1.2m)

♈ *Pittosporum tenuifolium 'Warnham Gold'* Best in winter. 5ft (1.5m)

Salvia officinalis 'Kew Gold' Evenly coloured; slightly miffy. 2ft (60cm)

---

† These are forms of privet, but don't let that put you off.

SILVER AND GREY LEAVES

Evergreens with silver or grey leaves tend to appreciate hot, dry conditions and some are also more tender than other evergreens. Most are best in a sunny place, in well-drained soil with shelter.

♀ *Acacia baileyana* Pretty divided leaves; yellow winter flowers. 12ft (3.6m)

♀ *Artemisia 'Powis Castle'* Shining silvery mound; no flowers. 2ft (60cm)

♀ *Brachyglottis 'Sunshine'* Floppy grey mound; yellow daisies. 3ft (90cm)

♀ *Calluna vulgaris 'Silver Queen'* Plus pink flowers; no lime. 2ft (60cm)

♀* *Convolvulus cneorum* Silky silver foliage; white trumpets. 18in (45cm)

♀ *Cytisus battandieri* Silver to brownish grey; yellow flowers. 15ft (4.5m)

Elaeagnus × *ebbingei* Leaves grey-green, silvery below; quick. 8ft (2.4m)

♀ *Eucalyptus gunnii* Silver and aromatic; prune hard annually. 6ft (1.8m)

♀ *Hebe pinguifolia 'Pagei'* Flat spreading growth; white flowers. 9in (23cm)

Helianthemum 'Wisley White' Slender leaves; white flowers. 1ft (30cm)

♀ *Ilex* × *meservae 'Blue Angel'* Dark, blue-green; best in sun. 6ft (1.8m)

Lavandula 'Richard Gray' Best for colour and hardiness. 2ft (60cm)

Lotus hirsutus Silver, clover-like leaves; self-sows if happy. 2ft (60cm)

Mahonia fremontii Neat, blue-grey leaves; red berries; spiny. 4ft (1.2m)

♀ *Olearia* × *macrodonta* Greyish holly-like leaves, silver below. 6ft (1.8m)

♀ *Rhododendron leptostylum* Blue-green; shade and no lime. 2ft (60cm)

♀ *Ruta graveolens 'Jackman's Blue'* Bushy, blue; yellow heads. 2ft (60cm)†

Salvia lavandulifolia Narrow grey leaves; purple-blue flowers. 2ft (60cm)

♀ *Santolina chamaecyparissus* Slender silver leaves; aromatic. 2ft (60cm)

Teucrium fruticans Neat leaf on straggly plant; best on wall. 6ft (1.8m)

---

† Rue. This may cause a severe allergic reaction if leaves touch skin.

PURPLE AND BRONZE LEAVES

There are relatively few purple or bronze evergreens and they should be used sparingly to avoid creating a gloomy atmosphere.

Calluna vulgaris 'Winter Chocolate' Chocolate, tipped red. 2ft (60cm)

Cordyline australis 'Purpurea' Palm-like; almost a small tree. 6ft (1.8m)

Daphne × *houtteana* Dark purple; pink flowers; slow and rare. 2ft (60cm)

Nandina domestica 'Nana Purpurea' New leaves red all year. 2ft (60cm)

Osmanthus heterophyllus 'Purpureus' Purple, greening later. 6ft (1.8m)

♇ *Phormium tenax* 'Purpureum' Long, purple, sword-like leaves. 6ft (1.8m)

Pittosporum tenuifolium 'Purpureum' Green turning purple. 6ft (1.8m)

♇ *Pittosporum tenuifolium* 'Tom Thumb' Green then purple. 2ft (60cm)

Rhododendron 'Elizabeth Lockart' Dark bronzy purple. 2ft (60cm)

♇* *Salvia officinalis* 'Purpurascens' Velvety purple; blue spikes. 2ft (60cm)

MULTICOLOURED LEAVES†

Evergreens with leaves in mixtures of green, pink, yellow, cream and white make interesting features but need careful positioning.

♇ *Euonymus fortunei* 'Emerald Gaiety' Cream edge goes pink. 2ft (60cm)

* *Hebe speciosa* 'Tricolor' Cream edge; new leaves purple. 4ft (1.2m)

Leucothoë fontanesiana 'Rainbow' Yellow, cream and pink. 4ft (1.2m)

Nandina domestica 'Firepower' Yellow-green to orange-red. 2ft (60cm)

♇ *Phormium cookianum* 'Tricolor' Green, cream, red edge. 4ft (1.2m)

Photinia davidiana 'Palette' Green, creamy white and pink. 5ft (1.5m)

♇ *Pittosporum* 'Garnettii' Grey-green, edged white, spotted pink. 8ft (2.4m)

Salvia officinalis 'Purpurascens Variegata' Purple and cream. 2ft (60cm)

Salvia officinalis 'Tricolor' Grey, cream and pink; rather weak. 2ft (60cm)

Pseudowintera colorata Crimson, pink and yellowish green! 3ft (90cm)

---

† Many of these are difficult to establish or slow-growing.

AROMATIC LEAVES

Many herbs and Mediterranean shrubs, along with shrubs from other regions
with similar climates, have aromatic foliage.

♈ *Artemisia 'Powis Castle'* Silver leaf, powerfully aromatic. 2ft (60cm)

  Chamaecyparis lawsoniana forms All resinously aromatic. 1–30ft
    (30cm–9m)

♈ *Cistus* × *cyprius* Leaves produce sweetly fragrant gum; hardy. 4ft (1.2m).

♈ *Cistus ladanifer 'Palhinhae'* Pure white; large sticky leaves. 5ft (1.5m)

♈ *Cupressus arizonica 'Pyramidalis'* Grey-blue leaves; elegant. 12ft (3.6m)

  Drimys lanceolata Peppery taste and aroma; purple shoots. 4ft (1.2m)

  Escallonia rubra var. macrantha Pink flowers; balsam scent. 10ft (3m)

  Helichrysum italicum ssp. serotinum Strong curry smell. 2ft (60cm)

  Lavandula dentata Finely cut silvery leaf; unusually rich scent. 2ft (60cm)

  Lavandula 'Loddon Pink' All varieties aromatic; pink spikes. 2ft (60cm)

♈ *Myrtus communis* Neat, dark; sweet aroma; sun and shelter. 6ft (1.8m)

♈ *Phlomis fruticosa* Aroma like weak sage; yellow flower-heads. 3ft (90cm)

  Rhododendron cinnabarinum 'Roylei' Bluish leaf; elegant. 6ft (1.8m)

  Rosmarinus officinalis 'Majorca' The most intense blue. 4ft (1.2m)

  Rosmarinus officinalis 'Majorca Pink' Pink rosemary. 3ft (90cm)

  Salvia lavandulifolia Confusingly lavender-scented sage. 2ft (60cm)

* *Salvia officinalis 'Berggarten'* All sagey; this has big leaves. 2ft (60cm)

  Santolina pinnata 'Sulphurea' Very pungent; clip annually. 18in (45cm)

  Seriphidium tridentatum Rare artemisia relative; grey leaf. 6ft (1.8m)†

  Umbellularia californica Strongly pungent; beware overdoses. 6ft (1.8m)

  Vestia foetida Pretty yellow flowers; aroma horridly foetid. 3ft (90cm)

---

†   The leaves are at their most aromatic after rain; worth seeking out.

BOLD FOLIAGE†

Bold foliage, either rounded or divided, makes a strong impression when used as a feature and looks good surrounded by lacier leaves.

Aucuba japonica 'Hillieri' Huge deep green leaves; red fruits. 5ft (1.5m)

Chamaerops humilis Dwarf hardy palm; deeply divided fans. 2ft (60cm)

Daphniphyllum macropodum Like a large rhododendron. 6ft (1.8m)

♈ × *Fatshedera lizei* Large, leathery, maple-shaped leaves; flops. 4ft (1.2m)

♈* *Fatsia japonica* Huge, exotic, divided leaves; good in shade. 10ft (3m)

Ilex latifolia Huge glossy leaves; orange fruits; likes shelter. 12ft (3.6m)

Magnolia grandifolia Leaves like rubber plant; huge flowers. 10ft (3m)

Mahonia lomariifolia Long ranks of holly-like leaves; tender. 8ft (2.4m)

Prunus laurocerasus 'Latifolia' The most impressive laurel. 20ft (6m)

♈ *Rhododendron macabeanum* Stately and stunning; no lime. 8ft (2.4m)

DISTINCTIVE FOLIAGE

This section includes evergreens whose foliage has some other valuable ornamental features; each must be treated on its merits.

♈ *Eriobotrya japonica* Huge wrinkled leaves; winter flowers. 10ft (3m)

Gevuina avellana Glossy divided leaves, edged with hairs. 8ft (2.4m)

Hebe cupressoides Looks and even smells like a cypress. 3ft (90cm)

Ilex aquifolium 'Ferox' Spines round edge and on leaf blade. 4ft (1.2m)

Osmanthus yunnanensis Bold leaves; *some* wavy and toothed. 9ft (2.7m)

♈ *Ozothamnus ledifolius* Dark green, curls showing silver below. 4ft (1.2m)

Poncirus trifoliata Bright green stems and thorns all year. 6ft (1.8m)

Pseudopanax ferox Long, thin, drooping, toothed and greyish. 8ft (2.4m)

Rhododendron rex Grey, beige, brown or rusty below; no lime. 6ft (1.8m)

* *Viburnum rhytidophyllum* Distinctive deeply veined leaves. 10ft (3m)

---

† Shrubs with large leaves are best sheltered from damaging wind.

───────────────── **Attractive berries** ─────────────────

Shrubs with attractive berries bring colour at a season when it is most
valuable; some need male and female plants (see page oo).

RED BERRIES

Red berries tend to be favourite with birds and are often eaten first but, as far
as it is possible to tell, these varieties remain the longest.

Aucuba japonica 'Nana Rotundifolia' The most prolific; short. 3ft (90cm)†

♀ *Cotoneaster frigidus 'Cornubia'* Best of the taller varieties. 15ft (4.5m)

♀ *Gaultheria mucronata 'Bell's Seedling'* Deep red; self-fertile. 2ft (60cm)

Gaultheria × *wisleyensis 'Wisley Pearl'* Blood-red; no lime. 18in (45cm)

♀ *Ilex aquifolium 'J. C. van Thol'* Berries without male variety. 12ft (3.6m)

Ilex cornuta 'Burfordii' Compact habit, very free fruiting. 2ft (60cm)†

Photinia davidiana Huge bunches line shoots; vigorous plant. 8ft (2.4m)

* ♀*Pyracantha 'Waterei'* Dense bunches; compact; good hedge. 8ft (2.4m)

Ruscus aculeatus Tough and tolerant; a few are self-fertile. 2ft (60cm)†

Skimmia japonica 'Veitchii' Large bunches, long lasting. 2ft (60cm)†

YELLOW AND ORANGE BERRIES

It is sometimes the case that orange or yellow berries are less attractive to
birds, but often they are also smaller and less prolific.

Cotoneaster salicifolius 'Fructu Luteo' Bright yellow fruits. 15ft (4.5m)

♀ *Cotoneaster salicifolius 'Rothschildianus'* Creamier yellow. 15ft (4.5m)

Eleagnus × *ebbingei* Orange, slightly speckled; silver leaves. 6ft (1.8m)

Euonymus fortunei var. vegetus Small, orange; green leaves. 2ft (60cm)

Ilex aquifolium 'Amber' Large, slightly bronzed yellow berries. 12ft
(3.6m)†

Ilex aquifolium 'Bacciflava' Bright yellow berries; lasts well. 12ft (3.6m)†

* *Photinia davidiana 'Fructoluteo'* Bright yellow; vigorous. 8ft (2.4m)

♀ *Photinia 'Redstart'* Orangey-yellow, very prolific; superb. 8ft (2.4m)

Pyracantha 'Saphyr Orange' Upright habit; disease-resistant. 10ft (3m)

Pyracantha 'Soleil d'Or' Golden yellow; shorter than many. 8ft (2.4m)

───

† 　This is a female plant and needs a male nearby to produce berries.

PINK AND WHITE BERRIES

Pink and white berries are often said to be of little appeal to birds, but they all go in the end; pink can show up poorly in the garden.

Aucuba japonica 'Fructu Albo' White, with a touch of yellow. 5ft (1.5m)†

Azara lanceolata White fruits, unpredictably produced. 6ft (1.8m)

Cotoneaster × watereri 'Pink Champagne' Pinky yellow. 15ft (4.5m)

Euonymus tingens Pink fruits opening to show red seeds. 10ft (3m)

♀ *Gaultheria cuneata* White fruits, antiseptic smell; no lime. 1ft (30cm)

Gaultheria miqueliana White or pink, edible; creeps slowly. 6in (15cm)

* *Gaultheria mucronata 'Lilian'* (pernettya) Soft lilac-pink. 2ft (60cm)

Gaultheria mucronata 'Rosie' (pernettya) Two-tone pink. 2ft (60cm)

Gaultheria mucronata 'White Pearl' (pernettya) Pure white. 2ft (60cm)

Margyricarpus pinnatus White; creeping alpine shrub for sun. 1ft (30cm)

Viscum album Mistletoe; difficult to grow but worth trying. 2ft (60cm)

PURPLE, BLUE AND BLACK BERRIES

Dark-berried varieties show up least well and this may be why birds tend to leave them; set them at the front where you can see them.

Berberis replicata Blackish purple; leaves silvery below. 2ft (60cm)

♀ *Daphne pontica* Darkest blue-black; fragrant greenish flowers. 18in (45cm)

Dichroa febrifuga Blue; like a blue-flowered hydrangea. 5ft (1.5m)

Gaultheria fragrantissima Bright blue; scented white flowers. 2ft (60cm)

♀ *Gaultheria mucronata 'Mulberry Wine'* (pernettya) Purple. 2ft (60cm)

♀ *Ilex crenata 'Convexa'* Black; like a neat dark-leaved box. 18in (45cm)†

Mahonia repens Blue-black; yellow flowers; good leaves. 2ft (60cm)

Osmanthus decorus Purplish-black; scented white flowers. 10ft (3m)

♀ *Viburnum davidii* Turquoise-blue; low, dome-shaped habit. 3ft (90cm)†

♀* *Viburnum tinus 'Gwenllian'* Blue-black; good white flowers. 5ft (1.5m)

---

† This is a female plant and needs a male nearby to produce berries.

DECIDUOUS

In addition to a huge variety of flowers, deciduous shrubs bring constant change from unfolding spring leaves to autumn colour.

Spring-flowering

In spring the freshness and brightness of flowering shrubs is a joy in itself as well as partnering the spring flowers of perennials and bulbs.

Tall   These shrubs should all reach about 6ft (1.8m) in height after ten years, or sooner if planted in sheltered positions and looked after carefully.
℞ *Cercis siliquastrum* Mauve pea flowers on new and old shoots.
* *Chaenomales speciosa 'Nivalis'* Pure white; the most vigorous.†
  Corylopsis spicata Pale yellow, like strings of cowslips; no lime.
℞ *Exochorda* × *macrantha 'The Bride'* Pure white; arching habit.
℞ *Forsythia* × *intermedia 'Lynwood'* The most colourful variety.†
℞ *Magnolia* × *soulangiana 'Lennei'* Sumptuous mauve goblets.
℞ *Rhododendron 'Irene Koster'* Rose and cream; deciduous azalea.
℞ *Ribes sanguineum 'Pulborough Scarlet'* Deep red; vigorous.†
℞ *Stachyurus praecox* Long strings of cream flowers; broad habit.†
  Weigela 'Bristol Ruby' Deep crimson; tough and reliable.†

Medium   These shrubs should all reach between 2ft (60cm) and 6ft (1.8m) in height after ten years depending on the variety and how they are grown.
℞ *Chaenomeles* × *superba 'Knap Hill Scarlet'* Orange, not scarlet.†
  Cytisus 'Killiney Red' Rusty-red flowers line shoots; short-lived.†
℞ *Enkianthus campanulatus* Dainty pink and white bells; no lime.
  Forsythia × *intermedia 'Minigold'* Prolific, very bright; dwarf.†
℞ *Magnolia stellata* White starry flowers; may be damaged by frost.
℞ *Prunus triloba 'Multiplex'* Bright pink, tightly double flowers.†
  Rhododendron (deciduous azaleas) Huge range of colours.
℞ *Salix hastata 'Wehrenhnii'* Silver catkins in purplish red stems.

---

†   It is especially important to prune immediately after flowering.

♈ *Spiraea thunbergii* Heads of small white flowers line branches.
* *Viburnum × carlesii* White flowers; all forms exquisitely fragrant.

Small These shrubs should all reach no more than 2ft (60cm) in height after about ten years, except perhaps in mild gardens or on rich soil.

♈ *Berberis thunbergii 'Atropurpurea Nana'* Yellow; purple leaves.
   Betula nana Short catkins; neat, twiggy habit; likes moisture.
♈ *Cytisus × kewensis* Small, cream pea flowers make a low cloud.
   Daphne alpina Fragrant white flowers; orangey red berries.
   Deutzia 'Nikko' White flowers; makes a low arching mound.
♈ *Genista lydia* Bright yellow; good tumbling over rocks; likes sun.
♈ *Prunus tenella 'Fire Hill'* Pink flowers line the stems; stunning.
* *Rosa 'De Meaux'* Pink pompons; neat, scented, unusually early.
♈ *Salix repens var. argentea* Clouds of small catkins; silvery leaves.
♈ *Spiraea japonica 'Nana'* Pink heads on neat, spreading mounds.

──────────────── **Summer-flowering** ────────────────

Summer-flowering shrubs need to be bright and bold to balance the bright colours from other summer garden plants.

Tall These shrubs should reach at least 6ft (1.8m) in height after ten years, or sooner if planted in sheltered positions and looked after carefully.

♈* *Buddleja davidii 'Empire Blue'* Violet-blue with an orange eye.†
♈ *Buddleja globosa* Bright orange flowers in balls, not spikes.
♈ *Ceanothus 'Gloire de Versailles'* Clouds of sky blue into autumn.†
♈ *Hoheria lyallii* Pure white cherry-like flowers offset by grey foliage.
♈ *Lavatera 'Barnsley'* Flared pink-eyed white flowers; long season.†
   Rosa moyesii Deep red single flowers; large scarlet hips later.
   Rubus ulmifolius 'Bellidiflorus' Double pink; extremely vigorous.†
♈ *Spartium junceum* Large bright yellow pea flowers; sunny site.
   Spiraea × billiardii 'Triumphans' Dense rosy spikes; suckers.†
♈ *Tamarix ramosissima 'Rubra'* Fluffy spikes of deep rosy-red.†

---

† Best pruned in spring as the new growth is just beginning.

Medium   These shrubs should all reach between 2ft (60cm) and 6ft (1.8m)
in height after ten years, depending on the variety and how they are grown.

♈ *Buddleja davidii 'Nanho Blue'* Purple-blue spikes; compact plant.
   Caryopteris × *clandonensis 'Kew Blue'* Dark blue; spring prune.
   Deutzia setchuensis Clouds of small white starry flowers; slow.
   Hydrangea 'Hamburg' Pink on lime; blue on acid soil; mophead.†

♈* *Perovskia atriplicifolia 'Blue Spire'* Long slender blue spikes.
   Phygelius aequalis 'Yellow Trumpet' Elegant yellow spikes.

♈ *Potentilla fruticosa 'Elizabeth'* Yellow flowers for months.
   Rosa Take your pick from the lists starting on page 249.

♈ *Spiraea japonica 'Anthony Waterer'* Flat, deep pink heads.
   Viburnum plicatum 'Nanum Semperflorens' White lacecaps.

Small   These shrubs should all reach no more than 2ft (60cm) in height
after about ten years, except perhaps in mild gardens or on rich soil.

   Genista hispanica Yellow pea flowers on tight mound; spiny.
   Helichrysum thianschanicum Yellow flowers; white felted leaves.
   Hypericum empetrifolium Yellow saucers; tiny twiggy shrublet.
   Jasminum parkeri Yellow flowers; makes a tight mound; sun.

♈* *Philadelphus 'Manteau d'Hermine'* Double white; prune to size.
   Potentilla fruticosa 'Manchu' White flowers; grey leaves; low.
   Potentilla fruticosa 'Sunset' Orange flowers; spreading habit.
   Rosa County Series Range of low, spreading ground cover roses.
   Spiraea japonica 'Little Princess' Deep rose; neat mound.
   Stephanandra incisa 'Crispa' Greenish white spikes; low mound.

---

†   Use a bluing agent if you want to keep it blue on limy soil.

Autumn-flowering

Unfortunately although many summer shrubs extend their season into autumn, the range of autumn-only shrubs is rather small.

Tall   These shrubs should all reach about 6ft (1.8m) in height after ten years, or sooner if planted in sheltered positions and looked after carefully.

♀ *Aralia elata* Clouds of small white flowers; huge leaves; suckers.

Buddleja auriculata Small creamy spikes; delicious scent; tender.

Buddleja caryopteridifolia Purple scented flowers; prune in spring.

Clerodendron trichotomum White fragrant flowers, purple buds.

♀* *Eucryphia glutinosa* Wonderful white flowers; starts late summer.

Hamamelis virginiana The autumn witch hazel; delicate scent.

♀ *Hibiscus syriacus 'Diana'* Huge, white, slightly crimped trumpets.

♀ *Hibiscus syriacus 'Hamabo'* Blushed white single, deep red eye.

♀ *Hibiscus syriacus 'Oiseau Bleu'* Single, purplish blue trumpets.

Hydrangea 'Otaksa' Cream, then pink or blue; tallest mophead.

Medium   These shrubs should all reach between 2ft (60cm) and 6ft (1.8m) in height after ten years, depending on the variety and how they are grown.

♀ *Abelia × grandiflora* Blushed white flowers on arching shoots.

♀ *Ceratostigma willmottianum* Blue flowers amid reddening leaves.

Clethra alnifolia Scented white spikes; starts in late summer.

♀ *Disanthus cercidifolius* Small purple flowers amid crimson leaves.

♀ *Fuchsia 'Mrs Popple'* Red and purple; the hardiest fuchsia of all.

Hydrangea paniculata 'Pink Diamond' White, fading to pink.

Hydrangea paniculata 'Tardiva' Cream spikes; the latest form.

♀ *Hypericum 'Rowallane'* Golden yellow but appreciates shelter.

♀ *Indigofera heterantha* Deep rosy red pea flowers; hot sites.

♀* *Lespedeza thunbergii* Rosy purple flowers weigh down branches.

Small   These shrubs should all reach no more than 2ft (60cm) in height after about ten years, except perhaps in mild gardens or on rich soil.

*   *Elscholtzia stauntonii* Rosy-purple spikes; fragrant foliage.

♀   *Fuchsia 'Lady Thumb'* Red and white semi-double; very tight.

Fuchsia 'Sleepy' Carmine and mauve; tough, but not the toughest.

♀   *Fuchsia 'Tom Thumb'* Red and violet; prolific; tight and compact.

♀   *Hydrangea involucrata 'Hortensis'* Double white, turning pink.

Sphaeralcea fendleri Reddish orange; low spreading habit.

Ulex minor Golden pea flowers; spiny bush; starve for best show.

Zauschneria californica 'Albiflora' White tubular flowers; sun.

♀   *Zauschneria californica 'Dublin'* Brilliant scarlet; good drainage.

Zauschneria californica 'Solidarity Pink' Pink; all slightly tender.

Long-flowering

Shrubs with an unusually long flowering season help provide the maximum amount of colour, especially important in small gardens.

Abelia schumanii Mauvey-pink, scented; summer and autumn. 4ft (1.2m)

♀   *Buddleja × weyeriana 'Sungold'* Orange; summer and autumn. 8ft (2.4m)

♀   *Fuchsia 'Corallina'* Red and violet; summer and autumn. 3ft (90cm)

Hydrangea 'Forever Pink' Deep pink; summer and autumn. 2ft (60cm)

♀   *Hypericum 'Hidcote'* Bright yellow; summer and autumn. 6ft (1.8m)

♀*   *Lavatera 'Barnsley'* Dark-eyed blush; summer and autumn. 8ft (2.4m)

Potentilla fruticosa 'Goldstar' Bright yellow; spring-autumn. 3ft (90cm)

Potentilla fruticosa 'Red Robin' Brick-red; spring-autumn. 2ft (60cm)

Rosa 'Perdita' Apricot blush, quartered; wonderful scent. 3ft (90cm)†

♀   *Syringa microphylla 'Superba'* Rosy-pink; spring-autumn. 6ft (1.8m)

---

†   Many other English roses have a long season; see page 262.

Winter-flowering†

Winter-flowering varieties are even fewer than those which flower in autumn and they tend to be concentrated in relatively few species, some of which feature quite a number of good varieties.

℧ *Chaenomeles* × *superba* 'Rowallane' Bright red, early; thorny. 6ft (1.8m)

℧ *Cornus mas* Small yellow fragrant flowers; red berries. 12ft (3.6m)

℧ *Daphne bholua* 'Gurkha' Purple and white, highly fragrant. 3ft (90cm)

Daphne jezoensis Golden yellow, scented; tricky to grow. 2ft (60cm)

Daphne mezereum Purple and white forms; sweetly scented. 2ft (60cm)

Forsythia viridissima 'Bronxensis' Earliest forsythia; dwarf. 2ft (60cm)

Hamamelis × *intermedia* 'Advent' Bright yellow, the earliest. 6ft (1.8m)

℧ *Hamamelis* × *intermedia* 'Jelena' Coppery orange; less scent. 6ft (1.8m)

℧* *Hamamelis* × *intermedia*'Pallida' Yellow, fragrant, spidery. 6ft (1.8m)

℧ *Jasminum nudiflorum* Bright yellow on green stems; tough. 6ft (1.8m)

Lonicera fragrantissima Small, creamy white; red berries. 6ft (1.8m)

℧ *Lonicera* × *purpusii* 'Winter Beauty' Extra prolific; vigorous. 8ft (2.4m)

℧ *Rhododendron* 'Emasculum' Lilac-pink, reliable; acid soil. 2ft (60cm)

Rhododendron mucronulatum Bright purplish pink; acid soil. 4ft (1.2m)

℧ *Salix daphnoides* 'Aglaia' Yellow catkins, red stems; 4ft (1.2m) if pruned.

Salix × *rubra* 'Eugenei' Greyish pink catkins; vigorous. 10ft (3m)

℧ *Stachyurus praecox* Long strings of creamy bells; red stems. 10ft (3m)

℧ *Viburnum* × *bodnantense* 'Charles Lamont' Pink; scented. 8ft (2.4m)

℧ *Viburnum* × *bodnantense* 'Dawn' Blushed white, sweet scent. 8ft (2.4m)

Viburnum farreri 'Candidissimum' Pure white; scented. 5ft (1.5m)

---

† Many are scented; shelter helps prevent the scent dispersing.

Attractive flowers†

There is a great profusion of deciduous shrubs with good flowers, but as most of us garden in relatively modest gardens we have space for only a few. None of those listed here will disappoint.

WHITE FLOWERS

Some white-flowered shrubs are actually slightly creamy, others may be a little blushed but they all bring brilliance and clarity.

℣ *Amelanchier lamarckii* Pure flowers with new coppery leaves. sp
   Buddleja davidii 'Peace' Long spikes; deadhead promptly. su
   Chaenomeles speciosa 'Nivalis' One of the finest chaenomeles. sp
   Cytisus praecox 'Albus' Fountain of scented white pea flowers. sp
   Deutzia scabra 'Candidissima' Pure white, double; scented. su
℣ *Exochorda macrantha* 'The Bride' Fleeting but spectacular. su
℣ *Hibiscus syriacus* 'Diana' Pure white, crimped, single flowers. au
℣ *Hydrangea paniculata* 'Grandiflora' Huge spikes; prune hard. su
℣ *Lonicera* × *purpusii* 'Winter Beauty' Creamy and fragrant. wi
℣ *Magnolia* × *soulangeana* 'Lennei Alba' Huge white chalices. sp
℣ *Magnolia stellata* Ragged white stars; compact and twiggy. sp
℣ *Philadelphus* 'Belle Etoile' Single white, deep pink at the base. su
℣ *Potentilla fruticosa* 'Abbotswood' Pure white; greyish leaves. su
℣ *Rubus* 'Benenden' Like big gold-eyed roses; good in shade. su
   Spiraea japonica var. albiflora Flat heads of fluffy flowers. su
℣ *Spiraea thunbergii* Heads of small white flowers line branches, sp
℣ *Syringa vulgaris* 'Madame Lemoine' Double; cream buds. sp
   Viburnum × *carlesii* 'Charis' Pink buds open white; fragrant. sp
   Viburnum farreri 'Candidissimum' Pure white, sweet scent. wi
℣* *Viburnum plicatum* 'Mariesii' Lacecaps line horizontal shoots. sp

---

†   In this section sp=spring, su=summer, au=autumn, wi=winter.

PINK FLOWERS

Fixing the lines between pink and red, pink and mauve, pink and lilac is not easy and there are so many different shades from blushed white to deep rose to salmon that this list is a mixed one.

♈ *Buddleja 'Pink Delight'* Unusually long spikes of bright pink. su
   Ceanothus × *pallidus 'Marie Simon'* The only pink ceanothus. su
♈ *Chaenomeles speciosa 'Moerloosei'* Pink, paling to white. sp
♈ *Deutzia* × *elegantissima 'Rosealind'* Carmine pink; fragrant. su
♈ *Hibiscus syriacus 'Hamabo'* Very pale pink, darker eye. su/au
   Hydrangea macrophylla 'Mariesii' Lacecap; blue on acid soil. su
♈ *Hydrangea 'Preziosa'* Shining rose pink, steadily deepening. su
♈ *Kolkwitzia amabilis 'Pink Cloud'* Pink with a yellow throat. su
   Lonicera tatarica 'Zabelii' Small, pale pink clusters; tough. su
♈* *Magnolia* × *loebneri 'Leonard Messel'* Pale lilac rose; tall. sp†
   Phygelius × *rectus 'Pink Elf'* Long pale trumpets, red lips. su
   Potentilla fruticosa 'Princess' Soft pink; best in half shade. su
♈ *Prunus tenella 'Fire Hill'* Brilliant thicket former; suckers. sp
♈ *Prunus triloba 'Multiplex'* Double rose; prune after flowers. sp
   Rubus ulmifolius 'Bellidiflorus' Double pink spikes; vigorous. su
♈ *Syringa* × *hyacinthiflora 'Esther Staley'* The best pink lilac. sp
   Tamarix ramosissima 'Pink Cascade' Feathery plumes. su
♈ *Viburnum* × *bodnantense 'Dawn'* Tough and sweetly scented. wi
♈ *Viburnum* × *carlesii 'Aurora'* Exquisite penetrating scent. sp
   Weigela 'Boskoop Glory' The palest readily available form. su.

---

†   This is one of the few magnolias to thrive on both acid and chalk.

RED FLOWERS

Here too there is a difficult dividing line between red and pink and between red and purple. There are few real scarlet varieties but sultry crimson shades more than make up for their absence.

℣ *Abutilon 'Ashford Red'* Deep pink-tinted red; rather tender. su/au†
  Buddleja colvilei 'Kewensis' Deep red drooping spikes. su†
℣ *Buddleja davidii 'Royal Red'* Huge, slightly purplish spikes. su
  Calycanthus occidentalis Unusual reddish-brown; scented. su/au
  Chaenomeles × superba 'Firedance' Brilliant scarlet; spiny. sp
℣ *Clerodendrum bungei* Flat heads, slightly pink-tinted; scented. su
  Cornus florida f. rubra Bold rosy red bracts; often spectacular. sp
  Cytisus 'Killiney Red' Rich, slightly chestnut-red; full sun. sp/su
℣ *Erythrina crista-gallii* Huge spikes of scarlet flowers; tender. su†
  Fuchsia 'Rufus' Entirely red; very prolific; not the hardiest. su/au
℣ *Hydrangea macrophylla 'Geoffrey Chadbund'* Brick red. su
  Lonicera tatarica 'Hack's Red' Darkest form; very striking. su
℣ *Paeonia delavayi* Crimson-red tree peony; sumptuous foliage. sp
  Potentilla fruticosa 'Red Robin' Slightly bricky shade; fades. su
* *Ribes sanguineum 'King Edward VII'* Crimson; darkest form. sp
℣ *Ribes speciosum* Small, scarlet, fuchsia-like flowers; spiny. sp†
  Salvia microphylla var. neurepia Slightly rosy red; tender. su/au
℣ *Spiraea japonica 'Anthony Waterer'* Glowing pale crimson. su
℣ *Tamarix ramosissima 'Rubra'* Slender red feathery plumes. su
  Weigela 'Bristol Ruby' Deep red; upright; tough and reliable. sp

---

†   Best grown either trained on a wall or sheltered by a wall.

YELLOW FLOWERS

Yellow covers varieties in rich cream, orange tinges and also gold, although this is a word much overused to describe flowers; in fact it often pays to beware of words like cream, primrose and gold.

♀ *Berberis thunbergii* Dainty yellow flowers with red streaks. sp

♀ *Buddleja globosa* Bright orange balls; 'Lemon Ball' is yellow. su

♀ *Cornus mas* Clusters of small, fragrant greeny yellow flowers. wi

♀ *Corylopsis pauciflora* Most colourful of this valuable group. wi

♀ *Corylus avellana 'Contorta'* Yellow catkins on twisted shoots. wi

♀ *Cytisus* × *beanii* Rich yellow pea flowers on low mound. sp

♀* *Cytisus* × *praecox 'Allgold'* Bright yellow, arching shoots. sp†

♀ *Forsythia 'Lynwood'* Buttercup yellow and very tough. sp

♀ *Fothergilla major* Tufts of fluffy creamy white flowers. wi

   Genista hispanica Yellow pea flowers; long season; spiny. sp/su

♀ *Hamamelis* × *intermedia 'Pallida'* Spidery and fragrant. wi

♀ *Kerria japonica 'Pleniflora'* Double rich yellow, green stems. sp

♀ *Paeonia delavayi var. ludlowii* Buttercup-yellow tree peony. sp

♀ *Phlomis fruticosa* Whorls of bright yellow amid grey leaves. su

   Phygelius aequalis 'Yellow Trumpet' Long yellow trumpets. su

♀ *Potentilla fruticosa 'Elizabeth'* Bright buttercup yellow. sp-au

   Ribes odoratum Clusters of rich yellow, clove-scented flowers. sp

♀ *Stachyurus praecox* Small yellow bells; spreading habit. wi

   Syringa vulgaris 'Primrose' As near to yellow as lilacs come. sp

   Weigela middendorffiana Yellow, orange markings in throat. su

---

† Pruning back hard soon after flowering helps prevent lank growth.

BLUE FLOWERS

So many blues are either purple, lavender or lilac that finding true blues is rather difficult and it turns out that there are not very many.

- ♀ *Buddleja davidii 'Empire Blue'* A gem among buddleias. su†
- *Buddleja davidii 'Nanho Blue'* Superb, rounded, compact form. su†
- *Caryopteris × clandonensis 'Kew Blue'* Prolific bright blue. su/au†
- ♀* *Ceanothus × delileanus 'Gloire de Versailles'* Clouds of blue. su/au
- ♀ *Ceratostigma willmottianum* Sparkling blue, helpfully late. au
- ♀ *Hibiscus syriacus 'Oiseau Bleu'* Best single blue hibiscus. su/au
- ♀ *Hydrangea macrophylla 'Altona'* Blue on acid soil; likes shade. su
- ♀ *Hydrangea macrophylla 'Mariesii Perfecta'* Superb lacecap. su
- ♀ *Perovskia atriplicifolia 'Blue Spire'* Elegant slender spikes. su/au†
- ♀ *Syringa vulgaris 'Firmament'* Nearest to true blue; scented. su

PURPLE FLOWERS

Many purple flowers have too much red in them to qualify and those that belong here need careful placing to reveal their dark beauty.

- ♀ *Buddleja davidii 'Black Knight'* Deep, sultry slender spikes. su†
- ♀* *Buddleja davidii 'Dartmoor'* Rather pinky but huge flat heads. su†
- *Cercis siliquastrum 'Bodnant'* Rich purple pea flowers. su
- *Daphne mezereum* Small, highly fragrant flowers line shoots. wi
- *Hibiscus syriacus 'Violet Clair Double'* The richest form. su/au
- ♀ *Indigofera heterantha* Clouds of pea flowers at a useful season. au†
- ♀ *Magnolia liliflora 'Nigra'* Huge deep purple goblets; acid soil. sp
- ♀ *Rhododendron dauricum 'Midwinter'* Good colour; acid soil. wi
- *Rubus odoratus* Large, fragrant, slightly rosy; vigorous. su
- ♀ *Syringa vulgaris 'Charles Joly'* Richest purple, fragrant. sp

---

†   Prune back very hard every year just as growth starts.

SCENTED FLOWERS

Scented shrubs are essential features of any garden and varieties are available for all seasons. They are best planted in sheltered places, so the scent lingers, and near paths, gates and doorways.

Abeliophyllum distichum Vanilla scent; like a white forsythia. wi

♀ *Aesculus parviflora* Heavy sweet scent from white candles. su

Buddleja davidii All forms are honey-scented; many colours. su

♀ *Clethra alnifolia 'Paniculata'* Pleasing scent; white spikes. su

♀ *Corylopsis sinensis* Fragile cowslip scent from yellow strings. sp

♀ *Cytisus × praecox 'Warminster'* Heavy, even overpowering. sp

Daphne All are scented to some extent, many very sweetly. wi/sp

♀ *Elaeagnus 'Quicksilver'* Very sweet; tiny flowers; silver leaves. su

♀ *Fothergilla major* Slightly hoppy scent; fluffy white flowers. wi

♀ *Hamamelis mollis* All are sweet, sometimes slightly fruity. wi

Lonicera fragrantissima Best scented shrubby honeysuckle. wi

♀ *Philadelphus 'Belle Etoile'* Essential familiar fragrance; white. su

Rhododendron Deciduous azaleas, especially Ghent group. sp

Ribes odoratum Slightly clove-scented yellow flowers. sp

Rosa Vast range of perfumes from both old and modern types. su†

Rubus odoratus Summer scent from vigorous suckering shrub. su

♀ *Spartium junceum* Vanilla-scented yellow pea flowers; tall. sp

Syringa Scent varies but tall and bushy forms are invaluable. sp/su

Viburnum × bodnantense All forms are invaluable and hardy. wi

* *Viburnum carlesii* Penetrating sweet, clovish scent; all superb. sp

---

†   For list of scented roses see page 000.

--------------------------- **Attractive foliage** ---------------------------

The foliage of deciduous shrubs is especially valuable, as not only does it have
its variegations and colourings but it has the additional feature of changing
through the season from unfurling to leaf drop.

VARIEGATED LEAVES – EDGED

Varieties in which the leaves are edged in yellow, cream or white depend for
their effect on the width of the border; those with wide margins look very
bright, those with a narrow edge create a softer, more subtle effect.

℞ *Aralia elata 'Variegata'* Fine pale line around bold leaves. 7ft (2.1m)
  Buddleja davidii 'Harlequin' Cream-edged 'Royal Red'. 6ft (1.8m)†
  Buddleja davidii 'White Harlequin' Cream-edge; white spikes. 6ft (1.8m)†
℞ *Cornus alba 'Elegantissima'* White-edged, grey-green leaves. 6ft (1.8m)
℞ *Cornus alba 'Spaethii'* Gold-edged; red stems in winter. 6ft (1.8m)
℞ *Cornus alternifolia 'Argentea'* White-edged; tiered habit. 10ft (3m)
℞ *Cotoneaster atropurpureus 'Variegata'* Cream rim; spreading. 2ft (60cm)
  Daphne × burkwoodii 'Carol Mackie' Deep yellow to cream. 2ft (60cm)
  Fuchsia magellanica 'Sharpitor' Grey-green, edged white. 4ft (1.2m)
  Hibiscus syriacus 'Meehanii' Cream edge; flowers mauve. 4ft (1.2m)
  Kerria japonica 'Picta' Cream edge; single yellow flowers. 3ft (90cm)
  Ligustrum ovalifolium 'Argenteum' Pale green, cream edge. 6ft (1.8m)
℞ *Philadelphus coronarius 'Variegatus'* Cream edge; shade. 3ft (90cm)
  Philadelphus 'Innocence' Cream edge; white, scented; strong. 5ft (1.5m)
  Potentilla fruticosa 'Abbotswood Silver' White edge; reverts. 3ft (90cm)
  Sambucus nigra 'Marginata' Creamy edge; best pruned hard. 6ft (1.8m)
  Symphoricarpus orbiculatus 'Foliis Variegatus' Yellow edge. 6ft (1.8m)
  Syringa emodi 'Aureovariegata' Yellow edge; poor scent. 8ft (2.4m)
* *Weigela 'Florida Variegata'* Cream edge; pink flowers; superb. 5ft (1.5m)
℞ *Weigela 'Praecox Variegata'* Yellow edge fading to white. 5ft (1.5m)

----

† 'Harlequin' is quite stable, 'White Harlequin' throws green shoots.

VARIEGATED LEAVES — SPLASHED

Not all gardeners appreciate shrubs with splashed leaves, and they often look better seen from a distance rather than from close to.

* * *Acer crataegifolium* 'Veitchii' Small leaves, speckled white. 8ft (2.4m)
* *Acer palmatum* 'Asahai-zuru' Best of many speckled forms. 8ft (2.4m)
* *Berberis thunbergii* 'Silver Beauty' Green, speckled cream. 4ft (1.2m)
* *Euonymus europaeus* 'Aucubifolius' Mottled cream and white. 8ft (2.4m)
* *Hoheria populnea* 'Variegata' Slightly greenish yellow centre. 8ft (2.4m)
* *Lavatera* 'Wembdon Variegated' Yellow splashes; pink bowls. 6ft (1.8m)
* *Ribes americanum* 'Variegatum' Mottled cream and pale green. 3ft (90cm)
* *Sambucus nigra* 'Pulverulenta' Dark green, tiny white spots. 10ft (3m)
* *Spiraea japonica* 'Pink Ice' White-marbled; purplish flowers. 2ft (60cm)
* *Stachyurus chinensis* 'Magpie' Creamy edge plus speckles. 8ft (2.4m)

MULTICOLOURED LEAVES†

These are the love 'em or hate 'em plants which some gardeners drool over but which others refuse to allow into their garden.

* ♉ *Acer negundo* 'Flamingo' Grey, pink and white; pollard. 6ft (1.8m).
* *Berberis thunbergii* 'Golden Ring' Purple, narrow gold rim. 5ft (1.5m)
* *Cornus florida* 'Welchii' Green, cream edge, flushed pink. 6ft (1.8m)
* ♉ *Fuchsia magellanica* 'Versicolor' Grey-green, white and pink. 3ft (90cm)
* *Hydrangea macrophylla* 'Quadricolor' Green, cream, yellow. 3ft (90cm)
* *Hypericum* 'Gladys Brabazon' Pink, white, green; weak. 2ft (60cm)
* * *Hypericum* × *moserianum* 'Tricolor' Gold edged, tinged pink. 2ft (60cm)
* *Salix integra* 'Hakuru-nishiki' Green and white, flushed pink. 6ft (1.8m)
* *Sambucus racemosa* 'Plumosa Aurea' Bronze then yellow. 12ft (3.6m)
* ♉ *Spiraea japonica* 'Anthony Waterer' Splashed pink, cream. 2ft (60cm)

---

† These are often slower and trickier than green-leaved sorts.

GOLD AND YELLOW LEAVES

Most yellow-and gold-leaved varieties fade to green during the season, some keep their colour longer than others. Some are best in partial shade to prevent scorch, others will happily take full sun.

♡ *Acer shirasawanum 'Aureum'* Keeps colour well; shade. 6ft (1.8m)

Berberis thunbergii 'Aurea' Spectacular; best in some shade. 3ft (90cm)

Cornus alba 'Aurea' Soft yellow; usually scorches in full sun. 6ft (1.8m)

Cornus mas 'Aurea' Yellow, then lime; yellow winter flowers. 8ft (2.4m)

Corylus avellana 'Aurea' Bold yellow leaves if pruned often. 8ft (2.4m)

Hypericum inodorum 'Ysella' Gold, fades to green; scorches. 2ft (60cm)

♡ *Philadelphus coronarius 'Aureus'* Yellow or limy; scorches. 6ft (1.8m)

♡ *Physocarpus opulifolius 'Dart's Gold'* Very bright; prolific. 6ft (1.8m)

Ribes alpinum 'Aureum' Yellow then green; spreading habit. 2ft (60cm)

♡ *Ribes sanguineum 'Brocklebankii'* Soft yellow; light shade. 3ft (90cm)

* *Rubus cockburnianus 'Golden Vale'* Yellow; white stems. 6ft (1.8m)

Rubus idaeus 'Aureus' Yellow-leaved raspberry; some fruit. 4ft (1.2m)

Rubus parviflorus 'Sunshine Spreader' Gold all season. 2ft (60cm)†

♡ *Sambucus nigra 'Aurea'* Greeny gold; best pruned each spring. 5ft (1.5m)

♡ *Sambucus racemosa 'Sutherland Gold'* Resistant to scorch. 8ft (2.4m)

♡ *Spiraea japonica 'Gold Mound'* Rich, slightly orangey gold. 2ft (60cm)

Syringa vulgaris 'Aurea' Yellow then green; lilac flowers. 10ft (3m)

Viburnum opulus 'Aureum' Yellow, then lime; light shade. 4ft (1.2m)

Weigela 'Looymansii Aurea' Pale yellow then green; shade. 3ft (90cm)

Weigela 'Olympiade' Yellow sport of 'Bristol Ruby'; shade. 3ft (90cm)

---

† A new plant which doesn't scorch and makes good ground cover.

SILVER AND GREY LEAVES

Many silver-leaved deciduous shrubs are adapted to grow in relatively hot and dry conditions although this is less universal than with evergreens so the planting site must be considered carefully.

Amorpha canescens Grey acacia-like leaves; violet flowers. 5ft (1.5m)

Atriplex halimus Good grey leaves; sometimes semi-evergreen. 4ft (1.2m)

♈ *Berberis dictyophylla* Spectacular grey leaves; upright growth. 6ft (1.8m)

Buddleja alternifolia 'Argentea' Silky, silvery leaves; weeping. 6ft (1.8m)

♈ *Buddleja fallowiana 'Alba'* Woolly foliage; slightly tender. 8ft (2.4m)

Caryopteris × *clandonensis* Grey-green, aromatic; blue spikes. 2ft (60cm)

♈ *Elaeagnus angustifolia* Grey, willowy foliage; vigorous, spiny. 6ft (1.8m)

♈ *Hippophaë rhamnoides* Clear silver; any soil; suckers. 12ft (3.6m)

Lotus hirsutus Small silver leaves; white flowers; full sun. 2ft (60cm)

♈ *Perovskia atriplicifolia* Grey, deeply cut leaves; blue spikes. 2ft (60cm)

♈* *Potentilla fruticosa 'Beesii'* Silver leaves, yellow flowers. 2ft (60cm)

Potentilla fruticosa 'Manchu' Silver leaves, white flowers. 2ft (60cm)

Rosa fedtschenkoana Sea-green foliage; single white flowers. 6ft (1.8m)

♈ *Rosa glauca* Red-tinted, grey leaves on red stems; pink flowers. 6ft (1.8m)

Rubus thibetanus 'Silver Fern' Small dissected silvery leaves. 4ft (1.2m)

Salix exigua Slim, silver leaves on slender brown branches. 10ft (3m)†

♈ *Salix lanata* Downy grey leaves; yellow catkins in spring. 2ft (60cm)

Salix lapponum Downy grey leaves; dwarf, spreading shrub. 18in (45cm)

Sibiraea altaiensis Sea-green leaves on spiraea-like plant; rare. 4ft (1.2m)

Zauschneria californica ssp. mexicana Grey leaf; red flowers. 2ft (60cm)

---

† Although a lovely plant, this can sucker alarmingly at times

PURPLE AND BRONZE LEAVES

Purple-leaved shrubs must be used with caution and the larger they grow the more caution is required; too many can make the garden look funereal yet one or two strategically placed are invaluable.

♈ *Acer palmatum 'Bloodgood'* Richest colour; red in autumn. 10ft (3m)

* *Acer palmatum 'Dissectum Nigrum'* Purplish red, finely cut. 4ft (1.2m)

♈ *Berberis thunbergii 'Bagatelle'* Neat, rounded purple balls. 18in (45cm)†

Berberis thunbergii 'Dart's Red Lady' Arching habit. 2ft (60cm)†

Berberis thunbergii 'Helmund Pillar' Narrow purple pillar. 4ft (1.2m)†

♈ *Berberis × ottawensis 'Superba'* Wine red; yellow flowers. 10ft (3m).†

♈ *Cercis canadensis 'Forest Pansy'* Purple then red in autumn. 10ft (3m)

♈ *Corylus maxima 'Purpurea'* Rich colour; can be too dark. 12ft (3.6m).

♈ *Cotinus coggygria 'Royal Purple'* The darkest; pinky flowers. 8ft (2.4m)

♈ *Cotinus 'Grace'* Soft purple, scarlet in autumn; pink flowers. 10ft (3m)

Hoheria populnea 'Foliis Purpureus' Purple below leaves. 12ft (3.6m).

Hypericum × inodorum 'Albury Purple' Also yellow flowers. 3ft (90cm)

♈ *Prunus × blireana* Coppery purple; fragrant pink flowers. 12ft (3.6m)

♈ *Prunus × cistena* Purple leaves; white flowers; black fruits. 5ft (1.5m)

Prunus persica 'Rubira' Dark reddish purple; pink flowers. 6ft (1.8m)

Prunus spinosa 'Purpurea' Purple white flowers; choice. 6ft (1.8m)

♈ *Sambucus nigra 'Guincho Purple'* Purple, greening later. 12ft (3.6m)

♈ *Viburnum sargentii 'Onondaga'* Bronzed; white lacecaps. 5ft (1.5m)

♈ *Weigela florida 'Foliis Purpureis'* Purple; pretty pink flowers. 3ft (90cm)

Weigela 'Victoria' Darker leaves and flowers than above form. 3ft (90cm)

---

† The purple-leaved berberis are the finest and easiest of them all.

AUTUMN-COLOURING LEAVES

Autumn-colouring shrubs bring character to the autumn garden and associate well with autumn flowers like Michaelmas daisies and sedums; unfortunately quality of colour varies from year to year.†

♀ *Acer japonicum 'Aconitifolium'* Stunning crimson; reliable. 6ft (1.8m)

♀* *Acer palmatum 'Ozakazuki'* Best form for scarlet colour. 10ft (3m)

♀ *Aesculus parviflora* Red in spring, bright yellow in autumn. 10ft (3m)

♀ *Amelanchier lamarckii* Genuinely fiery foliage; red fruits. 15ft (4.5m)

♀ *Berberis thunbergii* All have good red or orange colour. 1–8ft
(30cm–2.4m)

♀ *Berberis wilsoniae* Coral and orange; berries in similar shades. 4ft (1.2m)

♀ *Ceratostigma willmottianum* Red; superb with blue flowers. 3ft (90cm)

Cornus kousa Orange, red and crimson; best on acid soil. 8ft (2.4m)

♀ *Cotinus coggygria* All forms turn scarlet; many good forms. 10ft (3m)

♀ *Cotoneaster horizontalis* Red; looks good with its red berries. 2ft (60cm)

♀ *Enkianthus campanulatus* Red, orange and yellow; acid soil. 8ft (2.4m)

♀ *Euonymus alatus* Vivid pinky scarlet; dependable; adaptable. 5ft (1.5m)

Fothergilla monticola Yellow and orange; best autumn species. 6ft (1.8m)

♀ *Hamamelis mollis* Orangey-yellow; yellow, scented flowers. 10ft (3m)

Rhododendron Mainly Ghent and Occidentalis azaleas. 4–8ft (1.2–2.4m)

♀ *Rhus hirta* Drips with orange and yellow; females often best. 10ft (3m)

Ribes odoratum Pink and yellow; clove-scented flowers. 6ft (1.8m)

Rosa rugosa Clear yellow; many good flower forms; tough. 4–6ft
(1.2–1.8m)

Stephanandra incisa 'Crispa' Pale orange; white flowers. 2ft (60cm)

Viburnum opulus Yellow; red or yellow fruits; many forms. 10ft (3m)

---

† Heavy soil and long spells of cool but not frosty weather is best.

AROMATIC LEAVES

Evergreens have the edge when it comes to aromatic foliage but there are still some deciduous types worth considering.

Abelia × *grandiflora* Pungent when crushed; blushed flowers. 4ft (1.2m)

*   *Aloysia triphylla* Lemon verbena; strong lemon-scented leaves. 3ft (90cm)

Artemisia arbrotanum Southernwood. Sweet, grey-green leaf. 2ft (60cm)

Caryopteris × *clandonensis* Noticeably aromatic; blue spikes. 2ft (60cm)

♀ *Clerodendrum bungei* Pungent, perhaps, rather than aromatic. 3ft (90cm)

Elscholtzia stauntonii Delightful minty aroma; purple spikes. 3ft (90cm)

Myrica gale Strongly aromatic; poor flowers; loves bogs. 6ft (1.8m)

♀ *Perovskia atriplicifolia* Silvery aromatic leaves; blue spikes. 2ft (60cm)

♀ *Ptelea trifoliata* Intense bitter aroma; fragrant flowers too. 12ft (3.6m)

Ribes sanguineum Aromatic foliage; less than fragrant flowers. 6ft (1.8m)

BOLD FOLIAGE

The boldness and opulence of large luxuriant foliage is always worth treasuring and worth planting where winds will not shred it.

♀ *Aesculus parviflora* 5 or 7 red-tinted leaflets up to 9in (23cm) long. 10ft (3m)

♀ *Aralia elata* Vast, elegant, twice divided and often greyish. 10ft (3m)

Clerodendron trichotomum Large, oval and slightly purplish. 8ft (2.4m)

Decaisnea fargesii 2ft (60cm) long, divided like roses; rather greyish. 10ft (3m)

♀ *Hydrangea quercifolia* Like dark, soft, veined 8in (20cm) oak leaves. 5ft (1.5m)

♀ *Paeonia delavayi* Large, deeply divided and red tinted in spring. 8ft (2.4m)

♀ *Paulownia tomentosa* 2ft (60cm), heart-shaped; prune hard in spring. 6ft (1.8m)†

♀* *Rhus hirta 'Laciniata'* 18in (45cm) long, regularly divided, lacily cut. 12ft (3.6m)

Sambucus canadensis 'Maxima' 18in (45cm) long; huge white heads. 6ft (1.8m)

♀ *Sorbaria tomentosa* Long rows of toothed leaflets; suckers. 10ft (3m)

---

†   This and other shrubs will produce larger leaves if cut back hard.

LACY AND DIVIDED FOLIAGE

To balance bold foliage and create lighter effects, foliage which is repeatedly or neatly divided is useful though it can be scorched.

℣ *Acer palmatum 'Dissectum'* Entrancing lacy-leaved maple. 4ft (1.2m)

Amorpha canescens Neat and regularly divided; violet flowers. 8ft (2.4m)

℣ *Artemisia abrotanum* Grey-green and a foam of slivers. 2ft (60cm)

Lupinus arboreus Small, lupin-like leaves on rounded shrubs. 5ft (1.5m)

Perovskia atriplicifolia Small, silvery, stiff and neatly divided. 2ft (60cm)

Rubus thibetanus 'Silver Fern' Silvered, sharply cut leaves. 6ft (1.8m)

Sambucus nigra 'Laciniata' Finely divided, almost fern like. 8ft (2.4m)

Sambucus racemosa 'Tenuifolia' Like a tough cut-leaved acer. 3ft (90cm)

Stephanandra incisa 'Crispa' Prettily divided and crinkled. 18in (45cm)

Tamarix gallica Feathery sea-green leaves; pink flowers. 8ft (2.4m)

Attractive fruits

With evergreen shrubs, the berries are set off by a background of good green foliage; deciduous foliage colours sympathetically.

RED BERRIES

Red berries often have the greatest initial impact and harmonize well with autumn leaves, but they may also be a first course for birds.

Berberis × *carminea 'Buccaneer'* Huge berries in fat clusters. 6ft (1.8m)

℣ *Cornus 'Norman Hadden'* Large, strawberry-shaped fruits. 8ft (2.4m)

Cotoneaster frigidus Deep red berries weigh down branches. 15ft (4.5m)

Daphne mezerum Bright red, crowding shoots; but poisonous. 2ft (60cm)

℣ *Euonymus europaeus 'Red Cascade'* Slightly rosy red. 10ft (3m)

℣ *Rosa 'Geranium'* Huge crimson flagons follow red flowers. 7ft (2.1m)†

Rosa rugosa Single forms especially have huge bright hips. 6ft (1.8m)†

℣ *Sambucus racemosa 'Sutherland Gold'* Best left unpruned. 10ft (3m)

* *Viburnum betulifolium* Bare shoots drip with glistening beads. 8ft (2.4m)

℣ *Viburnum opulus 'Compactum'* Perfect fruiter for tiny garden. 4ft (1.2m)

---

† For other roses with good fruits see page 000.

YELLOW AND ORANGE BERRIES

Orange and yellow are often the second preferences for the birds, so especially in mild years may stay uneaten until well into winter.

    Chaenomeles japonica Round yellow aromatic quinces. 8ft (2.4m)

    Citrus × *sinensis* 'Meyer' Hardiest but needs wall protection. 4ft (1.2m)

♕ *Cydonia oblonga* 'Vranja' Large pear-shaped yellow quinces. 12ft (3.6m)

    Daphne caucasica Yellow berries follow white spring flowers. 2ft (60cm)

♕ *Elaeagnus angustifolia* Orange berries on mature plants; spiny. 6ft (1.8m)

♕* *Hippophaë rhamnoides* Orange-yellow; both sexes needed. 12ft (3.6m)

    Poncirus trifoliata Fruits like small lemons; not fully hardy. 6ft (1.8m)

♕ *Rosa macrophylla* 'Master Hugh' Orange; largest of rose hips. 6ft (1.8m)

    Rubus phoenicolasius Wineberry; very sweet orangey fruits. 6ft (1.8m)†

♕ *Viburnum opulus* 'Xanthocarpum' Clear golden-yellow. 10ft (3m)

PINK AND WHITE BERRIES

Progressing through the colours they become increasingly ignored by birds; pinks and whites seem to both last well and show up well.

♕* *Berberis* 'Rubrostilla' Unusually large berries in dark coral. 5ft (1.5m)

♕ *Berberis wilsoniae* Coral pink with orange and pink leaves. 4ft (1.2m)

    Callicarpa japonica 'Leucocarpa' Small white; best in groups. 6ft (1.8m)

    Cornus stolonifera White fruits when not pruned annually. 4ft (1.2m)

    Daphne mezereum 'Bowles Variety' White fruits and flowers. 2ft (60cm)

    Euonymus hamiltonianus ssp. sieboldianus Pink, prolific. 10ft (3m)

    Myrica pensylvanica White; best in dry acid soil; good by sea. 6ft (1.8m)

♕ *Sorbus reducta* White flushed pink; dwarf, usually suckers. 2ft (60cm)

    Symphoricarpus × *doorenbosii* 'Magic Berry' Pink; neat. 6ft (1.8m)

    Symphoricarpus × *doorenbosii* 'White Hedge' White; upright. 8ft (2.4m)

---

†   There are also two yellow raspberries, 'Golden Everest' and 'Fallgold'.

PURPLE, BLUE AND BLACK BERRIES

Sometimes gobbled with unseemly haste yet sometimes left to rot, berries in dark shades may be less noticeable than other colours.

♀ *Amelanchier lamarckii* Early black berries; very reliable. 15ft (4.5m)

♀ *Callicarpa bodinieri 'Profusion'* Small, violet; best in groups. 6ft (1.8m)

♀* *Clerodendrum trichotomum var. fargesii* Brilliant blue. 6ft (1.8m)

   Cornus amomum Small, pale blue; purple winter stems; rare. 6ft (1.8m)

   Leycesteria formosa Reddish purple berries; often eaten early. 5ft (1.5m)

   Rhamnus frangula Red turning to black; good in damp sites. 8ft (2.4m)

   Ribes odoratum Black, after yellow clove-scented flowers. 6ft (1.8m)

   Rosa pimpinellifolia Black, or sometimes purplish black, hips. 4ft (1.2m)

   Symplococus paniculata Bright blue; best in groups; acid soil. 10ft

   Viburnum lantana Red at first, then black; good on chalk. 10ft (3m)

FRUITS WITH OTHER DECORATIVE FEATURES

Berries may be the most obvious form of decorative fruits but many shrubs have fruits with other features or unusual colouring.

   Colutea arborescens Curious, inflated, red-tinted bladders. 8ft (2.4m)

   Coriaria terminalis var. xanthocarpa Yellow fleshy petals. 3ft (90cm)

   Cotinus coggygria 'Purpureus' Fluffy pink seed heads. 10ft (3m)

*   *Decaisnea fargesii* Strange, metallic blue, broad bean pods. 10ft (3m)

   Lotus hirsutus Small reddish pea pods follow white flowers. 2ft (60cm)†

♀ *Ptelea trifoliata* Large clusters of flat, green winged fruits. 12ft (3.6m)

♀ *Rhus hirta* Heads of deep red fruits at branch tips on females. 12ft (3.6m)

♀ *Staphylea colchica* Fat grey-green bladders; white flowers. 8ft (2.4m)

   Staphylea holocarpa 'Rosea' Inflated pods; soft pink flowers. 8ft (2.4m)

   Viburnum opulus 'Fructuluteo' Yellow berries tinted pink. 10ft (3m)

---

†   The fruits look lovely set against the grey foliage. Self-sows.

CLIMBERS AND WALL SHRUBS

This section covers true climbers and a certain number of shrubs which are especially suited to growing on walls, fences and trellis.

Spring-flowering

As well as the clematis, listed separately, many early-flowering shrubs appreciate the shelter of a warm wall.

Climbers

Spring is a good season for twining and clinging climbers with three large groups at their best, plenty of others and many scented.

Akebia quinata Scented reddish purple flowers; good in trees. 15ft (4.5m)

Akebia trifoliata Dark purple flowered twiner; mauve fruits. 15ft (4.5m)

Clematis large-flowered Late spring, early summer; list page 266.

* *Clematis small-flowered* Specialities of spring; see list page 265.

Jasminum beesianum Unexpectedly deep red; fragrant. 10ft (3m)

♈ *Jasminum* × *stephanense* Pink, fragrant, prolific; south wall. 10ft (3m)

Lonicera periclymenum All forms good and fragrant; twiners. 12ft (3.6m)

Schisandra rubriflora Crimson flowers then scarlet fruits. 10ft (3m)

♈ *Wisteria sinensis 'Alba'* Fragrant, pure white; exquisite. 25ft (7.5m)†

Wisteria sinensis 'Caroline' Genuinely early; mauve flowers. 30ft (9m)

Wall shrubs

Some spring wall shrubs need the shelter of a wall for themselves or their flowers, while tougher species just look good on walls.

Abeliophyllum distichum Like a small, pretty, white forsythia. 4ft (1.2m)

Abeliophyllum distichum 'Roseum' Pink version of above. 4ft (1.2m)

♈ *Camellia 'Jupiter'* Single, rich rose flowers; moist, acid soil. 6ft (1.8m)†

♈ *Ceanothus 'Delight'* Long spikes of rich blue; very hardy. 10ft (3m)†

♈ *Chaenomeles 'Pink Lady'* Prolific rose pink; for cold walls. 8ft (2.4m)†

Choisya ternata White scented flowers; best on warm wall. 6ft (1.8m)

Coronilla valentina All forms flower for longer on walls. 6ft (1.8m)

† There are many other excellent varieties of this plant which are suitable.

*   *Forsythia suspensa* 'Nymans' Primrose flowers; purple stems. 10ft (3m)
      Forsythia suspensa var. sieboldii Elegant drooping habit. 8ft (2.4m)
      Rosmarinus 'Sissinghurst' Good blue; prolific on warm wall. 4ft (1.2m)†

Attractive flowers

WHITE FLOWERS

Few white-flowered climbers and wall shrubs are pure white, most take on
pinky tints as they fade but are none the worse for that.

      Abeliophyllum distichum Blushes eventually; best in hot sun. 4ft (1.2m)
♀   *Camellia japonica* 'Nuccio's Gem' Neat double; compact. 4ft (1.2m)
      Chaenomeles speciosa 'Nivalis' Pure white, but not prolific. 12ft (3.6m)
♀   *Choisya* 'Aztec Pearl' Slightly pink-flushed white; fragrant. 6ft (1.8m)
♀   *Choisya ternata* Pure white, highly scented; very long season. 6ft (1.8m)
      Clematis alpina 'White Moth' Large, double; late, restrained. 6ft (1.8m)††
      Clematis armandii 'Snowdrift' Pure white; unpredictable. 20ft (6m)††
      Clematis 'James Mason' Dark-centred, prolific; second crop. 8ft (2.4m)
♀   *Wisteria floribunda* 'Alba' Occasionally tinted mauve at edges. 30ft (9m)
♀* *Wisteria sinensis* 'Alba' Pure white, superb scent; essential. 25ft (7.5m)

PINK FLOWERS

Pink-flowered varieties need choosing carefully, in full awareness of the
colour of the wall or fence on which they are to be grown.

      Abeliophyllum distichum 'Roseum' Frilly pink; purple stems. 4ft (1.2m)
♀   *Camellia japonica* 'Apple Blossom' Blushed pink, darker rim. 6ft (1.8m)
♀* *Chaenomeles speciosa* 'Moerloosei' Pink and white; sparse. 10ft (3m)
      Clematis alpina 'Willy' Pale pink; modest growth; self-clings. 8ft (2.4m)††
      Clematis armandii 'Apple Blossom' Blush pink; evergreen. 20ft (6m)††
♀   *Clematis montana* 'Elizabeth' Pale pink; vigorous and unruly. 25ft (7.5m)††
♀   *Clematis* 'Nelly Moser' The most famous variety; prune lightly. 8ft (2.4m)
      Lonicera japonica var. repens White, blushed pink; fragrant. 15ft (4.5m)
      Schisandra chinensis Pale pink, scented; vigorous and twining. 25ft (7.5m)
♀   *Wisteria floribunda* 'Rosea' Pale pea flowers, tipped purple. 20ft (6m)

---

†   There are many other excellent varieties of this plant which are suitable.
††   If pruning is necessary, do it immediately after flowering.

RED FLOWERS

Here we find a mixture of the flamboyant and the demure, the rare and the familiar, with some unusually well-scented varieties.

Akebia quinata Scented reddish purple flowers; good in trees. 15ft (4.5m)

Akebia trifoliata Reddish-purple-flowered twiner; mauve fruits. 15ft (4.5m)

Camellia japonica 'Apollo' Large, semi-double; frost-resistant. 6ft (1.8m)

♀ *Camellia japonica 'Rubescens Major'* Crimson, fully double. 4ft (1.2m)

♀ *Chaenomeles × superba 'Rowallane'* Bright crimson; prolific. 10ft (3m)

Clematis alpina 'Ruby' Best red alpina; unusually vigorous. 10ft (3m)

Clematis 'Barbara Dibley' Purplish red striped darker; shade. 8ft (2.4m)

Clematis japonica Polished, pale-edged, purplish red bells. 6ft (1.8m)

* *Jasminum beesianum* Unusually deep red; highly scented. 10ft (3m)

Schisandra rubriflora Crimson flowers then scarlet fruits. 10ft (3m)

YELLOW AND ORANGE FLOWERS

While yellow is a colour which seems to predominate in spring, in climbers and wall shrubs the choice is unexpectedly thin.

Acacia armata Clouds of yellow on spiny branches; tender. 10ft (3m)

Azara dentata Scented orangey-yellow clusters; evergreen. 8ft (2.4m)

Camellia 'Jury's Yellow' White with yellow anemone centre. 6ft (1.8m)

Clematis 'Moonlight' Yellowest, but still cream; slow starter. 5ft (1.5m)

Clematis 'Wada's Memory' Very pale and creamy; vigorous. 7ft (2.1m)

Corokia cotoneaster Tiny flowers on distinctive twiggy bush. 3ft (90cm)

♀* *Coronilla valentina ssp. glauca* Long season of pea flowers. 6ft (1.8m)

Forsythia 'Minigold' Naturally shorter so better on a wall. 6ft (1.8m)†

Piptanthus laburnifolius Bold evergreen; bright pea flowers. 10ft (3m)

♀ *Sophora tetraptera* Clusters of yellow flowers; needs wall. 6ft (1.8m)

---

† Always keep in mind that plants grow taller with wall protection.

BLUE AND PURPLE FLOWERS

The blues and purples are even more restricted than the yellows, just three groups provide most of the most choice varieties.

♀ *Ceanothus 'Delight'* Rich blue; one of the hardiest evergreens. 12ft (3.6m)

♀ *Ceanothus* × *delileanus 'Topaz'* Deep indigo blue; deciduous. 6ft (1.8m)

♀* *Ceanothus 'Puget Blue'* Spectacular bright blue; evergreen. 12ft (3.6m)

Clematis double Intriguing spring specialities; see list page 267.

Clematis large-flowered Huge choice in these colours; list page 266.

♀ *Clematis macropetala 'Maidwell Hall'* Very deep blue. 8ft (2.4m)

Rosmarinus Rosemary; all best against south wall in cold areas. 4ft (1.2m)

♀* *Wisteria floribunda 'Multijuga'* Mauve spikes up to 3ft (90cm)! 35ft (10.5m)†

Wisteria floribunda 'Violacea Plena' Double dark purple. 20ft (6m)†

Wisteria sinensis 'Black Dragon' Rare, double, dark purple. 35ft (10.5m)†

SCENTED FLOWERS

Fragrance is a feature of a number of wall shrubs and climbers and the shelter of the wall often ensures that the scent is not dispersed.

Abeliophyllum distichum Vanilla-scented white on bare twigs. 5ft (1.5m)

♀ *Camellia 'Narumigata'* Single white, pink edge; sunny wall. 8ft (2.4m)

♀ *Choisya ternata* Scented white flowers with aromatic leaves. 6ft (1.8m)

Clematis montana 'Odorata' The best for scent; pale pink. 20ft (6m)

Coronilla valentina Yellow flowers; fruit scent, less in evening. 7ft (2.1m)

Drimys winteri White; indescribable scent; leaves poisonous. 10ft (3m)

♀ *Jasminum* × *stephanense* Pale pink, sweet scent, long season. 10ft (3m)

Lonicera periclymenum All are scented, usually only in evening. 12ft (3.6m)

* *Lonicera periclymenum 'Sweet Sue'* Scent day *and* evening. 12ft (3.6m)

Viburnum carlesii Superb on a wall; penetrating sweetness. 8ft (2.4m)

---

† To flower well, wisterias need pruning in summer and winter.

------------------------------ **Summer-flowering** ------------------------------

Summer climbers flower on growth which has developed earlier in the year; spring pruning and rich feeding encourages the best show.

Climbers

Summer climbers seem to be either exotic or unusually vigorous; some are a little difficult but others will run to the top of trees to create a spectacular display; there are also some good self-clingers.

    Aristolochia durior Strange green, yellow and brown flowers. 10ft (3m)

♀ *Campsis* × *tagliabuana 'Madame Galen'* Salmon-red, exotic. 20ft (6m)†

    Clematis double-flowered Only early-flowers double; list page 267.

    Clematis large-flowered Huge range of fine colours; list page 266.

    Clematis small-flowered Many forms and colours; list page 265.

    Decumaria sinensis Unremarkable cream flowers; super scent. 5ft (1.5m)†

    Eccremocarpus scaber 'Fireworks' Red, orange and yellow seed mix.
      6ft (1.8m)

♀ *Fallopia baldschuanica* Russian vine; startlingly rampant. 40ft

♀ *Hydrangea anomala ssp. petiolaris* White lacecap; clings. 20ft (6m)†

♀ *Jasminum officinale* White, heavy exotic scent; spring prune. 20ft (6m)

♀ *Lapegeria rosea* Rare twiner with waxy pink flowers; tricky. 10ft (3m)

♀ *Lonicera* × *tellmanniana* Coppery yellow, reddish in bud. 12ft (3.6m)

    Mutisia ilicifolia Yellow centred pink daisies; best in shrub. 4ft (1.2m)

♀ *Passiflora caerulea* Spectacular blue and white flowers. 15ft (4.5m)

♀ *Pilostegia viburnoides* Heads of creamy flowers; self-clinger. 6ft (1.8m)

    Schizophragma hydrangeoides Creamy lacecaps; self-clings. 10ft (3m)†

♀ *Schizophragma integrifolium* Larger flowers than above. 10ft (3m)

♀* *Solanum jasminoides 'Album'* Clouds of neat white flowers. 12ft (3.6m)

♀ *Trachelospermum jasminoides* White, highly scented; slow. 8ft (2.4m)†

♀ *Wisteria sinensis* Most will produce a few late flowers. 25ft (7.5m)

---

†   These plants all cling to walls by short roots on the stems.

Wall shrubs

These shrubs are ideal for training on walls and are not twining or otherwise self-supporting. Some may be grown as free-standing shrubs in mild areas but need wall protection in colder regions.

    Abutilon 'Patrick Synge' Lovely lanterns in burnt orange. 6ft (1.8m)

    Acca sellowiana Unique red and white edible flowers; tricky. 8ft (2.4m)

    Aloysia triphylla Strongly lemon-scented foliage; lilac spikes. 5ft (1.5m)

    Buddleia crispa Fragrant lilac spikes; grey leaves; warm wall. 12ft (3.6m)

    Ceanothus Mainly deciduous, some evergreens; most are blue. 8ft (2.4m)

☙ *Clianthus puniceus* Scarlet lobster-claw flowers; very tender. 6ft (1.8m)

☙ *Erythrina crista-galli* Dramatic scarlet flowers; slow to mature. 6ft (1.8m)

☙* *Fremontodendron 'California Glory'* Huge yellow bowls. 15ft (4.5m)

☙ *Itea ilicifolia* Long green fragrant tassels; hates cold winds. 6ft (1.8m)

☙ *Jasminum humile 'Revolutum'* Bright yellow flowers; bushy. 6ft (1.8m)

    Lomatia myricoides Small, white, scented; no lime; full sun. 8ft (2.4m)

☙ *Magnolia grandiflora 'Exmouth'* Huge, creamy, fragrant. 10ft (3m)†

☙ *Myrtus communis* White flowers; neat evergreen leaves. 8ft (2.4m)

☙ *Phlomis fruticosa* Bright yellow flowers; greyish leaves. 3ft (90cm)

☙ *Pyracantha 'Watereri'* White flowers, red berries; compact. 8ft (2.4m)

☙ *Rhaphiolepis umbellata* Pink-tinted white flowers; hates wind. 5ft (1.5m)

    Robinia hispida 'Macrophylla' Like a bristly pink wisteria. 12ft (3.6m)

    Rosa Climbers and ramblers are indispensable; see list page 000.

☙ *Solanum crispum 'Glasnevin'* Purple and yellow; prune yearly. 6ft (1.8m)

    Vitex agnus-castus Slender spikes of scented violet flowers. 6ft (1.8m)

---

†   Some varieties take many years to flower; this is the quickest.

Attractive flowers

WHITE FLOWERS

White flowers create a cool atmosphere in the heat of summer and make a good background for a pastel, or silver and white border.

    Abutilon vitifolium 'Album' Big white bowls; warm, dry site. 15ft (4.5m)†

    Carpenteria californica 'Ladham's Variety' Scented; sun. 6ft (1.8m)

    Clematis 'Huldine' Mauve-backed white; but unpredictable. 10ft (3m)

    Clematis 'John Huxtable' Cream-eyed; prolific and reliable. 8ft (2.4m)

♀* *Clematis viticella 'Alba Luxurians'* Dark-eyed pure white. 10ft (3m)

♀ *Hydrangea anomala ssp. petiolaris* White lacecaps; tough. 10ft (3m)

    Jasminum officinale 'Affine' Pink tinted white; heavy scent. 25ft (7.5m)

♀ *Pilostegia viburnoides* Creamy, foamy heads; self-clinger. 25ft (7.5m)

♀ *Rosa 'White Cockade'* Shapely, scented blooms; modest growth. 8ft (2.4m)

♀ *Solanum jasminoides 'Album'* Yellow-eyed white; likes sun. 18ft (5.4m)

PINK FLOWERS

Pink climbers must be chosen carefully; always choose the right shade of pink to suit the colour of the wall or fence behind.

♀ *Clematis 'Comtesse de Bouchaud'* Pure pink; spring prune. 8ft (2.4m)

    Clematis 'Miss Crawshay' Lovely slightly mauvish shade. 6ft (1.8m)

    Clematis texensis 'Princess of Wales' Deep pink; prune hard. 10ft (3m)

    Escallonia 'Donard Seedling' Pale pink; hardier than many. 8ft (2.4m)

♀ *Indigofera amblyantha* Long summer strings of rosy flowers. 6ft (1.8m)

♀ *Jasminum × stephanense* Pale pink, fragrant and vigorous. 20ft (6m)

♀ *Lapageria rosea* Waxy bells; needs shelter; unpredictable. 12ft (3.6m)

    Lavatera 'Pink Frills' Small, semi-double; greyish leaves. 6ft (1.8m)†

    Mutisia oligodon Salmony daisies, best guided through a shrub. 5ft (1.5m)

♀* *Rosa 'New Dawn'* Blush-pink, fragrant, restrained; unrivalled. 12ft (3.6m)

---

† This can be a short-lived plant, but it roots well from cuttings.

RED FLOWERS

Again, matching the shade of red in the flowers to the colour of the brick, stone, or fence background can enhance or devalue the plant.

℣ *Abutilon 'Ashford Red'* Deep bells; needs a warm sunny wall. 6ft (1.8m)
   Callistemon citrinus Cerise-red bottle brush flowers; needs sun. 8ft (2.4m)
℣* *Clematis 'Niobe'* Deep velvety red; best in some shade. 8ft (2.4m)†
   Clematis texensis 'Gravetye Beauty' Rich, ruby, spidery star. 8ft (2.4m)
℣ *Clematis viticella 'Royal Velours'* Purple-tinted, sultry red. 12ft (3.6m)
℣ *Clianthus puniceus* Lobster-claw; scarlet flowers; warm wall. 8ft (2.4m)
℣ *Crinodendron hookerianum* Dark red lanterns; hates limy soil. 6ft (1.8m)
℣ *Escallonia 'Crimson Spire'* Clusters of small red flowers. 10ft (3m)
℣ *Lonicera periclymenum 'Serotina'* Red, white inside; scented. 12ft (3.6m)
℣ *Rosa 'Dublin Bay'* Scented crimson flowers all summer. 10ft (3m)

YELLOW FLOWERS

These supreme summery colours look well with purple and bronze foliage and show up well in the competition of the summer garden.

℣ *Abutilon 'Canary Bird'* Bright buttery bells; for a south wall. 4ft (1.2m)
℣* *Clematis 'Bill MacKenzie'* Bright, fleshy petals; silvery seeds. 20ft (6m)
   Clematis 'Moonlight' Best in shade; flowers early and late. 5ft (1.5m)
℣ *Clematis rehderiana* Small, pale, cowslip-scented bells. 20ft (6m)
℣ *Cytisus battandieri* Pineapple-scented yellow flowers. 15ft (4.5m)
℣ *Eccremocarpus scaber 'Aureus'* Clusters of tubular flowers. 6ft (1.8m)
℣ *Fremontodendron 'California Glory'* Vigorous; short-lived. 20ft (6m)
℣* *Lonicera 'Graham Thomas'* Deep cream; very long season. 12ft (3.6m)
℣ *Phlomis fruticosa* Bold yellow flowers; soft evergreen leaves. 4ft (1.2m)
   Rosa 'Goldfinch' Short, colourful season of gold and primrose. 8ft (2.4m)

---

† Prune hard in spring for late flowers, or tip back for earlier display.

ORANGE FLOWERS

These rusty and coppery orange shades mark the transition between the brilliance of summer and the typical autumn shades.

    Abutilon 'Firebelle' Soft orange bells; usefully compact. 4ft (1.2m)†

    Abutilon 'Patrick Synge' Big rusty orange bells; dark leaves. 6ft (1.8m)†

♀ *Buddleja globosa* Compact balls; best on wall in cold areas. 10ft (3m)†

    Campsis grandiflora Red-tinted orange trumpets; exotic. 18ft (5.4m)†

    Clematis thibetana 'Orange Peel' The nearest to true orange. 20ft (6m)

♀ *Eccremocarpus scaber* Clings by tendrils; long season; sun. 6ft (1.8m)

    Lonicera × brownii 'Fuchsioides' Slim, fragrant and scarlet. 12ft (3.6m)

♀ *Lonicera sempervirens* Yellow-throated; lovely, but no scent. 15ft (4.5m)†

♀ *Lonicera × tellmanniana* Soft orange with coppery tints. 12ft (3.6m)

    Rosa 'Schoolgirl' Coppery-tinted, wonderful scent; odd name. 10ft (3m)

BLUE AND PURPLE FLOWERS

The darker blues and purples need planting close to the path or against a pale background to show up well; not so the paler shades.

    Abutilon × suntense Large mauve cups; needs sun and shelter. 15ft (4.5m)

♀ *Clematis 'Jackmanii'* Well known purple; prune hard in spring. 8ft (2.4m)

♀* *Clematis 'Perle d'Azur'* Clouds of exquisite, pale, silvery blue; 12ft (3.6m)

    Hedysarum multijugum Purple pea flowers, dark foliage. 10ft (3m)

♀ *Passiflora caerulea* Unique blue and white fragrant flowers. 15ft (4.5m)

♀ *Rhodochiton atrosanguineus* Distinctive purple bells; tender. 4ft (1.2m)

♀ *Solanum crispum 'Glasnevin'* Yellow-eyed purplish blue. 6ft (1.8m)

♀ *Sollya heterophylla* Small blue bells in pendulous clusters. 6ft (1.8m)

    Teucrium fruticans Pale blue flowers among silvery leaves. 8ft (2.4m)

    Vitex agnus-castus Slim, scented mauve spikes; spring prune. 7ft (2.1m)

---

†   A tender plant which may survive if given a warm sheltered wall.

SCENTED FLOWERS

The warmth of the summer sun often creates powerful fragrances from climbers and wall shrubs, especially those planted on walls which retain heat. This can be especially noticeable in the evening.

Actinidia deliciosa Kiwi fruit; sweet white flowers; vigorous. 30ft (9m)

Buddleja crispa Lilac, honey scent; grey woolly leaves. 10ft (3m)

♀ *Buddleja fallowiana* '*Alba*' White, honey scent; grey leaves. 10ft (3m)

Carpenteria californica '*Ladham's Variety*' White; sweet. 5ft (1.5m)

♀ *Ceanothus* '*Gloire de Versailles*' Blue; best of scented types. 6ft (1.8m)

♀ *Cestrum parqui* Greenish yellow; foetid by day, spicy at night. 8ft (2.4m)

Clematis '*Fair Rosamund*' Blush; light primrose scent. 8ft (2.4m)†

Clematis flammula Hawthorn scent; clouds of white stars. 15ft (4.5m)

♀ *Clematis* × *triternata* '*Rubromarginata*' White, edged red. 12ft (3.6m)

Decumaria sinensis Honey-scented; white fluffy heads. 10ft (3m)

♀ *Itea ilicifolia* Long, greeny white, honey-scented catkins. 10ft (3m)

♀ *Jasminum humile* '*Revolutum*' Yellow; shrubby; light scent. 5ft (1.5m)

♀* *Jasminum officinale* White, climber; familiar heavy scent. 20ft (6m)

Lonicera periclymenum '*Sweet Sue*' Scent day *and* evening. 12ft (3.6m)

♀ *Magnolia grandiflora* '*Exmouth*' Spicy citrus scent; exotic. 25ft (7.5m)

♀ *Myrtus communis* White; spicy and sweet; leaves aromatic. 8ft (2.4m)

♀ *Passiflora caerulea* Fragile and sweet; extraordinary flowers. 15ft (4.5m)

Rosa Many climbers and ramblers are scented; see lists page 254.

♀ *Trachelospermum jasminoides* White; captivating scent. 8ft (2.4m)

Vitex agnus-castus Sweet lilac spikes; leaves aromatic. 8ft (2.4m)

---

† This is the only large-flowered clematis with a noticeable scent.

---------------------- **Autumn-flowering** ----------------------

Many of the best autumn climbers and wall shrubs are either continuing to
flower from the summer or will continue into winter.

Climbers

Autumn climbers are a mixture of the choice, the tender, the tough and the
rampageous and their sites will need choosing carefully.

    Araujia sericifera Fragrant, waxy white flowers; rather tender. 6ft (1.8m)

♀ *Campsis* × *tagliabuana 'Madame Galen'* Orangey pink. 15ft (4.5m)

    Clematis A number of autumn specialities are listed on page ooo.

♀* *Eccremocarpus scaber* Orange, pink, yellow or red; tendrils. 8ft (2.4m)

♀ *Fallopia baldshuanica* Small white flowers; unstoppable. 30ft (9m)

♀ *Jasminum officinale* White; lasts into autumn from summer. 20ft (6m)

♀ *Lapageria rosea* Large, pink waxy flowers; temperamental. 6ft (1.8m)

    Lonicera japonica 'Hall's Prolific' White; feed for late show. 12ft (3.6m)

♀ *Lonicera periclymenum 'Graham Thomas'* Cream; reliable. 12ft (3.6m)

♀ *Pilostegia viburnoides* Cream; usually lasts from summer. 6ft (1.8m)

Wall shrubs

Wall and even fence protection helps summer species last into autumn and
encourages winter sorts into an earlier display.

♀ *Buddleja fallowiana 'Alba'* White; lasts well if dead-headed. 10ft (3m)†

♀ *Fremontodendron 'California Glory'* Bright yellow bowls. 12ft (3.6m)

♀* *Indigofera heterantha* Pink pea flowers; vigorous and prolific. 8ft (2.4m)†

♀ *Jasminum nudiflorum* Winter jasmine; starts in autumn. 15ft (4.5m)

    Lonicera fragrantissima Earliest scented shrubby honeysuckle. 8ft (2.4m)

♀ *Magnolia grandiflora 'Exmouth'* This and 'Goliath' last well. 10ft (3m)

♀ *Mahonia 'Lionel Fortescue'* Yellow spikes; bold leaves. 6ft (1.8m)

♀ *Solanum crispum 'Glasnevin'* Yellow-eyed blue; likes chalk. 15ft (4.5m)†

♀ *Viburnum* × *bodnantense 'Deben'* Pink, then white; fragrant. 8ft (2.4m)

    Vitex agnus-castus Fragrant lilac spikes last into autumn. 10ft (3m)†

---

†   This variety benefits from being pruned every spring.

Attractive flowers

WHITE FLOWERS†

In autumn clouds of pure white flowers seem refreshingly at odds with the season, while creamier shades fit well with other autumn shades.

♀ *Abelia* × *grandiflora* Elegant growth; long season on wall. 6ft (1.8m)

♀* *Buddleja fallowiana 'Alba'* White, scented; greyish leaves. 10ft (3m)

   Clematis flammula Small, hawthorn-scented stars; prolific. 25ft (7.5m)

   Clematis 'Huldine' Large flowers; sometimes temperamental. 20ft (6m)

♀ *Jasminum officinale* White; long season when growing well. 20ft (6m)

♀ *Magnolia grandiflora 'Exmouth'* Exotic yet dependable. 10ft (3m)

♀ *Pilostegia viburnoides* Cream; starts in summer; self-clings. 6ft (1.8m)

   Lonicera fragrantissima Flowers for months on sheltered wall. 8ft (2.4m)

   Lonicera japonica 'Hall's Prolific' White, fading to cream. 12ft (3.6m)

♀ *Viburnum* × *bodnantense 'Deben'* Pink buds open to white. 8ft (2.4m)

PINK AND RED FLOWERS

Reds and some pinks fit well into the autumn scene, making a good background to berries and autumnal shades in autumn borders.

♀ *Campsis* × *tagliabuana 'Madame Galen'* Stems cling. 15ft (4.5m)

   Clematis 'Madame Baron Veillard' Large, rosy mauve. 15ft (4.5m)

*   *Clematis texensis 'Gravetye Beauty'* Dark red bells; prolific. 10ft (3m)

♀ *Eccremocarpus scaber* Pink and red forms in seed mixtures. 8ft (2.4m)

♀ *Fuchsia 'Corallina'* Red and violet; dark leaf; best fan-trained. 8ft (2.4m)

♀ *Indigofera heterantha* Strangely uncommon; pink flowers. 8ft (2.4m)

♀ *Lapageria rosea* Bold, pink waxy flowers; unpredictable. 6ft (1.8m)

   Rosa 'Aloha' Fragrant deep rose climber with darker tints; 10ft (3m)

   Rosa 'Old Blush' 'Monthly rose', can flower all the year round. 6ft (1.8m)

♀ *Viburnum* × *bodnantense 'Charles Lamont'* Best pink form. 8ft (2.4m)

---

†   In addition to these suggestions, don't forget roses (page 249).

YELLOW AND ORANGE FLOWERS

These colours harmonize naturally with changing autumn foliage but most like warmer conditions than autumn colour shrubs.

℣ *Abutilon 'Kentish Belle'* Red-veined orange bells; hot wall. 6ft (1.8m)

℣ *Cestrum parqui* Yellowish green flowers, evening scented. 6ft (1.8m)

℣* *Clematis 'Bill MacKenzie'* Lemon peel with silver seeds. 20ft (6m)

℣ *Clematis rehderiana* Dainty, pale yellow, cowslip-scented. 15ft (4.5m)

℣ *Eccremocarpus scaber* Orange is usual, yellow also available. 8ft (2.4m)

℣ *Fremontodendron 'California Glory'* Buttercup bowls. 12ft (3.6m)

℣ *Jasminum nudiflorum* Winter jasmine; flowers for months. 15ft (4.5m)

℣ *Lonicera periclymenum 'Graham Thomas'* Cream, scented. 12ft (3.6m)

℣ *Mahonia 'Lionel Fortescue'* Long yellow spikes; good leaf. 6ft (1.8m)

   Rosa 'Princesse de Nassau' Sweet-scented creamy Musk rose. 10ft (3m)

BLUE AND PURPLE FLOWERS

Autumnals in these shades are few, and clematis could probably supply more if they were fed, pruned and dead-headed well.

   Buddleja fallowiana Honey-sweet, lavender-blue spikes. 10ft (3m)

℣* *Ceanothus 'Autumnal Blue'* Tough evergreen; long season. 12ft (3.6m)

℣ *Clematis 'Gipsy Queen'* Bold, deep purple; summer-autumn. 15ft (4.5m)

℣ *Clematis* × *jouiniana 'Praecox'* Blue and white; vigorous. 10ft (3m)†

   Clematis 'Lady Betty Balfour' Deep violet-blue; sunny wall. 15ft (4.5m)

℣ *Clematis 'Madame Grangé'* Purple, with red streaks. 10ft (3m)

℣ *Hebe 'Mrs Winder'* Bright blue spikes against purple leaves. 3ft (90cm)

℣ *Hibiscus syriacus 'Oiseau Bleu'* Dark-eyed violet-blue single. 6ft (1.8m)

℣ *Solanum crispum 'Glasnevin'* Blue 'potato' flowers; fan-train. 15ft (4.5m)

   Vitex agnus-castus Scented mauve spikes; aromatic leaves. 10ft (3m)

---

†   This small-flowered variety dies back to a woody base in winter.

SCENTED FLOWERS

Fragrance in autumn is perhaps less easy to find than at other seasons and may be curtailed by fierce early frosts and by gales.

Araujia sericifera Grow up vertical wires on a sunny wall. 6ft (1.8m)

Buddleja fallowiana That usual sweet, honey, buddleja scent. 10ft (3m)

♀ *Cestrum parqui* Yellowish green; good in open in warm places. 6ft (1.8m)

* *Clematis flammula* Pervasive hawthorn scent; good in trees. 25ft (7.5m)

♀ *Clematis rehderiana* Elegant, pale yellow bells; divided leaf. 15ft (4.5m)

♀ *Jasminum officinale* Best trained over an arch or doorway. 20ft (6m)

Lonicera fragrantissima Flowers through winter when mild. 8ft (2.4m)

Lonicera japonica 'Hall's Prolific' White; mild but valuable. 12ft (3.6m)

♀ *Lonicera periclymenum 'Graham Thomas'* Best in evening. 12ft (3.6m)

♀ *Magnolia grandiflora 'Exmouth'* Huge flowers; huge leaves. 10ft (3m)

♀ *Mahonia 'Lionel Fortescue'* May be ravaged by sparrows. 6ft (1.8m)

Passiflora caerulea Fascinating flowers, mildly scented. 12ft (3.6m)

Rosa 'Aloha' Deep rose-pink cupped flowers; reliable. 10ft (3m)†

Rosa 'Gloire de Ducher' Deep crimson ageing to purple. 6ft (1.8m)†

Rosa 'Mutabilis' Orange buds, opening coppery yellow. 8ft (2.4m)†

Rosa 'Old Blush' Rather loose pale pink flowers; loves shelter. 8ft (2.4m)†

Rosa 'Princesse de Nassau' Cream; unusually good in autumn. 10ft (3m)†

♀ *Viburnum* × *bodnantense 'Charles Lamont'* Pink; oddly rare. 8ft (2.4m)

♀ *Viburnum* × *bodnantense 'Deben'* White, from pink buds. 8ft (2.4m)

Vitex agnus-castus Sweet flowers; aromatic leaves; hot wall. 10ft (3m)

---

† These roses are often best in the shelter of a wall, not trained on it.

----------------- **Winter-flowering** -----------------

Most of the winter-flowering varieties for this section are shrubs rather than climbers and are also a little tender, so for most a west- or south-facing wall will give them the protection they need.

    Abeliophyllum distichum Like a dwarf, early white forsythia. 5ft (1.5m)

♀ *Acacia dealbata* Fluffy yellow flowers; silver foliage; tender. 10ft (3m)

♀ *Azara microphylla* Rich yellow, fluffy flowers; vanilla scent. 8ft (2.4m)

    Buddleja auriculata Creamy scented spikes; starts in autumn. 12ft (3.6m)

    Camellia japonica 'Otome' Large, pale pink single; erect habit. 6ft (1.8m)†

♀ *Camellia sasanqua 'Narumigata'* Pink-edged cream; scent. 6ft (1.8m)†

♀ *Chimonanthus praecox 'Luteus'* Yellow; best on south wall. 8ft (2.4m)

♀* *Clematis cirrhosa 'Freckles'* Cream flowers, dense red spots. 8ft (2.4m)

    Clematis cirrhosa 'Ourika Valley' Pale yellow; the hardiest. 8ft (2.4m)

    Clematis cirrhosa 'Wisley Cream' Cream; bronzed leaves. 8ft (2.4m)

♀ *Daphne bholua 'Jacqueline Postill'* Purple/white; super scent. 6ft (1.8m)

    Daphne odora Reddish-purple, scented; rounded habit. 3ft (90cm)

♀ *Garrya elliptica 'James Roof'* Long grey-green catkins. 12ft (3.6m)

    Garrya × *issaquaensis 'Pat Ballard'* Long red-green catkins. 8ft (2.4m)

♀ *Jasminum nudiflorum* Yellow flowers; lax green stems. 10ft (3m)

    Lonicera fragrantissima Small, sweet, creamy flowers; tough. 8ft (2.4m)

♀ *Lonicera* × *purpusii 'Winter Beauty'* White; new tips purple. 8ft (2.4m)

♀ *Mahonia* × *media 'Charity'* Yellow spikes; bold evergreen. 10ft (3m)†

    Prunus mume 'Beni-chidori' Dark, double pink; south wall. 8ft (2.4m)

    Viburnum × *bodnantense* West or south walls protect flowers. 8ft (2.4m)

---

†   Other varieties of this plant may also fit in here.

―――――――――――――― **Attractive foliage** ――――――――――――――

Wall shrubs and climbers are worth choosing with their foliage in mind to provide a long-season background to foreground flowers.

VARIEGATED LEAVES†

Most plants in this section are shrubs rather than true climbers; they are usually less vigorous than their green-leaved relations.

 Abutilon megapotamicum 'Variegatum' Spotted; south wall. 6ft (1.8m)

♀ *Aralia elata* 'Variegata' Edged in white, superb; best sheltered. 8ft (2.4m)

 Azara microphyllum 'Variegatum' Leaves edged with cream. 6ft (1.8m)

 Camellia sasanqua 'Variegata' Greyish green, edged white. 5ft (1.5m)

 Coronilla valentina 'Variegata' Leaves edged creamy white. 4ft (1.2m)

 Eleagnus × *ebbingei* 'Limelight' Yellow-splashed; north wall. 9ft (2.7m)

 Euonymus fortunei 'Silver Queen' Leaves edged with cream. 3ft (90cm)

 Fuchsia magellanica 'Sharpitor' Greyish green, edged white. 3ft (90cm)

 Hedera helix 'Goldheart' Yellow splashed; many others. 10ft (3m)

♀* *Jasminum officinale* 'Argenteovariegatum' Edged cream. 8ft (2.4m)

 Kadsura japonica 'Variegata' Rare climber; cream edges. 8ft (2.4m)

 Lonicera japonica 'Aureoreticulata' Pretty yellow veins. 10ft (3m)

 Lonicera periclymenum 'Harlequin' Broad yellow edge; 10ft (3m)

 Luma apiculata 'Glanleam Gold' Bright creamy yellow edge. 6ft (1.8m)

 Myrtus communis 'Variegata' Neat leaf finely edged cream. 6ft (1.8m)

 Pyracantha 'Harlequin' Leaves edged white; red berries. 6ft (1.8m)

 Rosa wichuraiana 'Variegata' White-flecked; white flowers. 15ft (4.5m)

 Rubus fruticosus 'Variegatus' Cream edged blackberry. 6ft (1.8m)

 Schizophragma hydrangeoides 'Moonlight' Grey flecks; rare. 8ft (2.4m)

♀ *Trachelospermum jasminoides* 'Variegatum' White margins. 7ft (2.1m)

―――――――――――――――――――――――――――――――――――――

†   If plain, green-leaved shoots appear they should be cut out.

GOLD AND YELLOW LEAVES

The choice of gold-leaved varieties is relatively small and some of those there are tend to have speckled rather than all gold foliage.

℣ *Choisya ternata 'Sundance'* Yellow leaves; white flowers. 4ft (1.2m)

   Elaeagnus pungens 'Frederici' Yellow splashed; rather slow. 6ft (1.8m)

   Fuchsia magellanica 'Aurea' Golden leaves; bright red flowers. 2ft (60cm)

℣ *Hedera helix 'Buttercup'* Yellow in winter; greener later. 15ft (4.5m)†

℣ *Humulus lupulus 'Aureus'* Bright yellow; dies back in winter. 12ft (3.6m)

   Jasminum nudiflorum 'Aureum' Yellow, or yellow spotted. 8ft (2.4m)

* *Jasminum officinale 'Aureum'* Edged and tinted with yellow. 8ft (2.4m)

℣ *Laurus nobilis 'Aurea'* Leaves yellow; likes warmth, shelter. 8ft (2.4m)

℣ *Phlomis chrysophylla* Rough leaves, yellow-tinted in summer. 4ft (1.2m)

℣ *Ribes sanguineum 'Brocklebankii'* Yellow; likes light shade. 3ft (90cm)

SILVER AND GREY LEAVES

Again, shrubs predominate here as there are few true climbers which fit the bill; most appreciate a sunny wall and good drainage.

   Artemisia 'Powis Castle' Mounds of lacy silver leaves; lovely. 3ft (90cm)

℣ *Buddleja fallowiana 'Alba'* Felted silver leaves; white flowers. 8ft (2.4m)

℣ *Cistus 'Peggy Sammons'* Grey-green; pale pink flowers. 4ft (1.2m)

   Clematis phlebantha Silver leaves; flowers cream; rare. 8ft (2.4m)

℣ *Convolvulus cneorum* Shining silver leaves; white flowers. 4ft (1.2m)

℣ *Cytisus battandieri* Bold, silver green leaves; yellow flowers. 15ft (4.5m)

℣ *Lavandula lanata* White, woolly; needs warmth and shelter. 2ft (60cm)

℣ *Lonicera caprifolium* Blue-green leaves; flowers creamy . 12ft (3.6m)

   Teucrium fruticans White underneath leaves; blue flowers. 6ft (1.8m)

* *Vitis vinifera 'Incana'* Downy, grey-green leaves; black fruits. 15ft (4.5m)

---

†   Looks especially good trained to grow up a tree trunk.

PURPLE, BRONZE AND MULTICOLOURED LEAVES

This final round-up of coloured-leaved climbers includes a number with pinkish tones in addition to their creamy variegations.

♀ *Actinidia kolomikta* Half white then pink, half green leaves. 12ft (3.6m)

Ampelopsis brevipedunculata 'Elegans' Pink/white splashed. 8ft (2.4m)

♀ *Clematis montana var. rubens* Purple shoots; pink flowers. 30ft (9m)

Cleyera japonica 'Tricolor' Green, grey, cream and pink. 8ft (2.4m)

Euonymus fortunei 'Coloratus' Green, then purple in winter. 6ft (1.8m)

♀ *Fuchsia magellanica 'Versicolor'* Pink, cream and grey; pretty. 3ft (90cm)

♀ *Leptospermum scoparium 'Nicholsii'* Purple; red blooms. 6ft (1.8m)

♀* *Parthenocissus henryana* White veins, green then red leaves. 10ft (3m)

Pseudowintera colorata Yellowish green, pink and crimson. 4ft (1.2m)

♀ *Vitis vinifera 'Purpurea'* Red to rich purple foliage; superb. 15ft (4.5m)

AROMATIC LEAVES†

The warmth and shelter of a wall or fence not only provides the shelter many aromatic shrubs need but also enhances that aroma.

Aloysia triphylla Powerful lemon scent; rather a sparse plant. 3ft (90cm)

♀* *Artemisia abrotanum* Sweet and pungent; grey-green leaves. 2ft (60cm)

♀ *Choisya ternata* Crush the leaves to release the aroma. 6ft (1.8m)

♀ *Cistus ladanifer* Leaves gummy; red-blotched white flowers. 6ft (1.8m)

♀ *Lavandula lanata* Lavender oils vaporize in hot situations. 2ft (60cm)

♀ *Myrtus communis* Delightfully pungent; scented white flowers. 6ft (1.8m)

♀ *Prostanthera rotundifolia* Minty aroma; purple flowers. 4ft (1.2m)

Pseudowintera colorata Crush the leaves for a spicy aroma. 4ft (1.2m)

Rosmarinus All grow and flower best in front of a sunny wall. 5ft (1.5m)

Umbellularia californica Pungent aroma, best from afar. 10ft (3m)

---

† Many aromatic sages also appreciate the shelter of a warm wall.

AUTUMN-COLOURING LEAVES

The best backdrop for an autumn border is a climber whose foliage develops fiery autumn colour; here there are many true climbers which can make a show in trees as well as on fences and walls.

    Actinidia deliciosa Kiwi fruit; yellow and pale orange leaves. 20ft (6m)

℗ *Actinidia kolomikta* Pink and green leaves turn yellow. 12ft (3.6m)

    Akebia quinata Good yellow autumn colour; violet fruits. 15ft (4.5m)

    Ampelopsis brevipedunculata Yellow to orange, blue berries. 12ft (3.6m)

    Ampelopsis megalophylla Best autumn colours in full sun. 20ft (6m)

    Campsis radicans Fine yellow colour follows orange flowers. 20ft (6m)

℗ *Ceanothus* × *delileanus 'Gloire de Versailles'* Yellow; blue flowers. 6ft (1.8m)

    Celastrus orbiculatus Brilliant yellow with orange fruits. 20ft (6m)†

    Chaenomeles Most varieties show some yellow autumn colour. 8ft (2.4m)

℗ *Cotoneaster horizontalis* Orange and red with red berries. 5ft (1.5m)

℗ *Hydrangea anomala ssp. petiolaris* Sheets of yellow. 20ft (6m)

℗ *Parthenocissus henryana* White-veined to purple to scarlet. 10ft (3m)†

℗ *Parthenocissus quinquefolia* Sparkling scarlet and orange. 15ft (4.5m)†

℗ *Parthenocissus tricuspidata* Rich scarlet and deep crimson. 15ft (4.5m)†

℗ *Ribes speciosum* Soft yellow, especially effective on walls. 5ft (1.5m)

    Vitis amurensis Blood red and purple; tiny fruits; vigorous. 20ft (6m)

℗ *Vitis 'Brant'* Purple and red, with yellow veins; tasty fruits. 20ft (6m)†

℗* *Vitis coignetiae* Crimson and scarlet; truly spectacular. 20ft (6m)†

    Vitis vinifera fruiting types Many have yellow autumn colour.

℗ *Vitis vinifera 'Purpurea'* Claret, blue below, become purple. 15ft (4.5m)†

---

†   Trained in a large tree this makes a stunning autumn show.

BOLD AND ARCHITECTURAL FOLIAGE

Forceful foliage is a great asset on a wall, as it makes such a good background for the lighter and airier shrubs or perennials in front.

Actinidia deliciosa Heart-shaped leaves up to 8in (20cm) across. 20ft (6m)

Ampelopsis megalophylla Doubly divided, up to 2ft (60cm) long. 25ft (7.5m)

* *Aristolochia durior* Variable, but often heart-shaped; 10in (25cm). 10ft (3m)

♀ × *Fatshedera lizei* Leathery, shiny, sycamore-shaped; to 10in. 4ft (1.2m)

♀ *Ficus carica* Fig; impressive, boldly lobed leaves up to 10in. 12ft (3.6m)†

♀ *Hedera colchica* 'Dentata' The largest-leaved of all ivies. 12ft (3.6m)

Magnolia delavayi Greyish green, to 14in (35cm); one of the largest. 12ft (3.6m)

Magnolia grandiflora Bright green, to 10in (25cm); white flowers. 12ft (3.6m)

Vitis amurensis Oval, lobed leaves to 10in (25cm); rarely seen. 20ft (6m)

♀ *Vitis coignetiae* Rounded leaves to 1ft (30cm); largest-leaved vine. 20ft (6m)

WELL-SHAPED FOLIAGE

It is not only bold rounded leaves which make an impact; foliage which is neatly divided or even finely laced is also valuable.

Ampelopsis aconitifolia Deeply cut leaves; orange berries. 20ft (6m)

Caesalpinia gallesii Doubly divided leaves; yellow flowers. 8ft (2.4m)

Clematis cirrhosa Prettily curled and divided; cream flowers. 10ft (3m)

♀ *Clianthus puniceus* Rich, regularly divided; red flowers. 6ft (1.8m)

Gevuina avellana Dark and glossy, edged with hairs; tender. 8ft (2.4m)

♀* *Mahonia lomariifolia* Impressive rows of holly-like leaflets. 8ft (2.4m)

♀ *Melianthus major* Superb, blue-green, toothed leaves; hot wall. 4ft (1.2m)

Sophora microphylla Neat divided leaves; yellow pea flowers. 6ft (1.8m)

Vitis vinifera 'Ciotat' Parsley-like leaf; fruits on warm wall. 15ft (4.5m)

♀ *Wisteria sinensis* Familiar divided leaves, elegant all summer. 20ft (6m)

---

† Leaves best if cut back each spring; fruits best if left and starved.

———————————— Ornamental fruits ————————————

Many plants, both climbers and wall shrubs, need warm walls to ripen their fruits and then produce most attractive, and sometimes tasty, crops. Fortunately some are less fussy as to their situation.

    Acca sellowiana Yellow, egg-like fruits; edible petals; hot wall. 6ft (1.8m)

    Actinidia deliciosa Kiwi fruit; green turning brown; tasty. 20ft (6m)

    Akebia trifoliata Mauve; sausage-shaped; best in hot summer. 15ft (4.5m)

    Akebia quinata Purple, sausage-shaped, 3in (7.5cm); two plants best. 15ft (4.5m)

*   *Ampelopsis brevipedunculata* Masses of bright blue berries. 12ft (3.6m)

    Celastrus orbiculatus Yellow fruits open to show red seeds. 20ft (6m)

    Citrus × *sinensis* 'Meyer' The most likely of all citrus to fruit. 4ft (1.2m)

    Clematis Small-flowered types produce feathery seeds; page 265

♀ *Cydonia oblonga* 'Vranja' Yellow quinces; pink flowers. 15ft (4.5m)†

    Holboelia coriacea Fat, purple pods 3in (7.5cm) long; best in sun. 15ft (4.5m)

♀ *Mahonia lomariifolia* Long strings of small blue-black berries. 8ft (2.4m)

    Parthenocissus himalayana Deep blue berries; self-clings. 20ft (6m)

♀ *Passiflora caerulea* Orange fruits, often with last flowers. 15ft (4.5m)

    Prunus Peaches and nectarines are perfect for sunny walls. 12ft (3.6m)

♀ *Pyracantha* 'Watereri' Outstanding for tight compact growth. 8ft (2.4m)

    Ribes Gooseberries, red and white currants good on fences. 6ft (1.8m)†

    Rubus Blackberries, hybrid berries superb on fences. 8ft (2.4m) per year.†

    Schisandra grandiflora Short strings of small red berries. 10ft (3m)

♀ *Vitis* 'Brant' Tasty, purplish black grapes; good autumn colour. 20ft (6m)†

    Vitis vinifera 'Fragola' Small grapes, musky strawberry taste. 15ft (4.5m)†

———————————————————————————————

†   To produce the best crop this should be pruned regularly.

--- **Self-clingers** ---

It is sometimes said that self-clinging climbers damage brickwork but usually only soft stone and crumbling mortar is at risk; in fact climbers often protect walls from the extremes of the weather.

 Asteranthera ovata Two-lipped red flowers; cool site; tender. 8ft (2.4m)

 Campsis radicans Orangey red trumpets summer and autumn. 20ft (6m)

♀ *Campsis* × *tagliabuana* '*Madame Galen*' Salmon; needs help. 20ft (6m)

 Decumaria barbara Creamy heads of small-flowers. 10ft (3m)

 Ercilla volubilis Short, fluffy pink spikes; rare but pretty. 10ft (3m)

 Euonymus '*Coloratus*' Leaves green in summer, purple later. 10ft (3m)

♀ *Euonymus* '*Silver Queen*' Pale shoot tips, leaves cream-edged. 6ft (1.8m)

♀ *Hedera algeriensis* '*Gloire de Marengo*' Edged cream. 10ft (3m)†

♀ *Hedera colchica* '*Sulphur Heart*' Irregular yellow splash. 14ft

 Hedera helix '*Green Ripple*' Neat, jagged green leaves. 12ft (3.6m)

♀ *Hydrangea anomala ssp. petiolaris* Fine in trees, eventually. 20ft (6m)

 Hydrangea serratifolia Creamy columns of flower; rare. 20ft (6m)

♀ *Parthenocissus henryana* Dark leaves, veined white; lovely. 15ft (4.5m)

 Parthenocissus himalayana May need support at first. 20ft (6m)

♀ *Parthenocissus quinquefolia* Virginia creeper; red in autumn. 16ft

♀* *Parthenocissus tricuspidata* Boston ivy; crimson in autumn. 15ft (4.5m)

♀ *Pilostegia viburnoides* Creamy spikes; good on north walls. 6ft (1.8m)

 Schizophragma hydrangeoides '*Roseum*' Pink lacecaps; rare. 10ft (3m)

♀ *Schizophragma integrifolia* Cream lacecaps 12in (30cm) across. 10ft (3m)

♀ *Trachelospermum jasminoides* White, fragrant; warm wall. 8ft (2.4m)

---

†   This may be damaged by severe frost in colder parts of the country.

Exceptionally vigorous

Sometimes you need to cover a shed or other eyesore quickly and these will do the job; but remember they will keep on growing.

    Ampelopsis brevipedunculata Clings by tendrils; reliable. 12ft (3.6m)

    Aristolochia durior Strange yellowish flowers; twines. 10ft (3m)

    Ceanothus Evergreens are especially quick on warm walls. 12ft (3.6m)

    Clematis montana Pink spring flowers; can be hard to control. 30ft (9m)

♈* *Fallopia baldshuanica* The quickest of all; white flowers. 40ft (12m)

    Hedera algeriensis Large, leathery leaves; the fastest ivy. 15ft (4.5m)

♈ *Parthenocissus quinquefolia* Gallops once it gets a hold. 16ft (4.8m)

♈ *Passiflora caerulea* In cold areas may be killed back by frost. 16ft (4.8m)

    Rosa – ramblers Some can reach 30ft (9m) easily; see list page 254.

♈ *Wisteria sinensis* Flowers poorly when left to run up; twines. 35ft (10.5m)

Good growing through trees†

Careful planning is required before putting a climber in a tree; many need a large host, some will break branches of weak trees.

♈ *Actinidia kolomikta* Colourful pink and white leaves; twines. 12ft (3.6m)

    Clematis Vigorous small-flowered species best; see list page 263.

♈ *Hedera helix 'Buttercup'* Climbs trunk; yellows in autumn. 15ft (4.5m)

♈ *Hydrangea anomala ssp. petiolaris* Requires a stout host. 20ft (6m)

♈ *Parthenocissus henryana* Looks best in dark-leaved host. 15ft (4.5m)

♈ *Pilostegia viburnoides* Tough, evergreen, adaptable but slow. 6ft (1.8m)

* *Rosa – ramblers* Many are ideal; cling by thorns; see list page 257.

♈ *Schizophragma integrifolia* The best 'climbing hydrangea'. 10ft (3m)

♈ *Vitis vinifera 'Purpurea'* Superb in grey trees or large shrubs. 15ft (4.5m)

♈ *Wisteria sinensis* Stunning when mature; slow to flower well. 30ft (9m)

---

†   These may need a good start in rich soil to cope with tree roots.

Good growing through shrubs

Many climbers are at their best when trained through mature shrubs; varieties needing spring pruning are easiest to control.

Ampelopsis brevipedunculata 'Elegans' Tolerates pruning. 5ft (1.5m)

Clematis 'Arabella' Rare blue hybrid, prolific and easy. 8ft (2.4m)

Clematis integrifolia Blue and pink forms; dies down in winter. 2ft (60cm)

♀ Clematis texensis 'Duchess of Albany' White-eyed pink. 8ft (2.4m)†

Clematis texensis 'Gravetye Beauty' Silky rich, deep red. 8ft (2.4m)†

♀* Clematis viticella 'Alba Luxurians' Lovely dark-eyed white. 10ft (3m)†

♀ Clematis viticella 'Etoile Violette' Very prolific deep purple. 10ft (3m)†

Clematis 'Jackmanii Superba' Familiar rich purple; red tint. 10ft (3m)†

♀ Clematis 'Niobe' Deep red; good grown in a variegated shrub. 8ft (2.4m)†

♀ Clematis 'Perle d'Azur' Silvery blue; good in a silver shrub. 8ft (2.4m)†

♀ Eccremocarpus scaber Clings well by tendrils on leaves. 8ft (2.4m)

♀ Ipomoea 'Heavenly Blue' Pale blue annual; plant large plants. 6ft (1.8m)

♀ Lathyrus latifolius Pink and white; no scent, but prolific. 8ft (2.4m)

Lathyrus odoratus 'Galaxy' Scented annual; many colours. 6ft (1.8m)

Lathyrus rotundifolius Brick red; good in pink shrub roses. 6ft (1.8m)

Lonicera japonica 'Aureoreticulata' Pretty shoots peep out. 10ft (3m)

Solanum dulcamara 'Variegata' Gold-edged leaf; blue flowers. 5ft (1.5m)

♀ Solanum jasminoides 'Album' White flowers; spring prune. 12ft (3.6m)

Tropaeolum peregrinum Yellow annual; sow under shrubs. 6ft (1.8m)

♀ Tropaeolum speciosum Flame flower; spreads once established. 6ft (1.8m)

---

† This is best cut back hard in spring to keep it in control.

-------------------- Herbaceous climbers --------------------

Although the number of perennial climbers is few, those there are can be
trained through stout shrubs, or even smaller ones, very effectively. Over half
fall under clematis and lathyrus.

    Aconitum hemslyanum Spikes of hooded mauve flowers. 10ft (3m)

    Adlumia fungosa Biennial; watery purple lockets; prolific. 10ft (3m)†

    Clematis fusca Purple or brownish hairy bells; variable. 3–5ft
      (90cm–1.5m)

    Clematis hirsutissima Nodding purple bells, shade varies. 2ft (60cm)†

*   *Clematis integrifolia 'Olgae'* Blue flowers, silver seeds. 2ft (60cm)

    Clematis viorna Nodding, cream-lipped, purplish bells. 8ft (2.4m)†

♀ *Codonopsis convolvulacea* Pretty, flared pale blue flowers. 4ft (1.2m)

    Dicentra scandens Yellowish lockets and lacy leaves; tricky. 5ft (1.5m)†

♀ *Humulus lupulus 'Aureus'* Bright yellow leaves; vigorous. 10ft (3m)

    Lathyrus grandiflorus Unusually large, deep pink flowers. 6ft (1.8m)

♀ *Lathyrus latifolius* Bold magenta pink; the most common form. 8ft (2.4m)

    Lathyrus latifolius 'Blushing Bride' White, with pink streaks. 8ft (2.4m)

    Lathyrus latifolius 'Pink Pearl' Pale pink; none have scent. 8ft (2.4m)

♀ *Lathyrus latifolius 'White Pearl'* Exquisite pure white. 8ft (2.4m)

    Lathyrus nervosus Rare blue for sunny spot; seed now listed. 4ft (1.2m)

    Lathyrus pubescens Lavender-blue flowers; slightly tender. 6ft (1.8m)

    Lathyrus rotundifolius Short spikes of brick red flowers. 8ft (2.4m)

    Thladiantha dubia Yellow flowers, red fruits; need two sexes. 10ft (3m)†

♀ *Tropaeolum speciosum* Delicate scarlet nasturtium; tricky. 6ft (1.8m)

---

†   Rare, but worth looking for; check *The Plant Finder* for sources.

Annual climbers†

Annual climbers may be few, but they are invaluable for adding height and for training through summer shrubs for later colour.

Asarina 'Jewel' Blues, pinks and white; sow early. hha. 6ft (1.8m)

Cajophora laterita Orange stars fade white; leaves sting! hha. 5ft (1.5m)

Cardiospermum halicacabanum Strange inflated pods. hha. 6ft (1.8m)

♀ *Cobaea scandens* Blue or white bells; sow early; strong. hha. 10ft (3m)

Dolichos lablab 'Ruby Moon' Purple leaf, pod, flower. hha. 6ft (1.8m)

Eccremocarpus 'Fireworks' Mixture in six shades. hha. 6ft (1.8m)

♀* *Ipomoea 'Heavenly Blue'* Cool, pale blue trumpets; tricky. hha. 6ft (1.8m)

Ipomoea purpurea Good *annual* convulvulus; rich shades. ha 8ft (2.4m)

Lagenaria 'Small Fruited' Small gourds; all shapes/sizes. hha. 8ft (2.4m)

Lathyrus odoratus Many superb varieties; see list page 155. ha

Lathyrus sativus Small, azure blue flowers; slender plant. ha. 4ft (1.2m)

Lathyrus tingitanus Large, cerise and purple; dead head. ha. 5ft (1.5m)

Mina lobata Red sprays turning orange, yellow then white. hha. 5ft (1.5m)

Phaseolus 'Painted Lady' Red/white bicolour runner bean. ha. 8ft (2.4m)

♀ *Rhodochiton atrosanguineus* Unique purple bells; best as hha. 4ft (1.2m)

Thunbergia 'Susie Mixed' Black-eyed orange or yellow. hha. 4ft (1.2m)

Tropaeolum peregrinum Canary creeper; frilly yellow. ha. 6ft (1.8m)

Tropaeolum 'Spitfire' Classy and elegant red nasturtium. ha. 12ft (3.6m)

Tropaeolum 'Tall Mixed' Fiery nasturtium; poor soil best. ha. 8ft (2.4m)

Vicia sativa Purple, pink or two-tone vetch; self-sows. ha. 5ft (1.5m)

---

† ha = hardy annual, sow direct; hha = half hardy annual, sow in heat.

HARDY PERENNIALS

Hardy perennials have no woody growth above ground and die back to the ground at the end of each season. The leaves of the few which remain green during the winter die as new growth emerges. Hardy perennials are usually grown for their flowers, though some have good leaves and while most are at their best in summer, there are varieties for all seasons.

Spring-flowering

Spring brings the first real surge of flowering amongst perennials, and although many are woodland plants there are also sun lovers.

Medium† These perennials should reach between 1ft (30cm) and 3ft (90cm) in height, although some may grow taller in warm gardens and in rich soil.

♀ *Aquilegia 'Music Mixed'* Bright, multi-coloured, seed-raised mix.
   Bergenia 'Ballawley' Magenta-pink flowers above bold leaves.
♀ *Dicentra spectabilis* Pink or white lockets on arching stems.
♀ *Doronicum 'Miss Mason'* Brilliant yellow daisies; easy and tough.
   Euphorbia characias 'Humpty Dumpty' Dwarf, bushy form.
♀ *Euphorbia polychroma* Gold heads at soil level, streching up.
   Geranium phaeum Open heads of small, dark purple flowers.
   Geranium sylvaticum 'Amy Doncaster' White-eyed blue; lovely.
   Geum 'Leonard's Variety' Coppery pink; appreciates shade.
   Helleborus Orientalis Hybrids Most colours, some spotted.
   Iris 'Florentina' White, flushed palest blue; grown for centuries.
   Iris Intermediate Bearded Type Huge range of colours; full sun.
♀ *Paeonia mlokosewitchii* Elegant lemon bowls on broad leaves.
* *Phlox carolina 'Bill Baker'* Succession of candy pink flowers.
   Polemonium foliosissimum Blue; starts early, best dead-headed.
   Polemonium 'Hopleys' Pale lavender; upright habit; very prolific.
♀ *Primula japonica* Candelabras of orange, yellow, red or white.

---

† For tall-growing spring perennials, see page 000.

℣ *Trillium grandiflorum* Cool white flowers; slow but elegant.

℣ *Trollius* × *cultorum* 'Superbus' Deep yellow; hates drought.

℣ *Veronica gentianoides* Slender, sky-blue spikes; long season.

Small   These perennials should grow no more than 1ft (30cm) high, although they may sometimes grow taller in warm gardens and in rich soil.

℣ *Caltha palustris* 'Flore Pleno' Neat, fully double yellow buttons.

Campanula carpatica 'Blue Clips' Big blue bells; bushy plant.

Corydalis flexuosa Bright blue; dainty and prolific; likes shade.

℣* *Dicentra formosa* 'Stuart Boothman' Red lockets; grey foliage.

℣ *Epimedium grandiflorum* Red, pink or white; like little spiders.

℣ *Erythronium dens-canis* Rosy flowers with reflexed petals.

Geranium traversii 'Elegans' Pink flowers; pretty silver leaves.

Geum 'Lionel Cox' Cream, tinged pink; flowers all summer.

Iris 'Cherry Garden' Dark purple. More good Dwarf Bearded.

Iris setosa var. arctica Purple blue irises on pretty, leafy clumps.

Lamium maculatum 'Album' Prolific white flowers; good leaves.

Omphalodes cappadocica 'Cherry Ingram' Brilliant blue stars.

℣ *Primula* 'Guinevere' Pink flowers; reddish leaves; the toughest.†

Pulmonaria 'Frühlingshimmel' Rich but pale blue; likes shade.

Ranunculus ficaria 'Collarette' Tiny double yellow flowers.

Symphytum ibericum Tubular cream flowers; runs freely.

Tiarella wherryi 'Bronze Beauty' Dark pink buds, paler flowers.

Veronica pedicularis 'Georgia Blue' Bright blue; bronze leaves.

℣ *Vinca minor* 'La Grave' Large blue flowers; cut back in winter.

℣ *Viola* 'Jackanapes' Deep mahogany red and bright yellow; smart.

---

†   This is best lifted, divided and replanted every couple of years.

Tall   These perennials should reach over 3ft (90cm) in height except in gardens which are unusually cold or in soil which is very low in nutrients.

*   *Aquilegia 'Adelaide Addison'* Tightly double, blue and white.

    Aquilegia 'McKana Giants' Long-spurred flowers, many colours.

♗ *Aquilegia 'Nora Barlow'* Pink and white flowers like tiny roses.

♗ *Euphorbia characias 'Lambrook Gold'* Dark-eyed yellow heads.

♗ *Euphorbia griffithii 'Dixter'* Fiery red and orange heads; runs.

    Lunaria rediviva Palest lilac, sweetly scented flowers; seed-heads.

♗ *Phalaris arundinacea 'Picta'* Sprays of tiny flowers; variegated.

    Symphytum × uplandicum Pink, blue or purple; rampageous.

    Thalictrum aquilegifolium Fluffy, cream heads; pretty leaves.

    Thermopsis montana Like a yellow lupin with a running root.

Summer-flowering

Summer is the high season for hardy perennials and with so many to choose from, narrowing it down to a selection is very difficult.

Tall   These perennials should reach over 3ft (90cm) in height except in gardens which are unusually cold or in soil which is very low in nutrients.

    Acanthus mollis Stately spikes of pink and white; good leaf.†

♗ *Aruncus dioicus* Foamy, creamy plumes of tiny flowers; imposing.

    Campanula latifolia Bold and impressive; blue or white flowers.

♗ *Crambe cordifolia* Huge, airy, open heads of tiny white flowers.

    Delphinium 'Southern Noblemen' Finest delphiniums from seed.

    Iris 'Jane Phillips' Soft blue. Many other good Tall Bearded types.

♗ *Iris sibirica 'Cambridge'* Neat blue flowers; slender leaves.

    Kniphofia 'Prince Igor' Tall, majestic and brilliant orange.

*   *Lupinus 'New Generation'* The finest lupin mix from seed.

♗ *Phlox paniculata 'Mother of Pearl'* Blush pink. Many more good.

---

†   Although often suggested for shade, this flowers better in sun.

Medium   These perennials should reach between 1ft (30cm) and 3ft (90cm) in height although some may grow taller in warm gardens and in rich soil.

♔ *Achillea 'Moonshine'* Flat heads of soft yellow flowers; grey leaf.

♔ *Alchemilla mollis* Foamy, almost lime-green flowers; self-sows.
  Anthemis 'E C. Buxton' Cool yellow daisies; split every year.

♔ *Astilbe 'Fanal'* Deep red spikes of tiny flowers; hates drought.†
  Astrantia 'Ruby Wedding' Rich ruby pincushions all summer.

♔ *Erigeron 'Dunkelste Aller'* Deep purple-blue daisies; honey eye.
  Eryngium bourgatii Blue, thistle-like heads; white-veined leaves.
  Gypsophila paniculata 'Compacta Plena' Double white in clouds.

♔ *Hemerocallis 'Golden Chimes'* Rich yellow flowers for months.

♔ *Kniphofia 'Samuel's Sensation'* Orange pokers in great profusion.

♔ *Lobelia 'Queen Victoria'* Deep red flowers; rich beetroot leaves.
  Lupinus 'Gallery' The very best dwarf lupin mixture from seed.

♔ *Monarda 'Cambridge Scarlet'* Bergamot; sweetly aromatic leaves.
  Nepeta × faassenii Catmint; lavender spikes over grey foliage.

♔ *Paeonia 'Bowl of Beauty'* Pink and cream. Many more good.
  Papaver orientale 'Curlilocks' Frilly orange-scarlet. Lots more.

♔ *Penstemon 'Garnet'* Deep garnet-red, long season. More good.

♔ *Persicaria bistorta 'Superba'* Bright pink spikes; prefers damp.

♔* *Salvia × superba* Violet-blue spikes then dark reddish stems; sun.
  Scabiosa caucasica 'Clive Greaves' Soft lavender-blue; sun.

---

†   There are many other forms in reds, pinks and white; all like damp.

Small   These perennials should grow no more than 1ft (30cm) high, although they may sometimes grow taller in warm gardens and in rich soil.

Aruncus aethusifolius Dense clouds of small creamy flowers.

♔* *Astilbe 'Sprite'* Pink sprays; lustrous blue foliage; hates drought.

♔ *Dianthus 'Doris'* Pale pink, dark eye; scented. Many more good.

♔ *Diascia 'Ruby Field'* Rich red flowers for months; short-lived.

Eryngium maritimum Small blue heads; grey-blue foliage.

Malva sylvestris 'Primley Blue' Blue dark-veined flowers; spreads.

♔ *Oenothera macrocarpa* Floppy lemon trumpets on red stems.

♔ *Persicaria affinis 'Superba'* Pale pink spikes, steadily darkening.

♔ *Prunella 'Loveliness'* Strong but soft lavender-blue flowers; easy.

♔ *Sedum 'Ruby Glow'* Flat crimson heads; greyish-purple leaves.

Autumn-flowering

By the autumn the number of flowering perennials is declining, and many varieties come from relatively few characteristic species.

Tall   These perennials should reach over 3ft (90cm) in height except in gardens which are unusually cold or in soil which is very low in nutrients.

Aconitum carmichaelii Pale blue spikes above glossy leaves.

♔* *Aster 'Ochtendgloren'* Superb pink daisies. Many more good.

♔ *Aster novae-angliae 'Alma Pötschke'* Shocking-pink; mildew-free.

Aster novi-belgii 'Climax' Lavender daisies; elegant classic.

Boltonia asteroides 'Snowbank' Arching sprays of white daisies.

♔ *Cimicifuga simplex 'Elstead'* Tall spires; purple buds open white.

Eupatorium cannabinum 'Flore Pleno' Fluffy rosy purple heads.

Eupatorium rugosum Flat fuffy white heads on rounded plant.

Helianthus salicifolius Heads of yellow daisies on vast 12ft (3.6m) plant.

♔ *Leucanthemella serotina* Bold white daisies which turn with sun.

---

†   Many tall white asters look tatty as they age, this is a good substitute.

Medium   These perennials should reach between 1ft (30cm) and 3ft (90cm) in height, although some may grow taller in warm gardens and in rich soil.

♀ *Anemone × hybrida* 'Honorine Jobert' Pure white; superb.

♀* *Aster × frikartii* 'Mönch' Single blue; one of the finest asters.

♀ *Aster* 'Monte Cassino' Small white daisies. Many more good.

Aster novi-belgii 'Marie Ballard' Double blue, tinted lilac.

Dendranthema 'Bronze Elegance' Small, neat, bronze pompoms.†

♀ *Gentiana asclepiadea* Blue flowers on arching stems; likes shade.

Helenium 'Wyndley' Rich yellow daisies streaked red; easy.

Hosta plantaginea Fragrant white trumpets; likes damp and heat!

♀ *Schizostylis coccinea* 'Jennifer' Pale pink iris-relative; vigorous.

♀ *Sedum* 'Herbstfreude' Flat heads in rich pink, turning coppery.

Small   These perennials should grow no more than 1ft (30cm) high, although they may sometimes grow taller in warm gardens and in rich soil.

Arctanthemum arcticum 'Schwefelglanz' Yellow daisies.

Aster novi-belgii 'Prof. A. Kippenberg' Blue; short but strong.

Aster novi-belgii 'Schneekissen' White; neat mounded habit.

♀* *Dendranthema yezoense* White daisies; prefers good drainage.

♀ *Gentiana septemfida* Blue; stems long but plants flop naturally.

♀ *Liriope muscari* Spikes of blue flowers like a grape hyacinth.

Liriope muscari 'Munroe White' Small white flowers; likes sun.

♀ *Ophiopogon planiscapus var. nigrescens* Mauve; black leaves.

Sedum spectabile 'Stardust' Flat, greeny white heads; pale leaves.

♀ *Sedum* 'Vera Jameson' Flat, dusky pink heads; smoky leaves.

---

†   Try also 'Mei Kyo' (pink) and 'Purleigh White' (white).

Winter-flowering

In winter, we are left with but few varieties from which to choose over an even narrower range of species; so each one is valuable.

    Adonis amurensis Like a big buttercup; lacy leaves; hates wet. 6in (15cm)

♈ *Bergenia × schmidtii* Pink; earliest bergenia; many are good. 1ft (30cm)

* *Helleborus 'Early Purple'* Tough, reliable; other colours. 15in (38cm)

♈ *Hepatica nobilis* Small, bright, blue, pink or white flowers. 3in (7.5cm)

♈ *Iris uguicularis* Blue or lavender; hot, well drained spot. 1ft (30cm)

    Pachyphragma macrophyllum Pure white flowers; big leaves. 1ft (30cm)

♈ *Pulmonaria rubra* Reliably early; brick red; later types blue. 1ft (30cm)

    Pulmonaria rubra 'Albocorollata' White form of above. 1ft (30cm)

    Vinca difformis Large white flowers; cut back in late autumn. 1ft (30cm)

    Vinca difformis 'Jenny Pym' Pink form of above; hates cold. 1ft (30cm)

Attractive flowers

WHITE FLOWERS†

There has long been a fashion for planting borders of white flowers but many are actually cream or pink; these are among the whitest.

Tall   These perennials should reach over 3ft (90cm) in height except in gardens which are unusually cold or in soil which is very low in nutrients.

♈ *Anemone × hybrida 'Honorine Joubert'* Pure white; runs. au

♈ *Aruncus dioicus* Huge feathery plumes of tiny cream flowers. su

    Aster novae-angliae 'Herbstschnee' Bushy; few good whites. au

♈* *Campanula latiloba 'Alba'* Flared cups in pure white; stunning. su

♈ *Cimicifuga simplex 'Elstead'* Purple buds open to white spikes. su

♈ *Delphinium 'Sandpiper'* Pure white, with a dark brown eye. su

    Iris 'Winter Olympics' Pure white tall bearded type; best in sun. su

♈ *Leucanthemella serotina* Off-white daisies with green eyes. au

♈ *Phlox paniculata 'Fujiyama'* Elegant heads; hates drought. su/au

    Veronicastrum virginicum Slender spikes, faintly tinted blue. su

---

†   In this section sp = spring, su = summer, au = autumn, wi = winter.

Medium   These perennials should reach between 1ft (30cm) and 3ft (90cm) in height, although some may grow taller in warm gardens and in rich soil.

  ♈   *Aquilegia vulgaris 'Nivea'* White columbine, may be tinted pink. su

*   *Campanula persicifolia 'Hampstead White'* Truly exquisite. su

       Delphinium 'Casa Blanca' Like a cloud of white butterflies. su

       Geranium phaeum 'Album' Small reflexed petals; likes shade. su

  ♈   *Leucanthemum × superbum 'Aglaia'* Shaggy Shasta daisy. su

  ♈   *Lupinus 'Pope John Paul'* The nearest to pure white in a lupin. su

       Paeonia 'White Wings' Pure white single, fluffy gold centre. su

  ♈   *Papaver 'Black and White'* Pure with black basal blotches. su

  ♈   *Penstemon 'White Bedder'* Slightly creamy; very prolific. su/au

  ♈   *Pulmonaria officinalis 'Sissinghurst White'* Best white. sp

Small   These perennials should grow no more than 1ft (30cm) high, although they may sometimes grow taller in warm gardens and in rich soil.

       Bergenia 'Beethoven' The best white bergenia; hardly blushes. sp

  ♈   *Dendranthema yezoense* Slightly greyish daisies; very late. au

       Dianthus 'White Ladies' Clouds of fragrant, frilly flowers. su†

       Dicentra 'Snowflakes' Small lockets for months; vigorous. sp/au

 ♈* *Dicentra spectabilis 'Alba'* Clean and elegant; hates spring frost. sp

  ♈   *Epimedium grandiflorum 'White Queen'* Like dainty spiders. sp

       Helleborus niger 'White Magic' Small-flowered, but prolific. wi

  ♈   *Lamium maculatum 'White Nancy'* Silver leaves; likes shade. sp

       Primula vulgaris 'Alba Plena' Double primrose, creamy centre. sp

  ♈   *Viola cornuta 'Alba'* Clean white violet; straggly but pretty. sp/su

---

†   Other white pinks like 'Devon Dove' have larger flowers but less scent.

PINK FLOWERS

Pink is a word which covers an unusually wide range of colours including everything from salmon to rose to bright candy shades.

Tall   These perennials should reach over 3ft (90cm) in height, except in gardens which are unusually cold or in soil which is very low in nutrients.

♀   *Anemone × hybrida 'Königin Charlotte'* Bright rose. su/au

♀   *Aster novae-angliae 'Alma Pötschke'* Lurid salmon rose. au

♀   *Aster 'Ochtendgloren'* Spectacular bright rose; very prolific. au

♀   *Campanula lactiflora 'Loddon Anna'* Slightly mauvey pink. su

♀*   *Delphinium 'Rosemary Brock'* Best pink variety; fat spikes. su

♀   *Filipendula rubra 'Venusta'* Vast feathery plumes; vigorous. su

Linaria purpurea 'Canon Went' Tiny soft flowers; long spikes. su

Lythrum salicaria 'Rosensaule' Deep pink; tallest of spikes. su

♀   *Phlox maculata 'Alpha'* Rich pink cylindrical heads; no mildew. su

♀   *Phlox paniculata 'Mother of Pearl'* Pale blush with dark band. su

Medium   These perennials should reach between 1ft (30cm) and 3ft (90cm) in height although some may grow taller in warm gardens and in rich soil.

Dendranthema 'Clara Curtis' Single chrysanth, yellow eye. au

Geranium × oxonianum 'Claridge Druce' Very reliable. sp/su

♀   *Lupinus 'Kayleigh Ann Savage'* Long dusky spikes; stocky. su†

♀   *Monarda didyma 'Croftway Pink'* Tiers of pale pink; aromatic. su

♀   *Paeonia 'Bowl of Beauty'* Classic variety; leave to mature. su

♀   *Papaver orientale 'Cedric Morris'* Palest grey-pink; unique. su

♀*   *Penstemon 'Evelyn'* Small-flowered but one of the hardiest. su/au

♀   *Sedum spectabile 'Brilliant'* Pale flat heads; butterfly caviar. au

Sidalcea 'Elsie Hugh' Spikes of pale shining pink; frilly petals. su

♀   *Tanacetum 'Eileen May Robinson'* Pale, yellow-eyed daisies. su

---

†   Special lupins like this are hard to find, but worth searching out.

Small   These perennials should grow no more than 1ft (30cm) high, although they may sometimes grow taller in warm gardens and in rich soil.

    Aster novi-belgii 'Little Pink Beauty' Dwarf, but vigorous. au

♀ *Astilbe 'Sprite'* Foamy shell pink plumes; metallic leaves. su

♀ *Dianthus 'Valda Wyatt'* Pale rose, tinted lavender; scented. su

    Diascia fetcaniensis Small-flowered but prolific; dark-eyed. su

* *Geranium 'Mavis Simpson'* Silver foliage; prostrate growth. su

    Geranium sanguineum 'Glenluce' Pure, cool pink; easy. sp/su

    Phuopsis stylosa Fluffy pink balls on short floppy shoots. su

♀ *Primula 'Guinevere'* Dark-eyed flowers; red tinted foliage. sp

    Saponaria × *lempergii 'Max Frei'* Spreading; long season; rare. su

    Silene dioica 'Minikin' Deep and shining; dwarf red campion. sp/su

RED FLOWERS

Scarlet, crimson, magenta, deep orange and some mahogany-tinted shades all come here; it pays to choose the exact shade carefully to avoid clashes.

Tall   These perennials should reach over 3ft (90cm) in height, except in gardens which are unusually cold or in soil which is very low in nutrients.

    Aster novae-angliae 'Septemberrubin' Pink-tinted; no mildew. au

    Helenium 'Feursiegel' Brownish gold and red; one of the tallest. au

    Hemerocallis fulva 'Flore Pleno' Fully double dusky orange. su†

    Kniphofia 'Atlanta' Bold orange-red pokers, yellow at base. su

* *Kniphofia 'Prince Igor'* Stupendous spikes, fading yellow. su

    Leonitis ocymifolia Tiers of claw-like, burnt orange flowers. su

♀ *Lychnis chalcedonica* Flat heads of small scarlet flowers. su

♀ *Papaver orientale var. bracteatum* Elegant crimson poppies. su

♀ *Persicaria amplexicaulis 'Firetail'* Slim, fiery, crimson spikes. su

    Verbascum 'Cotswold Queen' Soft burnt orange spikes. su

---

†   This and 'Golden Chimes' are better in the garden than newer types.

Medium   These perennials should reach between 1ft (30cm) and 3ft (90cm) in height, although some may grow taller in warm gardens and in rich soil.

  ♆   *Astilbe 'Fanal'* Compact but vivid scarlet plumes; likes damp. su

      Astrantia major 'Ruby Wedding' Dainty dark crimson heads. su

  ♆   *Dicentra spectabilis* Red and white lockets on arching stems. sp

  ♆   *Geranium psilostemon* Bold, dark-eyed magenta flowers. su

  ♆   *Geum chiloense 'Mrs J. Bradshaw'* Brilliant red; easy, reliable. su

  ♆*   *Lobelia 'Compliment Scarlet'* Brilliant scarlet spikes; vigorous. su†

      Paeonia 'Inspecteur Lavergne' Crimson double, tipped silver. su

      Papaver orientale 'Ladybird' Bright scarlet, black basal blotch. su

  ♆   *Penstemon 'Chester Scarlet'* Large-flowered, white throat. su/au

  ♆   *Potentilla 'Gibson's Scarlet'* Brilliant scarlet; floppy plants. su

Small   These perennials should grow no more than 1ft (30cm) high, although they may sometimes grow taller in warm gardens and in rich soil.

  ♆   *Dianthus 'Houndspool Ruby'* Reddish pink with ruby centre. su

      Epimedium grandiflorum 'Crimson Beauty' Dainty, deep red. sp

  *   *Geranium 'Ann Folkard'* Magenta; flat or sprawls into shrubs. su

      Lamium maculatum 'Beacon Silver' Purple tints; silver leaves. sp

      Lychnis arkwrightii 'Vesuvius' Vermilion; purple leaves. su

      Primula vulgaris 'Red Paddy' Double deep red primrose. sp

      Pulmonaria rubra 'Bowles Red' Bright brick red; green leaf. wi/sp

      Ranunculus ficaria 'Coppernob' Deep orange; bronze leaf. sp

  ♆   *Sedum 'Ruby Glow'* Flat ruby heads over smoky red leaves. su/au

      Viola 'Arkwright Ruby' Bronzed ruby with a black eye. sp

---

†   Unlike most of the varieties in this section, this is raised from seed.

YELLOW FLOWERS

Here I use yellow to cover rich cream and pale orange as well as primrose and buttercup shades; true gold is rare but also fits here.

Tall   These perennials should reach over 3ft (90cm) in height, except in gardens which are unusually cold or in soil which is very low in nutrients.

℣ *Achillea filipendulina 'Gold Plate'* Flat heads on stiff stems. su
    Alcea rugosa Lovely, pale satiny yellow, rust-free hollyhock. su
    Cephalaria gigantea Like a huge, pale yellow scabious. su
℣ *Euphorbia characias 'Lambrook Gold'* Rich yellow. wi/sp
    Helianthus 'Lemon Queen' Wonderful cool lemon daisies. au
℣ *Hemerocallis 'Marion Vaughn'* Lemon, with a paler midrib. su
    Kniphofia 'September Sunshine' Clear yellow; usefully late. au
℣ *Ligularia 'The Rocket'* Slim yellow spikes; superb dark leaves. su
    Thermopsis montana Spikes of yellow pea flowers; runs. sp
℣ *Verbascum 'Gainsborough'* Bright yellow; short-lived. su

Medium   These perennials should reach between 1ft (30cm) and 3ft (90cm) in height, although some may grow taller in warm gardens and in rich soil.
    Anthemis 'E. C. Buxton' Clear lemon daisies; divide regularly. su
℣ *Aster ericoides 'Golden Spray'* Small pale yellow; darker eye. au
    Doronicum orientale 'Magnificum' Spectacular early perennial. sp
℣ *Euphorbia polychroma* Expanding dome of greenish yellow. sp
℣ *Hemerocallis 'Golden Chines'* Small, deep yellow; prolific. su
    Iris 'Dresden Candleglow' Cool lemon flowers; very prolific. sp
℣* *Kniphofia 'Little Maid'* Slender spikes; green opening ivory. su
    Lupin 'Moonraker' Sumptuous sharp yellow spikes; stocky. su
℣ *Paeonia mlokosewitschii* Superb single cool lemon peony. sp†
℣ *Rudbekia fulgida 'Goldsturm'* Almost gold daisies, black eyes. su

---

† This is expensive and slow to settle down but worth the wait.

Small   These perennials should grow no more than 1ft (30cm) high, although they may sometimes grow taller in warm gardens and in rich soil.

ℙ   *Caltha palustris 'Flore Pleno'* Neat, bright buttons; likes wet. sp

   Geum × chiloense 'Georgenberg' Dainty bright yellow. su

ℙ* *Hemerocallis 'Stella d'Oro'* The finest dwarf hemerocallis. su

   Iris 'Eyebright' Yellow, with contrasting maroon flash. sp

   Lysichiton americanus 1ft (30cm), buttercup yellow, arum flowers. sp†

   Primula 'Double Sulphur' Double yellow primrose; tough. sp

   Ranunculus ficaria 'Flore Pleno' Pretty, double celandine. sp

   Solidago 'Tom Thumb' Yellow plumes; the shortest golden rod. su

   Symphytum ibericum Rich cream, tubular flowers; runs. sp/su

ℙ   *Viola 'Moonlight'* Small creamy yellow flowers on long stems. sp

BLUE FLOWERS

If flowers ranged only from sky-blue to navy-blue describing them would be easy, but many have pink, red or purple overtones.

Tall   These perennials should reach over 3ft (90cm) in height, except in gardens which are unusually cold or in soil which is very low in nutrients.

ℙ   *Aconitum × cammarum 'Bicolor'* Dark blue and white. su

   Aquilegia vulgaris 'Adelaide Addison' Blue and white double. su

ℙ   *Aster × frikartii 'Wunder von Stäfa'* Bluish lilacish daisies. su/au

ℙ   *Baptisia australis* Smoky blue pea flowers; blue-green leaves. su

ℙ   *Campanula lactiflora 'Prichard's Variety'* Violet-tinted. su

   Delphinium 'Alice Artindale' Densely double bright blue. su

ℙ* *Delphinium 'Blue Nile'* Brilliant blue with a white eye. su

   Iris 'Jane Phillips' Classic pale blue bearded iris; prolific. su

ℙ   *Meconopsis betonicifolia* Himalayan poppy; mauve on lime. su

ℙ   *Salvia uliginosa* Small blue and white flowers in airy sprays. au

---

†   Although only 1ft (30cm) in flower, the leaves which follow reach 3ft (90cm).

Medium   These perennials should reach between 1ft (30cm) and 3ft (90cm) in height, although some may grow taller in warm gardens and in rich soil.

♔ *Anchusa azurea 'Loddon Royalist'* Deep, rich and vibrant. su

♔ *Aster* × *frikartii 'Mönch'* Neat blue daisies; very long season. su/au

  Campanula persicifolia 'Telham Beauty' Unusually large. su

♔ *Eryngium alpinum* Deep blue stems, deep blue cones. su

♔ *Gentiana asclepiadea* Bright blue on slender arching growth. au

♔* *Geranium 'Johnson's Blue'* Lavender-tinted; long season. su

♔ *Iris sibirica 'Cambridge'* Pale Cambridge blue; veined throat. su

  Pulmonaria mollis 'Royal Blue' The most sparkling blue of all. sp

  Scabiosa 'Butterfly Blue' Neat, lavender-tinted cushions. sp/su

♔ *Veronica gentianoides* Upright spikes of palest grey blue. sp†

Small   These perennials should grow no more than 1ft (30cm) high, although they may sometimes grow taller in warm gardens and in rich soil.

  Campanula carpatica 'Blue Clips' Large cups on a small plant. su

♔ *Geranium wallichianum 'Buxton's Variety'* White eyed. su/au

  Iris 'Small Wonder' Pale blue dwarf bearded, yellow throat. sp

  Omphalodes cappadocica 'Cherry Ingram' Bright stars; shade. sp

♔ *Penstemon 'Catherine de la Mare'* Bright blue with a red spark. su

  Polemonium reptans 'Blue Pearl' Bright blue with a cream eye. su

  Primula 'Blue Riband' Blue single; red eye, yellow throat. sp

♔ *Veronica 'Shirley Blue'* Sparkling blue spikes; rather floppy. sp/su

♔ *Vinca minor 'Azurea Flore Pleno'* Sky blue, double; creeps. sp

♔* *Viola 'Ardross Gem'* Pale blue viola with gold eye; lovely. sp/su

---

† There is a very pretty variegated form of this plant, 'Variegata'.

PURPLE AND MAUVE FLOWERING

This section covers all the purple, violet and mauve shades which bring such
opulence and depth of colour to our borders.

Tall   These perennials should reach over 3ft (90cm) in height, except in
gardens which are unusually cold or in soil which is very low in nutrients.

Aster novae-angliae 'Purple Cloud' Lilac-purple; no mildew. au

Aster novae-angliae 'Violetta' Deepest purple; no mildew. au

Aster novii-belgii 'The Archbishop' Violet; suitably sultry. au

Astilbe 'Purpurlanze' Slim, upright, magenta-purple spikes. su

*   *Campanula latifolia 'Brantwood'* Bold bells; rich violet-purple. su

♀ *Delphinium 'Bruce'* Rich violet-purple, greyish brown eye. su

Galega orientalis Mauve pea flowers; bushy plant; needs support. su†

Linaria purpurea Slimline spikes of tiny purple snapdragons. su†

Strobilanthes atropurpureus Unusual arched purple flowers. au

Verbena bonariensis Flat reddish purple heads; self-supporting. su/au†

Medium   These perennials should reach between 1ft (30cm) and 3ft (90cm)
in height, although some may grow taller in warm gardens and in rich soil.

♀ *Aster amellus 'Veilchenkönigin'* Rich violet; butterfly's delight. au

Erigeron 'Dignity' The best violet erigeron; bushy habit. su

Geranium phaeum Small, dusky purple flowers in airy heads. su†

*   *Helleborus 'Early Purple'* The most reliable winter hellebore. wi

Iris 'Dusky Dancer' Richest deep purple flag, almost black. su

Lobelia 'Tania' Rich crimson purple; coppery young leaves. su

♀ *Penstemon 'Alice Hindley'* Lavender and white; long season. su/au

Phlox paniculata 'Border Gem' Purple; old and dependable. su

Pulmonaria 'Patrick Bates' Violet, slightly reddish at first. sp

Salvia × sylvestris 'Maincht' Deepest indigo, purple stems. su

---

†   Beware, this plant may smother its neighbours with self-sown seedlings.

Small These perennials should grow no more than 1ft (30cm) high, although they may sometimes grow taller in warm gardens and in rich soil.

    Aster novii-belgii 'Purple Dome' Deep purple, semi-double. au

    Campanula glomerata 'Joan Elliott' Violet-blue; floppy. su/au

    Geranium procurrens Purple flowers; ground hugging habit. su/au

    Iris 'Raspberry Jam' Rich reddish violet flag; very dwarf; sp

    Origanum 'Kent Beauty' Mauve bracts; loves sun, hates wet. su

    Phuopsis stylosa 'Purpurea' Round mauve heads; floppy. su

♀ *Polemonium 'Lambrook Mauve'* Soft shimmering mauve. sp

    Primula 'Miss Indigo' Deep purple-blue double; silver edge. sp

♀ *Vinca minor 'Atropurpurea'* Plum-purple; good ground cover. sp

♀* *Viola 'Maggie Mott'* Huge flowers in pale bluey mauve. sp

BICOLOURED FLOWERS

There are some lovely perennials which owe their appeal to a particularly bold combination of two different colours in one flower.

    Aquilegia 'McKana Hybrids' Mix of bright bicolours. 3ft (90cm) sp/su†

    Dianthus 'Prudence' Neat white, edged and eyed crimson. 1ft (30cm) su

    Dianthus 'Ursula le Grove' Lacy white, red eye and frills. 1ft (30cm) su

♀ *Euphorbia characias* Masses of maroon-eyed green flowers. 3ft (90cm) sp

♀ *Geranium psilostemon* Black-eyed, bright magenta bowls; 3ft (90cm) su

    Helleborus spotted forms White or pink with red spots. 18in (45cm) wi

♀ *Lupinus 'Helen Sharman'* Orange and yellow bicolour. 4ft (1.2m) su

♀ *Papaver 'Black and White'* White bowls, blotched black. 4ft (1.2m) su.

* *Viola 'Ardross Gem'* Prolific blue, with a neat gold eye. 9in (23cm) sp

♀ *Viola 'Jackanapes'* Yellow lower petals, maroon above. 9in (23cm) sp/su

---

† Raise afresh from seed every few years to ensure best colour range.

UNUSUAL FLOWER COLOURS

In this list I have gathered together a selection of varieties which are either dramatically bicoloured or whose unusual colouring does not fit in well with the main colour groups featured so far.

℞ *Acanthus spinosus* Hooded white flowers in purple bracts. 5ft (1.5m) su

Achillea 'Forncett Fletton' Bright brick orange then yellow. 3ft (90cm) su

Aconitum 'Ivorine' Creamy ivory flowers; likes it cool. 2ft (60cm) sp

℞ *Alchemilla mollis* Clouds of green foam above pretty leaves. 1ft (30cm) su

Eryngium eberneum Green and silver cones; spiny leaves. 5ft (1.5m) su

Ferula communis Big yellow-green umbrellas; lacy leaves. 6ft (1.8m) su

℞ *Geranium pratense 'Mrs Kendall Clark'* Grey, flushed rose. 3ft (90cm) su

℞ *Geum 'Leonard's Variety'* Browny, pinkish orange. 18in (45cm) sp/su

℞ *Helleborus argutifolius* Bright green cups; bold leaves. 3ft (90cm) wi

Hemerocallis 'Catherine Woodbury' Soft pink, green eye. 3ft (90cm) su

Iris 'Jitterbug' Deep yellow flag speckled in rusty brown. 2ft (60cm) sp†

Kniphofia 'Ice Queen' Green buds to cream and open white. 5ft (1.5m) au

Morina longifolia Tiers of flowers, open pink turning white. 3ft (90cm) su

* *Penstemon 'Sour Grapes'* Blue and purple shadings. 3ft (90cm) su/au

Polemonium pauciflorum Pale primrose, flushed pink. 1ft (30cm) su

Pulmonaria rubra 'Ann' Bright brick red, striped white. 1ft (30cm) wi/sp

Rheum alexandrae Creamy bracts, reddish later; tricky. 4ft (1.2m) su

Tricyrtis hirta Small white flowers, heavily speckled purple. 2ft (60cm) au

℞ *Verbascum 'Helen Johnson'* Coppery beigey pink spikes. 4ft (1.2m) su

Viola 'Irish Molly' Unique dusky brown and green pansy. 6in (15cm) su

---

†   There are a great many other good bearded irises in unusual colours.

SCENTED FLOWERS

Strong scents are concentrated in a number of familiar plants like pinks and peonies, with many more having lesser fragrance.

Tall   These perennials should reach over 3ft (90cm) in height, except in gardens which are unusually cold or in soil which is very low in nutrients.

Asphodeline lutea Stiff yellow spikes above grassy foliage. su
Clematis heracleifolia Small, sweet, blue flowers; big leaves. su
Clematis × *jouiniana* 'Praecox' Pale blue, sweet scrambler. su
Clematis recta 'Purpurea' Clouds of cream; purple leaves. su
Crambe cordifolia Honey-scented white clouds; needs space. su
Filipendula kamtschatica Large white plumes; bold foliage. su
Hemerocallis multiflora Small, orange-yellow; late. su/au
Phlox paniculata 'Prospero' Lilac pink; sweet, peppery scent. su†
Phlox paniculata 'White Admiral' Bold, pure white heads. su†
Verbena bonariensis Mauve, on stiff stems; phloxy scent. su

Medium†   These perennials should reach between 1ft (30cm) and 3ft (90cm) in height, some may grow taller in warm gardens and in rich soil.

   Aquilegia fragrans White, apple-scented flowers; bluish leaves. su
   Astilbe 'Deutschland' Pure white plumes; likes moisture. su
♥ *Dictamnus albus* Slightly lemony scent; white or purple. su
♥ *Hemerocallis lilioasphodelus* Clear yellow 'lilies'; very strong. sp
♥ *Hosta* 'Honeybells' Strongly scented lilac-tinted white flowers. su
* *Iris* 'Florentina' Orris root; greyish white; strong, sweet scent . sp
   Iris graminea Purple flowers; smells strongly of stewed plums. su
   Lunaria rediviva White perennial honesty; smells of stocks. sp
♥ *Paeonia* 'Duchesse de Nemours' Classic double white; very old. su
♥ *Phlox carolina* 'Miss Lingard' Pure white; mildew-free. su

---

†   Most border phlox are scented, though some gardeners can smell none of them.

Small   These perennials should grow no more than 1ft (30cm) high, although they may sometimes grow taller in warm gardens and in rich soil.

   Alyssum montanum Lemon-yellow, alyssum scent; flat growth. sp

♀* *Convallaria majalis* Unmistakable white bells; strong perfume. sp

   Dianthus 'Mrs Sinkins' Messy white flowers, but superb scent. su†

♀ *Iris unguicularis* Blue or mauve, deliciously scented; likes sun. wi

   Petasites fragrans White; heliotrope scent; seriously rampant. wi

♀ *Primula veris* Delicate yellow bells; characteristic cowslip scent. sp

   Primula vulgaris Primrose; many coloured forms unscented. sp

   Viola 'Luna' Pale yellow; most violas scented, this specially. sp

   Viola odorata 'Governor Herrick' Purple sweet violet. sp

   Viola 'Rebecca' Frilly cream flowers, flecked with purple. sp

---

Attractive foliage

Good foliage makes or mars a border, for although flowers provide the most colour, interesting foliage provides colour for far longer.

VARIEGATED LEAVES

Foliage which is striped, blotched or streaked in white, yellow or cream creates a haze of colour at a distance and is bolder close to.

Tall   These perennials should reach over 3ft (90cm) in height, except in gardens which are unusually cold or in soil which is very low in nutrients.

   Cortaderia selloana 'Albolineata' Edged white; best in autumn.

♀ *Cortaderia selloana 'Aureolineata'* Edged gold, all gold later.

   Glyceria maxima 'Variegata' Striped cream, young shoots pink.

♀ *Hosta fluctuans 'Variegated'* Edged cream; elegant but slow.

   Iris pseudacorus 'Variegata' Bright yellow stripes, greener later.

   Miscanthus sinensis 'Variegatus' Broad cream central stripe.

   Miscanthus sinensis 'Zebrinus' Unusual horizontal yellow stripes.

   Spartina pectinata 'Aureo-marginata' Edged yellow; subtle.

♀* *Symphytum × uplandicum 'Variegatum'* Bold cream edge.

---

†   A large number of other pinks are scented, often of cloves.

Medium   These perennials should reach between 1ft (30cm) and 3ft (90cm) in height, although some may grow taller in warm gardens and in rich soil.

Aegopodium podagraria 'Variegata' White-edged ground elder.†

Aquilegia vulgaris 'Vervaeneana' Delightfully yellow-marbled.

♀ *Astrantia 'Sunningdale Variegated'* White-edged; remove flowers.

Dendranthema 'Anastasia Variegated' White-edged; pink poms.

Eryngium bourgatii Grey leaves, veined silver; blue-green heads.

Euphorbia characias 'Emmer Green' Cream-edged; green heads.

♀ *Hosta 'Shade Fanfare'* Broad cream-edge in shade, yellow in sun.

Iris foetidissima 'Variegata' Bold pale cream stripes; no flowers.

*   *Iris pallida 'Argentea Variegata'* Bluish leaves, striped white.

Mentha × suaveolens 'Variegata' Erratic white stripes; apple scent.†

♀ *Molinia caerulea 'Variegata'* Slender cream-striped leaves; lovely.

♀ *Phalaris arundinacea 'Picta'* White-striped, biscuit in winter.†

Phlox paniculata 'Norah Leigh' White-variegated; mauve flowers.

Physostegia virginiana 'Variegata' White-edged; pink flowers.

Polemonium caeruleum 'Brise d'Anjou' Cream-edged; stunning.

Polygonatum falcatum 'Variegatum' Neat white edge; vigorous.

Scrophularia auriculata 'Variegata' Very bright cream-edge.

Sisyrinchum striatum 'Aunt May' Iris-like leaves, cream-striped.

Veronica gentianoides 'Variegata' White-splashed; blue flowers.

Vinca major 'Variegata' Splashed cream; blue flowers; runs.†

---

†   This plant can sometimes be a nuisance by spreading too much.

Small   These perennials should grow no more than 1ft (30cm) high, although they may sometimes grow taller in warm gardens and in rich soil.

 Agrostis canina 'Silver Needles' Dense mat of white and green.

 Ajuga reptans 'Variegata' Grey-green, edged white; blue flowers.

 Arabis caucasica 'Gillian Sharman' Edged cream; white flowers.

♈ *Arum italicum 'Marmoratum'* White-veined all through winter.

♈ *Brunnera macrophylla 'Hadspen Cream'* Irregular primrose rim.

 Carex conica 'Snowline' Narrow leaves edged white; looks silver.

 Carex morrowii 'Variegata' Dark leaves, edged and striped white.

 Chiastophyllum 'Jim's Pride' Cream-edged rosettes, cream bells.

 Diascia 'Katherine Sharman' Neat white edges; ruby flowers.

♈ *Hakenochloa macra 'Aureola'* Fountain of yellow-striped leaves.

 Hosta 'Ground Master' Cream-edged, wavy leaves; good cover.

 Lamium galeobdolon 'Florentinum' Silver-blotched; rampant.

* *Lamium galeobdolon 'Hermann's Pride'* Silver-veined; neat.

 Lamium maculatum Silver-blotched; red, pink or white flowers.

 Pulmonaria rubra 'David Ward' The only white-edged variety.†

 Symphytum 'Goldsmith' Irregular yellow edge; blue flowers.

 Trifolium pratense 'Susan Smith' Unique, yellow-veined clover.

 Vinca minor 'Silver Service' Greyish and white; double blue.

---

†   This variety is best planted in some shade to prevent scorch.

GOLD AND YELLOW LEAVES

Most yellow-leaved varieties need good light to bring out their colour but may scorch in full sun; some go green late in the season.

Medium   These perennials should reach between 1ft (30cm) and 3ft (90cm) in height, although some may grow taller; there are few really tall forms.

    Aquilegia 'Mellow Yellow' Soft yellow; flowers blue or white.†
    Centaurea montana 'Gold Bullion' Retains colour; blue flowers.
    Deschampsia flexuosa 'Tatra Gold' Neat tufts of golden yellow.
    Filipendula ulmaria 'Aurea' Bright yellow, scorches badly in sun.
♀ *Hosta 'Sum and Substance'* Chartreuse gold; almost slugproof.
    Hosta 'Zounds' Puckered gold; lavender flowers; for light shade.
    Luzula sylvatica 'Hohe Tatra' Yellow in winter, then greener.
    Melissa officinalis 'Allgold' Bright yellow; scorches in full sun.
* *Milium effusum 'Aureum'* Soft yellow; sun or shade; self-sows.
    Origanum 'Norton Gold' Bright yellow marjoram; no scorch.

Small   These perennials should grow no more than 1ft (30cm) high, although they may sometimes grow taller in warm gardens and in rich soil.

* *Acorus gramineus 'Ogon'* Pretty yellow fans; bright in winter.
♀ *Carex elata 'Aurea'* Bright yellow; best in full sun; likes damp.
    Hosta 'Golden Prayers' Dwarf gold for light shade; lilac flowers.
    Lamium maculatum 'Cannon's Gold' Neat yellow; good in sun.
    Luzula sylvatica 'Aurea' Good yellow; best in winter and not dry.
♀ *Lysimachia nummularia 'Aurea'* Very bright ground hugger.
    Ranunculus repens 'Joe's Golden' Leaves mottled yellow.
    Stachys byzantina 'Primrose Heron' Yellow-flushed grey leaves.
    Veronica prostrata 'Trehane' Brilliant yellow sets off blue spikes.
    Viola cornuta 'Tony Venison' Tinted yellow, best when happy.

---

†   Raise new plants from seed every few years to keep colour true.

SILVER AND GREY LEAVES

Silver, grey and pewtery leaves not only set off many flower colours well but often indicate plants which thrive in hot, dry sites.

Tall These perennials should reach over 3ft (90cm) in height, except in gardens which are unusually cold or in soil which is very low in nutrients.

♀ *Cynara cardunculus* Cardoon; bold and stately; needs space.
♀ *Helictotrichon sempervirens* Fountain of steely blue; best in sun.
♀* *Hosta 'Krossa Regal'* Huge blue-grey leaves; very striking.†
♀ *Kniphofia caulescens* Long grey leaves from fat stems.
  Leymus arenarius Slim, grey-blue leaves; outrageously rampant.
♀ *Macleaya microcarpa 'Coral Plume'* Rounded grey-green leaves.
♀ *Melianthus major* Sumptuous blue-green leaves, boldly divided.†
  Sanguisorba obtusa Elegant arching greyish leaves; runs too well.
  Thalictrum aquilegifolium Grey-green, columbine-like leaves.
♀ *Verbascum 'Gainsborough'* Dusky grey rosette; lemon spikes.

Medium These perennials should reach between 1ft (30cm) and 3ft (90cm) in height, although some may grow taller in warm gardens and in rich soil.

♀ *Achillea 'Moonshine'* Divided, pewtery grey leaves; yellow heads.
♀ *Anaphalis margaritacea var. yedoensis* Felted white; likes shade.
♀* *Anthemis punctata ssp. cupaniana* Grey and lacy; white daisies.
♀ *Artemisia ludoviciana 'Valerie Finnis'* Silvery white; tough.
♀ *Artemisia pontica* Fluffy and silvery green; pretty, but runs.
  Euphorbia nicaaënsis Startling, fleshy, blue-grey leaves; loves sun.
  Hosta 'Snowden' Bold, greyish-green mound; late white flowers.†
  Nepeta × faassenii Catmint; aromatic grey leaves; purple spikes.
  Potentilla atrosanguinea var. argyrophylla Striking bright silver.
  Veronica spicata 'Heidekind' Slender grey leaves; pink spikes.

---

† This plant makes an effective specimen when grown in a container.

Small   These perennials should grow no more than 1ft (30cm) high, although they may sometimes grow taller in warm gardens and in rich soil.

♀ *Anaphalis triplinervis 'Sommerschnee'* Grey; white everlastings.
Anthemis marschalliana Neatly cut silver leaves; yellow daisies.
Artemisia stelleriana Boldly lobed, almost white, leaves; flat.
Dianthus Most garden pinks have good, slim, grey-blue leaves.
♀ *Dicentra 'Langtrees'* Broadly divided silvery grey leaves; creeps.
Festuca valesiaca 'Silbersee' Neat tufted grass; almost blue.
♀* *Hosta 'Halcyon'* Bluish heart-shaped leaves; lilac autumn flowers.
Lamium maculatum 'Beacon Silver' Neat, almost white leaves.
Pulmonaria 'Tim's Silver' Bold silver leaves with thin green rim.
Stachys byzantina 'Silver Carpet' Felted silver; no flower spikes.

PURPLE AND BRONZE-TINTED LEAVES

Some perennials have very strongly coloured purple leaves but others, whose colouring is merely a tint, can be equally effective.

Tall   These perennials should reach over 3ft (90cm) in height, except in gardens which are unusually cold or in soil which is very low in nutrients.

Artemisia lactiflora 'Guizhou' Blackish green leaves and stems.
Canna 'King Humbert' Huge purple leaves; not really hardy!
Cimicifuga simplex 'Atropurpurea' Purple-tinted; rather variable.
* *Cimicifuga simplex 'Brunette'* Best deep purple; pinkish flowers.
Clematis recta 'Purpurea' Deep purple greening later; white stars.
Foeniculum vulgare 'Purpureum' Fine purple-tinted leaves. †
♀ *Ligularia dentata 'Desdemona'* Richly coloured leaf undersides.
Miscanthus sinensis var. purpurascens Brown, pink central line.
Rheum palmatum 'Atrosanguineum' Beetroot first, then greener.
♀ *Rodgersia pinnata 'Superba'* Bronze, deeply veined; likes damp.

---

†   When this plant self-sows some plants may come up almost green.

Medium   These perennials should reach between 1ft (30cm) and 3ft (90cm) in height, although some may grow taller in warm gardens and in rich soil.

*   *Bergenia 'Bressingham Ruby'* Superb, ruby-red winter colour.

    Carex comans 'Bronze Form' Long slender milk chocolate leaves.

♀   *Crocosmia 'Solfaterre'* Smoky bronze leaves; soft orange flowers.

    Euphorbia amygdaloides 'Rubra' Deep maroon-red; variable.

    Euphorbia dulcis 'Chameleon' Dusky purple, pinkish in autumn.

♀   *Heuchera micrantha 'Palace Purple'* Deep purple, best in spring.

    Imperata cylindrica 'Rubra' Red tips to grassy leaves; slow.

♀   *Lobelia 'Queen Victoria'* Purple stems and leaves; scarlet flowers.

    Lychnis 'Molten Lava' Matt purple leaves; orange-scarlet flowers.

    Sedum telephium 'Arthur Branch' Shining purple; pink flowers.

Small   These perennials should grow no more than 1ft (30cm) high, although they may sometimes grow taller in warm gardens and in rich soil.

♀   *Ajuga reptans 'Braunherz'* Best of many purple-leaved bugles.

♀   *Ophiopogon planiscapus 'Nigrescens'* Slim black leaves; creeps.

    Oxalis triangularis 'Cupido' Large, blackish purple, clover-like.

    Plantago major 'Rubrifolia' Matt purple, sometimes green-tinted.

♀   *Primula 'Guinevere'* Superb reddish purple leaves; pink flowers.

♀   *Tiarella wherryi* Small, dusky, purple, maple-like; cream flowers.

    Trifolium repens 'Wheatfen' Purple clover leaves; flat-growing.

    Uncinia rubra Tufts of orangey reddish brown; hates drought.

*   *Veronica peduncularis 'Georgia Blue'* Shining purple; blue stars.

    Viola riviniana 'Purpurea' Dusky greenish purple; purple violets.†

---

†   Self-sows when happy, but is rarely a nuisance and never throws greens.

MULTICOLOURED LEAVES

This small range of perennials with leaves in multiple colourings needs careful positioning; some also need need careful cultivation.

Ajuga reptans 'Multicolor' Red, bronze, pink, gold and cream! 3in (7.5cm)

♕ *Athyrium niponicum 'Pictum'* Silvery-grey, maroon and pink. 1ft (30cm)

Euphorbia amygdaloides 'Variegata' Cream, green, pink. 1ft (30cm)

Fallopia japonica 'Spectabilis' Green, pink and cream; romps. 5ft (1.5m)

Geranium phaeum 'Variegatum' Green, cream, reddish pink. 2ft (60cm)

Heuchera 'Pewter Moon' Ruby purple below, silvered above. 1ft (30cm)

Houttuynia cordata 'Chameleon' Green, yellow, scarlet. 1ft (30cm)

Lamium maculatum 'Elisabeth de Haas' Green, cream, white. 4in (10cm)

Persicaria virginiana 'Painter's Palette' Green, cream, pink. 2ft (60cm)

* *Phlox paniculata 'Harlequin'* Grey-green, cream and pink tips. 3ft (90cm)

ORNAMENTAL NEW FOLIAGE

Some perennials begin to show colour as soon as their shoots peep through the ground and this adds another dimension to the garden.

Aquilegia Most columbines are reddish or purplish as they emerge.†

Artemisia vulgaris 'Variegata' New growth edged cream. 3ft (90cm)

Crambe maritima Reddish purple, ageing to bluish green. 2ft (60cm)

♕ *Dryopteris erythrosora* Fronds pinkish bronze then green. 18in (45cm)

* *Euphorbia sikkimensis* Green, striped white; red tinted at first. 4ft (1.2m)

Geranium 'Ann Folkard' New leaves almost gold all season. 2ft (60cm)

Lamium album 'Pale Peril' Tips of shoots gold, green later. 18in (45cm)

Oenothera fruticosa 'Erica Robin' Yellow, pink and spots. 2ft (60cm)

Paeonia New shoots of most peonies have a strong red colouring.†

Valeriana phu 'Aurea' Bright yellow in spring, fades to green. 2ft (60cm)

---

† Interplant with dwarf bulbs to create an unusual spring effect.

AROMATIC LEAVES

Foliage aromas not only make weeding a pleasure, (brushing the plants releases their scent) but add interest when flowers are few.

    Achillea filipendulina 'Gold Plate' Sharp, sweet and pungent. 4ft (1.2m)

    Achillea millefolium Familiar sharp yarrow smell; many colours.
        2ft (60cm)

♀ *Artemisia abrotanum* Southernwood; sweet, greyish leaves. 3ft (90cm)

    Artemisia alba Strongly camphor-scented grey-green leaves. 3ft (90cm)

    Chamaemelum nobile 'Treneague' Non-flowering chamomile. 3in (7.5cm)

♀ *Dictamnus albus* Exudes flammable aromatic oil in strong sun. 3ft (90cm)

    Filipendula ulmaria Carbolic freshness; coloured leaf forms. 2ft (60cm)

    Foeniculum vulgare Fennel; strong aniseed scent in all forms. 5ft (1.5m)†

    Levisticum vulgare Lovage; sharp and biting; imposing plant. 6ft (1.8m)†

    Melissa officinalis 'Allgold' Strongly lemon; all yellow leaves. 2ft (60cm)†

    Mentha gracilis 'Variegata' Mild, supposedly ginger, mint. 1ft (30cm)†

* *Monarda didyma* Softly minty; many good flower colours. 3–5ft
        (90cm–1.5m)†

    Nepeta × *faassenii* Catmint; grey leaf; white or bluish flowers. 18in
        (45cm)

    Nepeta sibirica Catmint smell, on taller, colourful blue plant. 3ft (90cm)

♀ *Origanum vulgare 'Aureum'* Yellow form of true marjoram. 15in (38cm)†

    Phuopsis stylosa Some say new-mown hay, others foxes! 1ft (30cm)

    Salvia Most species have a variant on the familiar sage smell. 1–6ft
        (30cm–1.8m)

    Sanguisorba minor Slightly nutty or maybe cucumber smell. 18in (45cm)

    Tanacetum parthenium Feverfew; familiar powerful scent. 3in (7.5–60cm)

    Tanacetum vulgare Tansy; strong and pungent; yellow buttons. 3ft (90cm)

---

†   This is a useful plant for use as a flavouring in the kitchen.

AUTUMN-COLOURING LEAVES

Perennials are not known for their autumn colour but there are some which are very effective, especially among the grasses.

- ♀ *Arisaema candidissima* Broad lobed leaves turn bright yellow. 1ft (30cm)
  Deschampsia caespitosa 'Goldschleir' Gold and coppery. 3ft (90cm)
- * *Geranium × cantabrigense* Very bright orangey shades. 1ft (30cm)
  Geranium macrorrhizum Orange tints but partially evergreen. 1ft (30cm)
  Geranium wlassovianum Brilliant red, then turning purplish. 2ft (60cm)
- ♀ *Hosta 'Halcyon'* Uniform shiny biscuit-brown; very attractive. 1ft (30cm)
  Miscanthus sinensis var. purpurascens Purple, tinted red. 4ft (1.2m)
- ♀ *Molinia caerulea 'Variegata'* Whole leaf turns beigey brown. 18in (45cm)
  Panicum virgatum 'Rubrum' Superb fiery reddish crimson. 3ft (90cm)
  Schizachyrium scoparium Bluish in summer, foxy in autumn. 2ft (60cm)

BOLD FOLIAGE

Bold foliage can create a focal point, a solid centre to a border, can be used as a full stop to mark a corner and blends with other leaves.

Tall   These perennials should reach over 3ft (90cm) in height, except in gardens which are unusually cold or in soil which is very low in nutrients.

- * *Acanthus mollis 'Latifolius'* Glossy and sumptuous; few flowers.
  Anemone tomentosa Large vine leaves, grey below; pink flowers.
- ♀ *Crambe cordifolia* Dark, deeply lobed leaves; white flowers.
- ♀ *Gunnera manicata* Giant rhubarb; vast leaves, needs wet soil.
  Heracleum mantegazzianum Huge, cut leaves – but dangerous.†
- ♀ *Hosta 'Krossa Regal'* Blue-grey leaves; unique arching habit.
  Ligularia stenocephala Rounded basal foliage, boldly toothed.
- ♀ *Lysichiton americanus* Soft leaves, like huge green paddles.
- ♀ *Rheum palmatum* All forms have superb, rhubarb-like leaves.
- ♀ *Veratrum nigrum* Arched, fresh green, rippled leaves; shade.

---

†   The sap of this plant can cause terrifying rashes on some people.

Medium   These perennials should reach between 1ft (30cm) and 3ft (90cm) in height, although some may grow taller in warm gardens and in rich soil.

♈ *Darmara peltata* Circular leaves on central stems; waterside.
 Helleborus Orientalis Hybrids Stark incised leaves; shade.
 Heuchera americana Like a large, jagged-edged ivy; glossy.

♈* *Hosta sieboldiana 'Elegans'* Large, bluish, puckered and veined.†
 Petasites japonicus var. giganteus Soft, floppy leaves; rampant.

♈ *Primula japonica* Long lush leaves, especially on watersides.
 Ranunculus aconitifolius Dark and deeply divided; white flowers.

♈ *Rodgersia podophylla* Broad, sharply jagged, coppery leaflets.
 Symplocarpus foetidus Broad, oval leaves; best in damp soil.

♈ *Zantedeschia aethiopica* Glossy arrowhead foliage; white arums.

Small   These perennials should grow no more than 1ft (30cm) high, although they may sometimes grow taller in warm gardens and in rich soil.
 Bergenia 'Wintermärchen' Winter leaves like crimson butterflies.

♈ *Brunnera macrophylla* Rounded, rough; some forms variegated.
♈ *Caltha palustris* Rounded and glossy; yellow flowers; moist soil.
 Galax urceolata Dark green, rounded; coppery in winter; shade.

♈* *Geranium renardii* Round, lobed, softly felted leaves; best in sun.
♈ *Hosta 'Golden Tiara'* Heart-shaped, gold-edged; clumps up well.†
 Pulmonaria 'Tim's Silver' Broad, flat, green-edged, silvered leaf.

♈ *Saxifraga fortunei* Rounded and lobed, red below; white flowers.
 Tellima grandiflora Rounded and hairy; good ground cover.
 Trachystemon orientalis Leaves like hairy hostas; rather vigorous.

---

† Slug damage can ruin the effect of hosta leaves; take precautions.

LACY FOLIAGE

Plants with lacy or well-divided foliage have the invaluable advantage of being able to knit together well with their neighbours.

Tall   These perennials should reach over 3ft (90cm) in height, except in gardens which are unusually cold or in soil which is very low in nutrients.

Achillea grandiflora Grey-green, doubly divided; off-white heads.

Aruncus dioicus 'Kneiffii' Slim, thread-like leaflets; cream heads.

♀ *Dicksonia antarctica* Hardiest tree fern; still only for milder areas.†

♀ *Dryopteris wallichiana* Gold-tinted at first, then dark and lush.†

Ferula communis Billowing mound of lacy green; yellow heads.

* *Foeniculum vulgare 'Purpureum'* Smoky purple leaf and stem.

Megacarpaea polyandra Large and deeply divided; rarely flowers.

♀ *Polysticum setiferum* Soft green, luxurious; tough, tolerant fern.

♀ *Thalictrum delavayi* Delicate, rounded leaflets; lilac flowers.

♀ *Thalictrum flavum ssp. glaucum* Daintily divided, blue-green.

Medium   These perennials should reach between 1ft (30cm) and 3ft (90cm) in height, although some may grow taller in warm gardens and in rich soil.

Artemisia alba 'Canescens' Lacy, pewtery thread-like leaves; runs.

♀ *Athyrium felix-femina* Delicate and very classy fern; likes damp.†

Chaerophyllum hirsutum 'Roseum' Up-market cow parsley; pink.

Dennstaedtia punctilobula Bright and prettily divided; but runs.†

♀ *Dryopteris felix-mas* Tough fern with many forms; tall in shade.†

Myrrhis odorata Lacy, cow parsley leaves; clean cream heads.

Polemonium foliosissimum Neat, regularly divided; lilac flowers.

* *Polysticum setiferum 'Acutilobum'* Elegant fern; sun-tolerant.†

Selinum wallichianum Stiffly upright; divided leaves; white heads.

Thalictrum diffusiflorum Dusky green, daintily divided; lilac.

---

† This fern thrives best in moist soil and a shady site.

Small These perennials should grow no more than 1ft (30cm) high, although they may sometimes grow taller in warm gardens and in rich soil.

    Achillea abratanoides Fine, aromatic, grey leaves; white heads,

    Adonis vernalis Bright green, finely cut; yellow buttercups, sun.

♀ *Astilbe 'Sprite'* Metallic blue-green leaves under pink spikes.

    Athyrium felix-femina 'Minutissimum' Dwarf, elegant, lady fern.

* *Corydalis flexuosa* Fragile, often red tinted leaves; blue flowers.

♀ *Dicentra formosa 'Stuart Boothman'* Grey-blue fronds; shade.

    Hypolepis millefolium Like a miniature bracken and invasive too.

    Leptinella squalida Tiny, sometimes bronzed; deeply cut flowers.

    Polypodium vulgare Stiff, boldly cut fronds; best in damper areas.

    Thalictrum minus Tiny maidenhair leaves; fluffy cream flowers.

NARROW FOLIAGE

Narrow, sword-like or strap-like leaves are very useful as foils to lacy and broad foliage and for making a strong upright statement.

Tall These perennials should reach over 3ft (90cm) in height, except in gardens which are unusually cold or in soil which is very low in nutrients.

♀ *Chusquea culeou* Erect, then arching; very elegant. Can reach 20ft (6m).

♀ *Crocosmia 'Lucifer'* Boldest crocosmia; pleated; scarlet flowers.

    Dierama pulcherrima Slim, grassy, and arching; pinkish bells.

* *Eryngium eberneum* Arching, toothed leaves; green heads; hardy.

    Helianthus salicifolius A fountain of grassy leaves; yellow daisies.

    Hemerocallis fulva Broad arching leaves; orangey flowers; runs.

    Iris spuria Very tall, unfashionable irises in blue, yellow or white.

    Kniphofia 'Prince Igor' Tallest poker; stunning foliage and spikes.†

♀ *Miscanthus sinensis* Tough, graceful grasses; many good forms.

    Spartina pectinata 'Aureomarginata' Striped yellow leaves.

---

†   This statuesque plant may be tall but it still fits into smaller gardens.

Medium   These perennials should reach between 1ft (30cm) and 3ft (90cm) in height, although some may grow taller in warm gardens and in rich soil.

* *Carex comans 'Bronze Form'* Like a mass of milk chocolate hair.
  Dianella tasmanica Dark green clumps; bright blue berries; tender.
  Dierama dracomontanum Grassy upright clumps; pink flowers.
  Iris foetidissima Emerald evergreen leaves; orange winter berries.
  Iris sibirica Slim, upright foliage; usually blue flowers; damp soil.
  Juncus effusus 'Spiralis' Quirky rush with twisted leaves; damp.
♀ *Kniphofia 'Little Maid'* Best small poker; narrow leaves; yellow.†
♀ *Molinia caerulea 'Variegata'* Waterfall of cream-striped leaves.
  Morina longifolia Flat, toothed, aromatic leaves; pink spikes.
  Sisyrinchium striatum Upright iris-like fans; spikes of yellow.

Small   These perennials should grow no more than 1ft (30cm) high, although they may sometimes grow taller in warm gardens and in rich soil.
  Agrostis 'Silver Needles' Tiny, white-variegated, carpeting grass.
♀ *Carex hachijoensis 'Evergold'* Lax, yellow striped clumps; damp.
  Dianthus All garden pinks have stiff, bluish, grassy leaves; for sun.
  Festuca glauca 'Harz' Tiny, spiky, blue-leaved grassy tufts; rare.
  Holcus mollis 'Albovariegatus' Variegated Yorkshire fog; creeps.
* *Iris* Dwarf Bearded types; stiff, upright leaves; huge range of shades.
♀ *Liriope muscari* Tight grassy clumps; blue flowers in autumn.
♀ *Ophiopogon planiscapus 'Nigrescens'* Low clumps; black leaves.
  Schoenus pauciflorus Short, upright maroon leaves; for damp soil.
  Sisyrinchium 'Californian Skies' Miniature iris leaves; blue stars.

---

†   The 'Border Ballet' seed-raised mixture is also worth growing.

Colourful berries†

Many gardeners expect trees and shrubs to have berries but forget there are also some good perennials with attractive berries.

℣ *Actaea rubra* Tight clusters of fat red berries; best in shade. 18in (45cm)
℣ *Convallaria majalis* Strings of red beads follow white flowers. 1ft (30cm)
  Dianella tasmanica Unexpectedly brilliant blue; no lime. 3ft (90cm)
  Disporum smithii Striking orange berries follow cream bells. 1ft (30cm)
* *Iris foetidissima* Winter berries in orange, yellow or white. 18in (45cm)
℣ *Paeonia mlokosewitschii* Black and red seeds in red-lined pods. 2ft (60cm)
  Phytolacca polyandra Crowded heads of juicy black berries. 4ft (1.2m)
  Podophyllum hexandrum Orange-red plum-like fruits; shade. 18in (45cm)
℣ *Smilacina racemosa* Clusters of red berries after cream flowers. 2ft (60cm)
℣ *Uvularia grandiflora* Red berries after yellow flowers; shade. 2ft (60cm)

Interesting fruits

Some perennials, although they do not have colourful berries, have fruits which are attractive or ornamental in a variety of other ways.

  Acaena Rough burrs in coppery shades; many forms; creeps. 3–6in
℣ *Anaphalis margaritacea var. yedoensis* Silvery everlastings. 2ft (60cm)
  Asphodeline lutea Fat, bulbous pods line stiff vertical stems. 3ft (90cm)
℣ *Baptisia australis* Flat, grey seeds pods follow blue flowers. 4ft (1.2m)
  Clematis integrifolia Silvery seed heads follow blue flowers. 2ft (60cm)
  Cortaderia selloana Fine feathery plumes last into winter. 8ft (2.4m)
℣ *Hosta sieboldiana 'Elegans'* Flared pods remain into winter. 2ft (60cm)
  Papaver orientalis Fat poppy pots top stout stems; good to cut. 3ft (90cm)
  Physalis alkakengii var. franchetii Orange papery lanterns. 2ft (60cm)
℣ *Veratrum nigrum* Tall, slim, almost black seed spikes; shade. 4ft (1.2m)

---

†   Although few perennials have poisonous berries, assume they all have.

Fearsome runners

There are some perennials which look wonderful but which can rampage through a border in no time, smothering other plants.

Aegopodium podagraria 'Variegata' Variegated ground elder! 2ft (60cm)
Anemone hybrida Almost all are invasive once established. 4ft (1.2m)
Campanula takesimana Fine roots run freely; pink flowers. 2ft (60cm)
Carex riparia 'Variegata' Variegated sedge; quickly colonizes. 2ft (60cm)
Convolvulus altheoides Pink flowers, grey leaves; a real terror. 1ft (30cm)
Dicentra 'Snowflakes' Runs strongly in damp shade; white. 18in (45cm)
Leymus arenarius Rampageous, blue-leaved, seashore grass. 4ft (1.2m)
Fallopia japonica Japanese knotweed; breaks paving stones. 6ft (1.8m)
Petasites japonicus var. giganteus Rampant in wet soil. 3ft (90cm)
Symphytum ibericum Small pieces will run; pink or blue. 2ft (60cm)

Spreaders by seed†

While a tendency to self-sow can be an endearing feature, some perennials produce too many seedlings so should be dead-headed.

Achillea millefolium One of the worst, and seedlings rarely true.
Alchemilla mollis Seedlings don't pull out easily; cut back hard,
Aquilegia Columbines seed freely but almost never come true.
Aster novi-belgii Michaelmas daisies seed in many colours.
Astrantia major Seedlings can swamp borders and kill small plants.
Digitalis Many generous with seedlings, but smother other plants.
Euphorbia characias Pods pop on hot days; seedlings everywhere.
Geranium pratense Smothering seedlings, but most are inferior.
Helleborus Orientalis Hybrids Seedlings common, but rarely true.
Lamium maculatum Some true, but all smother smaller gems.

---

† Most named varieties will produce seedlings which are inferior.

ALPINES AND ROCK PLANTS

Alpines and rock plants are spring-flowering, generally small, mostly under 1ft (30cm), and prefer a sunny site with well-drained soil.

HABIT

In spite of their rather narrow height range, rock plants vary greatly in their habit of growth from trailers, to hummocks, to tufts.

Trailing

These trailing rock plants have long stems which grow out over the soil and hang down over rocks but rarely have creeping roots.

Artemesia stelleriana Superb mats of lobed, almost white foliage.

♀* *Euphorbia myrsinites* Blue-green leaves; yellow-green flowers.

♀ *Globularia cordifolia* Round, deep blue flowers above dark mats.

♀ *Gypsophila repens* Ground- or rock-hugging sheets; pink or white.

♀ *Iberis sempervirens* Dense mounded mat hangs over rocks; white.

♀ *Penstemon newberryi* Evergreen mat; cerise flowers in summer.

Phlox subulata and *P. douglasii* Carpeting phlox in many shades.

♀ *Potentilla* × *tonguei* Red-centred, apricot summer flowers; sprawls.

♀ *Saponaria ocymoides* Dark pink flowers; lovely on a slope.

Tropaeolum polyphyllum Bluish leaves; bright yellow flowers.

Creeping

These low mat-forming plants tend to root as they run across the soil, or the roots themselves spread, so they are more invasive.

℣ *Anagallis tenella* 'Studland' Deep pink; dislikes the driest places.

℣ *Androsace lanuginosa* Dense, grey-green foliage; pink heads.

℣ *Campanula portenschlagiana* Fresh green leaves; blue stars.†

Centaurea pulchra Rounded mauve heads; can be invasive.

Cerastium tomentosum Spreading silver mats; white flowers.†

Coronilla minima Low carpet with small yellow pea flowers.

℣ *Dryas octopetala* Rooting, evergreen mound; white flowers.

Nierembergia repens Pure white bells; dark-leaved rooting stems.

Raoulia hookeri Pale green, rooting regularly; pale yellow flowers.

℣* *Thymus serpyllum* 'Coccineus' Flat, aromatic mat; crimson.

Mound- or cushion-forming

Plants forming neat cushions or hummocks, even if slightly open in habit, often make intriguing specimens even when not flowering.

℣ *Armeria juniperifolia* Lilac-pink flowers over tight mounds.

Asperula gussonii Dark-leaved hummock with pink flowers.

℣ *Aubrieta deltoidea* 'Doctor Mules' Rich violet-blue; spectacular.

℣ *Aubrieta deltoidea* 'Red Carpet' Deep red; many others available.

Dianthus squarrosus Scented white flowers above loose cushions.

Draba aizoides Deep green mounds; heads of tiny yellow flowers.

℣ *Hebe cupressoides* 'Boughton Dome' Neat evergreen dome.

℣ *Saponaria* × *olivana* Compact, dark cushions; pink flowers.

* *Saxifraga* Mossy types Green mounds; flowers pink, red or white.

℣ *Sedum kamtschaticum* 'Variegatum' Open mound; white-edged.

---

† This is a vigorous plant which may smother choice neighbours.

Tufted

This group includes a wide variety of rock plants, most with a relatively compact rootstock and a cluster of upright stems.

♀ *Campanula carpatica* Large open white or blue bells; long season.
♀ *Crepis incana* Pink, dandelion heads over grey leaves; summer.
♀ *Dianthus 'Pike's Pink'* Semi-double, dark-eyed, pink flowers.
  Gentiana verna Piercing blue trumpets on neat plants; tricky.
♀* *Geranium cinereum 'Ballerina'* Silvered tufts; dark-eyed lilac.
  Linaria alpina Blue-grey leaves; orange-lipped purple flowers.†
♀ *Oxalis enneaphylla* Bluish lobed leaves; pale-eyed pink flowers.
♀ *Pulsatilla vulgaris* Purple, pink or white bells; fluffy seed-heads.
  Sisyrinchium 'Californian Skies' Neat iris-like leaves; blue stars.
  Soldanella villosa Fringed, bell-shaped blue flowers; moist soil.

Bushy

The bushier, shrubbier alpines are invaluable in providing solidity and structure, even if only through their twiggy winter growth.

♀ *Aethionema 'Warley Rose'* Neat shrublet with deep pink flowers.
  Alyssum spinosum Spiny mounded plant; white flowers summer.
♀ *Cytisus* × *beanii* Low, slow, arching shoots; buttery pea flowers.
♀ *Daphne cneorum 'Eximea'* Evergreen mound; pink and fragrant.
  Deutzia crenata 'Nikko' Arching stems; white summer flowers.
♀ *Erinacea anthyllis* Tight spiny tussock; bluish mauve pea flowers.
♀ *Genista lydia* Arching green shoots; yellow peas; best over a wall.
* *Helianthemum* Evergreen, grey- or green-leaved; many colours.
  Jasminum parkeri Tight dome; yellow summer flowers; tender.
♀ *Penstemon fruticosus var. scouleri* Mauve two-lipped flowers.

---

† This is usually a rather short-lived plant but produces lots of seed.

———— Rosette-forming† ————

Rosettes of foliage nestling at soil level make an interesting and attractive feature before and after the plants flower.

    Aciphylla aurea Spiky, yellowish green rosettes; yellow flowers.

♀ *Campanula garganica* Heart-shaped leaf; blue summer flowers.

    Cirsium acaule Flat spiny rosette; mauve, thistle flowers.

* *Lewisia 'Ashwood Strain'* Succulent rosettes; brilliant flowers.

    Lewisia 'Sunset Strain' Orange, yellow and biscuity shades.

    Morisia monanthos Neatly lobed leaves; bright yellow flowers.

♀ *Ramonda myconi* Like a hardy African violet; best in shady crack.

    Saxifraga cochlearis Silvered mound of rosettes; white flowers.

♀ *Saxifraga 'Tumbling Waters'* Silvered rosette; superb white spike.

    Sempervivum 'Lady Kelly' Unusually large, deep purple rosettes.

---

†   Remove fallen leaves from these plants in autumn or they may rot.

FLOWERING ALPINES

Sparkling alpines bring a real lift to the spirits, especially early in the year, and their neat habit allows a good collection to be grown in a small space.

Spring-flowering

In spring the range of varieties is enormous, but there is a definite preponderance of bright and pale shades and fewer dark colours.

WHITE FLOWERS

The many good, sharp and pure whites among the rock plants help create the spring sparkle with relatively few off-white shades

Achillea 'Huteri' Flat white heads; greyish white leaves; bushy.

Anacyclus pyrethrum var. depressus White daisies, backed red.

Arabis ferdinandi-coburgii Neat clean flowers; flat, dark rosettes.

Celmisia bellidioides Large white daisies over a dark green mat.

♈ *Clematis marmoraria* Neat shrublet with slightly creamy flowers.

Dianthus 'La Bourboule Albus' Pure fringed flowers; grey mat.

♈ *Dryas octopetala* Yellow-eyed white; neat evergreen hummock.

♈ *Iberis sempervirens* Familiar evergreen mound; pure white.

* *Phlox subulata 'Schneewittchen'* Low, creeping pure white carpet.

Saxifraga × apiculata 'Alba' White heads; very early and tough.

PINK FLOWERS

The pinks cover quite a range of diferent plant habits, from neat shrublets to widely spreading creepers and tight tussocks.

♈ *Armeria juniperifolia 'Bevan's Variety'* Deep rose; tussock.

Asperula gussonii Pale pink flowers set neatly on dark green tufts.

♈ *Daphne cneorum 'Eximea'* Red buds, pink flowers; flat habit.

♈* *Dianthus 'Pike's Pink'* Palest rose pink; very neat and compact.

♈ *Erinus alpinus* Annual or biennial; flowers sometimes white.†

♈ *Lewisia cotyledon* Many pink and salmon shades; good in walls.

♈ *Oxalis adenophylla* Lilac-tinted pink; lobed grey-blue leaves.

---

†   This plant will self-sow happily in dry walls and gritty soil.

♀ *Phlox subulata 'McDaniel's Cushion'* Bright rose; low carpet.
♀ *Potentilla* × *tonguei* Peach, red centre; spreading; long season.
♀ *Saponaria ocymoides* Rich pink sprays over dark green leaves.

RED FLOWERS

Brilliant reds are not common among spring alpines, but there is a range of excellent plants in deep, sometimes purple-tinted shades.

* *Aubrieta 'Red Carpet'* Rich crimson, with a touch of purple.
Daphne cneorum 'Ruby Glow' The darkest rock garden daphne.
♀ *Dianthus alpinus 'Joan's Blood'* Deep crimson; bronzed leaves.
Dianthus 'Fusilier' Vivid scarlet, blue-tinted leaves; long season.
Lewisia 'Ashwood Ruby' Superb ruby-red; succulent leafy rosette.
♀ *Penstemon newberryi* Slightly pinkish crimson; flat evergreen.
♀ *Phlox douglasii 'Red Admiral'* Crimson; vigorous yet tight.
♀ *Phlox subulata 'Red Wings'* Dark-eyed carmine red; low carpet.
Saxifraga 'Wisley' Short dark red spikes above silver rosettes.
Thymus serpyllum 'Ruby Glow' Deep ruby-red; aromatic mat.

YELLOW FLOWERS

There are some exceptionally bright, clear yellows among the spring alpines and they come in a great variety of growth habits.

Adonis amurensis Big, bronze-backed buttercups; dissected leaf.
♀* *Aurinia saxatile var. citrina* Lemon clouds, often to autumn.
Aurinia saxatile 'Goldkugel' Deep, bright yellow; grey leaf.
Coronilla minima Gold , sweet scented; greyish leaves; loves sun.
♀ *Cytisus* × *beanii* Compact, arching habit; gold pea flowers.†
♀ *Cytisus* × *kewensis* Arching, widely spreading; cream pea flowers.†
Erigeron aureus 'Canary Bird' Neat daisies on upright stems.
♀ *Hypericum olympicum 'Citrinum'* Pale lemon bowls; grey leaf.
Verbascum acaule Bright flowers tight on rough green rosettes.
♀ *Verbascum 'Letitia'* Pale spikes; grey leaves; tricky but lovely.

---

† This dwarf, bushy broom is ideal tumbling over a low, sunny rock.

BLUE FLOWERS

The blues are a mixture of vivid gentian shades and some with mauve or lilac overtones; at their purest they are captivating.

   Aubrieta 'Triumphante' The aubrieta closest to a true blue.†

♀ *Gentiana acaulis* Trumpet gentian; large, vivid – temperamental.

   Gentiana verna Stunning trumpets in penetrating blue; not easy.

♀ *Globularia cordifolia* Round, deep blue heads over woody mats.

♀ *Lithodora diffusa 'Heavenly Blue'* Deep azure stars; no lime.

♀ *Phlox douglasii 'Iceberg'* Flat carpet of blue-tinted white flowers.

*   *Phlox subulata 'G. F. Wilson'* Lilac-tinted blue; old and reliable.

♀ *Ramonda myconi* Tough, textured rosettes; lilac-tinted blue; shade.

   Viola cornuta 'Belmont Blue' Slightly starry pale blue; long show.

♀ *Viola cornuta 'Minor'* Compact, small-flowered, violet-tinted.

PURPLE AND LAVENDER FLOWERS

Purple, violet, lavender and lilac shades cover a large part of the spectrum, but most plants come from the paler part of the range.

♀ *Aster alpinus* Yellow-eyed purple daisies over green rosettes.

♀ *Aubrieta 'Doctor Mules'* The richest violet variety; easy.†

♀ *Haberlea rhodopensis* White-throated lilac; bright rosettes; shade.

*   *Linaria alpina* Deep violet flowers with orange lips; grey leaves.

   Phlox douglasii 'Violet Queen' Deep violet; flat green carpet.

♀ *Pulsatilla vulgaris* Shining purple orange-centred bells; loves lime.

♀ *Soldanella villosa* Fringed violet flowers; spreads when happy.

   Thymus serpyllum 'East Lodge' Good mauve; rich green carpet.

   Viola cornuta 'Emma Cawthorne' White-eyed violet; spreads.

   Viola gracilis 'Major' Violet flowers; an old but reliable variety.

---

† There is an unexpected variety of aubrietas, not just the usual mauve.

Summer-flowering

Rock gardens and raised beds would be dreary if the popular myth of all rock plants being for spring was true; fortunately, it's not.

WHITE FLOWERS

There are few pure whites among the better of the summer rock plants; most, except the poppy and oxalis, are slightly creamy.

Acaena buchananii Creamy spheres becoming brownish later.

* *Androsace lanuginosa var. leitchlinii* Pink-eyed; spreads well.

Carlina acaulis Creamy thistles tight on spiny rosettes; dries well.

Epilobium glabellum Succession of creamy flowers; restrained.

Eriogonum umbellatum Fluffy, creamy heads on greyish rosettes.

♉ *Helianthemum 'The Bride'* Large single flowers; grey foliage.

Helichrysum bellidioides White everlastings on dark green mat.

Nierembergia repens Upturned white bells; steady creeper.

Oxalis magellanica Delicate ground cover; ground-level flowers.

Papaver alpinum 'Album' Alpine poppy; lacy leaves; short-lived.

PINK FLOWERS

Many of these plants boast the pretty combination of pink flowers set against grey or silver foliage, but some have mauvey overtones.

Acantholimon glumaceum Rich colour; spiny evergreen dome.

♉ *Aethionema 'Warley Rose'* Neat, twiggy shrublet; deep pink.

♉ *Crepis incana* Sharp pink 'dandelions' over grey hairy leaves.

Diascia fetcaniensis Soft pink spikes for months; propagate often.†

♉ *Geranium cinereum 'Ballerina'* Dark-eyed, lilac pink; silver leaf.

♉* *Helianthemum 'Rhodanthe Carneuum'* Soft rose; grey leaves.

Pelargonium endlicherianum Bright pink; unexpectedly hardy.

♉ *Petrorhagia saxifraga* Upward-facing flowers; greyish leaves.

♉ *Saponaria 'Bressingham'* Deep pink; red stems; flat growth.

♉ *Silene schafta* Deep pink flowers on clumps of dark leaves.

---

† Look out too for *Diascia vigilis* and *Diascia cordata*.

YELLOW AND ORANGE FLOWERS

The spark of an alpine summer comes in gold, buttercup and lemon and in a variety of flower shapes with not too many daisies.

Andryala agardhii Buttery daisies on twiggy, grey-leaved shrub.

Arnica montana Golden daisies over hairy rosettes; hates lime.

* *Diascia 'Blackthorn Apricot'* Almost orange; absolutely stunning.

♈ *Euryops acraeus* Neat, round, silver shrub; yellow daisies – again.

Genista pilosa 'Procumbens' Pea flowers; truly flat growth.

♈ *Helianthemum 'Jubilee'* Pretty, double yellow; dark green leaves.

Jasminum parkeri Small, twiggy mound or mat; bright yellow.

♈ *Oenothera macrocarpa* Huge yellow bowls on trailing stems.

Papaver alpinum Spectacular crimped flowers; choose from mix.†

Penstemon pinifolius 'Mersea Yellow' Slender and bright.

BLUE FLOWERS

There are many valuable blue summer alpines, like the mass of campanulas, which seem to be good pure colours without mauve.

Aphyllanthes monspeliensis Deep blue stars; neat rushy clump.

* *Campanula cochleariifolia 'Elizabeth Oliver'* Double; runs well.

Campanula 'E. K. Toogood' Pale-eyed starry flowers; easy.

Codonopsis clematidea Pale blue bells, beautifully marked inside.

Delphinium grandiflorum 'Blue Butterfly' Neat and bushy.

♈ *Gentiana septemfida* Deep blue trumpets, paler within; arching.

♈ *Lithodora oleifolia* Pink buds open pale sky-blue; likes lime.

♈ *Parochetus communis* Clover leaves and blue pea flowers; tender.

♈ *Phlox 'Chattahoochee'* Bright blue trailer with a neat cerise eye.

♈ *Platycodon grandiflorus 'Apoyama'* Large bells, short plant.

---

† Brilliantly coloured but short-lived; self-sows in gritty soil.

PURPLE AND RED FLOWERS

There are so few good red summer alpines, and not a vast range of purple ones, that rather than give two short lists they are together.

℞ *Campanula 'G. F. Wilson'* Deep violet-blue bells; yellowish leaf.
Centaurea bella Pretty mauve thistles over fine silvery foliage.

℞ *Diascia 'Ruby Field'* Deep reddish pink spikes; divide regularly.
Helianthemum 'Ben Dearg' Brilliant red; trim after flowering.

℞ *Penstemon pinifolius* Long, slim, scarlet flowers; fine leaves.
Phlox nana 'Mary Maslin' Brilliant red; hot, dry site; tricky.

℞ *Physoplexis comosa* Spherical pinkish lilac heads, tipped violet.
Pterocephalus perennis Mauve scabious heads on neat grey mats.
Scutellaria indica var. parvifolia Purple skullcap; greyish leaves.

* *Verbena peruviana* Bright scarlet; flat, bright green carpet; tender.

Autumn-flowering

By autumn the range of alpines has diminished greatly but there are still a few fine species to carry on the rock garden display.

Daphne jezoensis Neat shrub; yellow fragrant flowers into winter.
Dendranthema weyrichii Pink, yellow-eyed flowers; lacy leaf.

℞ *Erodium glandulosum* Mauve with dark purple spots; aromatic.
Erodium guttatum White, blotched deep purple; spreading habit.

℞ *Gentiana sino-ornata* Spectacular royal blue trumpets; no lime.

℞ *Gentiana × stevenagensis* Dark, silky blue; tough, but no lime.
Oxalis lobata Clovery leaves, yellow flowers; summer dormant.

℞ *Persicaria affinis 'Superba'* Pink spikes, then russet; creeping.†

℞* *Persicaria vaccinifolia* Neat pink spikes, browning later; creeps.†

℞ *Rhodanthemum hosmariense* White daisies over pewtery leaves.

---

† The pink spikes turning russet fit perfectly into the autumn garden.

--------   ## Unusual colours and combinations   --------

There are some colours and colour combinations which do not fit well into the above categories so they are grouped together here.

   Alchemilla alpina Fluffy greenish yellow heads over neat leaves.

♀ *Aquilegia flabellata* Short, dainty white-centred blue columbine.

   Aurinia saxatilis 'Dudley Nevill' Clouds of strange orangey buff.

   Erysimum 'Jacob's Jacket' Flowers bronze, to orange, then lilac.†

   Helianthemum 'Raspberry Ripple' Red and white single flowers.

♀ *Mimulus* 'Andean Nymph' Creamy pink, yellow throat; damp.

   Papaver miyabeanum Creamy yellow flowers; yellowish leaves.

   Phlox nana 'Paul Maslin' Yellow, with neat purple marks.

♀* *Viola* 'Jackanapes' Deep red upper petals, bright yellow below.

♀ *Viola* 'Molly Sanderson' The best of a number of black pansies.

--------   ## Long-flowering varieties   --------

In small gardens, a display of alpines which bursts out brightly in spring then vanishes can be dissatisfying; these flower for months.

♀ *Anagallis monellii* Deep blue trailer with a neat red eye.

♀* *Aurinia saxatilis* var. *citrina* Pale lemon; may self-seed darker.

♀ *Campanula* 'Birch Hybrid' Bold blue; vigorous but not invasive.

♀ *Diascia* 'Ruby Field' Deepest pink; roots easily; hates sogginess.

   Epilobium glabellum Pure white on green foliage; runs gently.

♀ *Erysimum* 'Constant Cheer' Russet turning purple; short-lived.

♀ *Geranium cinereum* 'Ballerina' Dark veined pink; tight rootstock.

   Persicaria affinis 'Superbum' Neat pink, fades brown; lasts well.

♀ *Rhodanthemum hosmariense* White daisies; appreciates shelter.

♀ *Viola cornuta* Grown well, most forms will flower for months.

----

†   This perennial wallflower is dwarfer than the spring bedding types.

FOLIAGE

Some purists among enthusiasts for rock plants will not admit that coloured leaved forms have a place in the garden; I disagree.

VARIEGATED LEAVES

The best variegated alpines tend to be concentrated among just a few different types, but fortunately all are relatively easy to grow.

Arabis albida 'Variegata' Cream-edged leaves; white flowers.†

Arabis ferdinandii-coburgii 'Old Gold' Yellow-edged green.†

Aubrieta 'Aurea Variegata' Yellow edge; lavender flowers.†

Aubrieta 'Silberrand' Leaves edged creamy white; blue flowers.†

Aurinia saxatilis 'Dudley Nevill Variegated' Cream-edged.

Chiastophyllum oppositifolium 'Jim's Pride' Cream-edged.

Diascia 'Katherine Sharman' Neat, white variegation; red flowers.

Phlox 'Chattahoochee Variegated' Cream-edged; acid soil, shade.

Phlox × *procumbens 'Variegata'* Cream and pink; pink flowers.

Saxifraga 'Bob Hawkins' Cream variegation; white flowers.

GOLD AND YELLOW LEAVES

Catalogues list very few yellow-leaved alpines, perhaps because purist alpine growers dislike them so much they throw them away.

*   *Campanula garganica 'Dickson's Gold'* Bright mound; blue stars.†

Lysimachia nummularia 'Aurea' Brilliant; for wide cool spots.†

Sagina subulata 'Aurea' Flat, yellow foliage mat; white flowers.

Salvia officinalis 'Kew Gold' Yellow-leaved sage; small and tight.

Saxifraga 'Cloth of Gold' Yellow mossy mounds; likes some shade.

Thymus × *citriodorus 'Archer's Gold'* Very bright, best in winter.†

♀   *Thymus* × *citriodorus 'Bertram Anderson'* Gold all year round.†

Veronica prostrata 'Trehane' Bright yellow; blue spikes.†

Viola cornuta 'Tony Venison' Yellow leaves; palest blue flowers.†

Viola cornuta 'Variegata' Yellow fading to green; blue flowers.†

---

†   This will also thrive at the front of borders on soils which are not wet.

SILVER, BLUISH AND GREY LEAVES†

Grey- and silver-leaved varieties, which thrive in hot, dry summer conditions of rock gardens and raised beds, are well represented.

♀* *Artemisia schmidtiana 'Nana'* Silky, silvery mats; delightful.
　Dianthus Many rock gardens pinks have good blue-grey leaves.
♀ *Euphorbia myrsinites* Distinctive blue-grey leaves; green flowers.
♀ *Geranium cinereum 'Ballerina'* Silky silver leaves; pink flowers.
♀ *Helianthemum 'The Bride'* Grey, evergreen leaf; white flower.
♀ *Oxalis adenophylla* Neat, blue-green lobed leaves; pink flowers.
　Raoulia australis Pewtery silver mat hugging the soil tightly.
　Saxifraga 'Silver Cushion' Name says it all; pink/white flowers.
♀ *Sedum spathulifolium 'Cape Blanco'* Fleshy, grey-white leaves.
　Tanacetum densum ssp. amani Soft, pewtery grey; hates wet.

PURPLE AND BRONZE LEAVES

Darker shades are invaluable in the rock garden to set off all those brighter, more sparkling colours, but too much can look dour.

　Acaena 'Copper Carpet' Bronzed in shade, coppery in sun.
♀ *Ajuga reptans 'Braunherz'* Deepest, blackest purple; OK in sun.
　Geranium sessiliflorum 'Porter's Pass' Beetroot-red; vigorous.
　Geranium 'Stanhoe' Unusual pale greyish brown; pink flowers.
　Sedum spurium 'Purple Carpet' Purple leaves; cerise flowers.
　Sempervivum 'Crispyn' Succulent, green, purple-tipped rosettes.
　Sempervivum 'Lady Kelly' Unusually large, misty purple rosettes.
　Thymus serpyllum 'Russetings' Bronze-tinted; mauve flowers.
* *Trifolium repens 'Wheatfen'* Purple-leaved clover; pink flowers.
　Viola riviniana 'Purpurea' Purple leaves; violet-blue flowers.

---

† These varieties are especially susceptible to winter wet.

GROUND COVER PLANTS

Ground cover plants are those which cover the ground so densely that weeds cannot take hold; always plant them in clean ground.

FLOWERS

Smothering weeds is the first requirement of a ground cover plant but fortunately many have the extra benefit of attractive flowers.

WHITE FLOWERS

Sheets of white flowers can be rather garish on a low-growing carpet, so it pays to choose white-flowered plants with character.

♀* *Anthemis punctata ssp. cupaniana* Spreading mound; likes sun.†
♀ *Aruncus dioicus* Dark, spreading foliage; tall creamy plumes.
♀ *Bergenia 'Bressingham White'* Bold evergreen; spreads steadily.
♀ *Choisya ternata* Rounded evergreen shrub; scented; likes sun.†
♀ *Cistus* × *dansereaui 'Decumbens'* White, red blotch; loves sun.
♀ *Geranium renardii* Dense felted mound; blue-veined flowers.
♀ × *Halimiocistus wintonensis* Red streaks; grey leaves; likes sun.
♀ *Potentilla 'Abbotswood'* Spreading but bushy; long season; sun.†
Pratia treadwellii Very low mat; long season; hates drought.
Tiarella 'Eco Slick Rock' Dense but delicate; neat leafy mat.

PINK FLOWERS

Some pinks can be strident, and as ground covers are sometimes used in broad swathes the right shade must go in the right place.

Bergenia 'Ballawley' Very bold leaf; deep cerise flower; vigorous.

♀* *Diascia vigilis* Soft shade; quick to spread; hates fierce winters.†

♀ *Dicentra formosa 'Stuart Boothman'* Dusky pink; only in shade.

Fragraria 'Pink Panda' Bright, clear colour; spreads by runners.

♀ *Geranium* × *oxonianum 'Wargrave Pink'* Salmony; long season.†

Mimulus 'Old Rose' Soft shade; best in slightly moist places.

Osteospermum 'Blackthorn Seedling' Rich rosy magenta; sun.

♀ *Darmara peltata* Leaves like umbrellas follow short spikes; damp.

Persicaria campanulata Pale pink bells; for wide empty spaces.

Symphytum 'Hidcote Pink' Pretty pink comfrey; very persistent.

---

†   This plant has an especially long season, which is always useful.

RED FLOWERS

The softer, richer reds make attractive, warm carpets but the more brilliant scarlet shades must be used with a little circumspection.

Armeria maritima 'Ruby Glow' Ruby pink; green tussocks.

Astrantia 'Ruby Wedding' Deepest crimson; dense dark foliage.

Campanula 'Elizabeth' Large, long misty red bells; unusual.

♀ *Diascia 'Ruby Field'* Soft, deep red; vigorous, but split regularly.

* *Euphorbia griffithii 'Fireglow'* Gingery red; strong, running roots.

Mimulus 'Wisley Red' Deep blood-red; strong, but no thug; damp.

♀ *Persicaria affine 'Superba'* Pink spikes turning crimson; sun.

Persicaria amplexicaule 'Inverleith' Slim, crimson spikes; bold.

♀ *Pulmonaria rubra* Small brick-red bells before bright leaves.

Verbena peruviana Scarlet heads; rich, bright green carpet.

YELLOW FLOWERS

A yellow ground-covering carpet can be a real spectacle, although it may detract from other plants; specimen shrubs can look superb.

♀ *Brachyglottis 'Sunshine'* Grey shrub; broad habit; yellow daisies.

Coreopsis verticillata 'Moonbeam' Dark, threadlike leaves; runs.

Helichrysum 'Schweffellicht' Tiny yellow everlastings; sun.

Inula ensifolia 'Compacta' Exquisite yellow daisies; damp soil.

Mimulus 'Puck' Red-throated yellow; damp soil, spreads well.

♀ *Oenothera macrocarpa* Huge upturned chalices over red stems.

Phlomis anatolica 'Lloyd's Variety' Imposing greyish shrub; sun.

♀ *Potentilla fruticosa 'Longacre Variety'* Unique spreading habit.

♀* *Viola 'Aspasia'* Cream and yellow; unusually widely spreading.†

Waldsteinia ternata Like a yellow-flowered strawberry; fruit poor.

---

† Violas are fine, compact ground coverers and come in many colours.

BLUE FLOWERS

Blue often makes a fine ground cover, especially as there are few blue shrubs, so yellow, pink and red shrubs should associate well.

♀ *Brunnera macrophylla* Leaf like a rough hosta; sharp blue stars.
    Campanula poscharskyana Neat, running clumps; very bright.
♀ *Ceanothus thyrsiflorus 'Repens'* Unique spreading blue clouds.
♀* *Geranium 'Johnsons Blue'* Long season; pretty leaves; dark veins.
♀ *Liriope muscari* Grassy foliage; tight clumps; spikes of blue balls.
    Pratia pedunculata Low carpet; runs well in damp soil; beware.
    Symphytum 'Hidcote Blue' Vigorous comfrey; very hard to kill!
    Vinca major Blue stars; undulating carpet; cut back in late winter.†
♀ *Vinca minor 'La Grave'* Small periwinkle; large blue flowers.†
    Viola sororia 'Freckles' Pretty speckled violet; leafy clump.

PURPLE FLOWERS

In ground cover the real purples are colours which tend to recede, but those with pink, blue or lavender tints will stand out more.

*   *Aubrieta 'Hartswood Purple'* Rich deep violet; very vigorous.
♀ *Daboecia* × *scotica 'William Buchanan'* Dark bells; no lime.
    Geranium × *cantabrigiense 'Cambridge'* Pinky mauve; shade.
    Geranium clarkei 'Kashmir Purple' Pink-veined; deep violet.
    Hebe 'Youngii' Short violet and white spikes; loves sun.
♀ *Lavandula 'Hidcote'* The deepest purple lavender; greyish leaves.
    Nepeta × *faassenii* Lavender catmint; aromatic, good around roses.
    Verbena 'Homestead Purple' New, hardy, rich purple variety.
♀ *Vinca minor 'Atropurpurea'* Plum purple; cut back in late winter.†
♀ *Viola 'Huntercombe Purple'* Violet with white eye; old favourite.

---

†   All vincas are valuable, including the many variegated ones.

FLOWERS IN MANY COLOURS

There are some plants which come in a wide variety of flower colours, all of which are suitable for ground cover in the right situation.

Astilbe Plumes in reds, many pinks and white; moist soil in sun.

Calluna vulgaris Red, purple, pink, lilac or white; sun; acid soil.

Epimedium Delicate sprays in reds, pinks, yellows, white; shade.†

Erica species Vast range in reds, pinks and white; sun; acid soil.

Helianthemum All colours but blue, single and double; sun.

Helleborus Orientalis Hybrids Plum, pink, white; many spotted.†

Phlox douglasii and P. subulata Red, pink, blue, lavender, white.

Pulmonaria Blue, red, pink, white; leaves with silver spots.†

Rhododendron All colours; dense evergreen foliage; very effective.†

Rosa County Series Ground cover roses named after counties.

FOLIAGE

Foliage actually does the job of covering the ground to prevent weed growth, so choosing varieties with good leaves is important.

GREEN LEAVES

Leaves which are green are not necessarily boring; some shrubs and perennials have green foliage which is among the finest of all.

*   *Acanthus mollis 'Latifolius'* Huge, glossy, arching, rich green leaf.

♀ *Dryopteris filix-mas* Repeatedly divided fronds; sun or shade.

   Euonymus 'Dart's Blanket' Deep green, bronzing in winter.

♀ *Hedera hibernica* Very dense dark cover; good in deep shade.†

♀ *Hosta lancifolia* Narrow and glossy; like overlapping fish-scales.†

   Lonicera pileata Ranks of narrow leaves on spreading evergreen.

♀ *Matteuccia struthiopteris* Shuttlecock fern; spreads by runners.†

   Prunus laurocerasus 'Zabeliana' Very glossy; spreading habit.

   Rubus 'Betty Ashburner' Dark, deeply veined; vigorous runners.

♀ *Taxus baccata 'Dovastoniana'* Yew, very much broader than high.

---

†   This is especially valuable in shady parts of the garden.

VARIEGATED LEAVES

Variegated foliage is the most familiar form of foliage colour; many variegated plants look better from a distance than close up.

℣ *Astrantia 'Sunningdale Variegated'* Cream and green mound.

℣ *Brunnera macrophylla 'Hadspen Cream'* Broad, white-edged.

℣ *Euonymus fortunei 'Emerald 'n' Gold'* Deep green, edged gold.

Hosta 'Thomas Hogg' Vigorous, and cheap; white-edged; shade.

Lamium maculatum 'Album' White-centred leaf; white flowers.

Luzula sylvatica 'Marginata' Fine cream edge to grassy leaf.

Mentha × *suaveolens 'Variegata'* White-edged mint; runs gently.

℣ *Phalaris arundinacia 'Picta'* Cheerful white-edged greyish grass.

* *Pulmonaria 'Roy Davidson'* Narrow leaves, heavily silver-spotted.†

Symphytum 'Goldsmith' Yellow and cream markings; shade.

GOLD AND YELLOW LEAVES

It is important to choose gold-and yellow-leaved varieties that will not scorch, as a scorched carpet looks horrid and distracts attention.

Calluna vulgaris 'Golden Feather' Gold in summer, orange later.

℣ *Choisya ternata 'Sundance'* Dense rounded evergreen shrub.

℣ *Erica erigena 'Golden Lady'* Golden leaves; white flowers.

Geranium 'Ann Folkard' New leaves gold through to autumn.

Hosta 'Zounds' Large, slightly puckered, greeny yellow leaves.

* *Juniperus* × *media 'Gold Sovereign'* Delicate-leaved conifer.

Lamium maculatum 'Cannon's Gold' Pure yellow; pink flower.

℣ *Lysimachia nummularia 'Aurea'* Yellow leaf and flower; flat.

Origanum vulgare 'Norton's Gold' No-scorch yellow marjoram.

Rubus cockburnianus 'Golden Vale' Ferny leaf; white stems.

---

† Many pulmonarias have attractive silver-spotted leaves.

SILVER, BLUE AND GREY LEAVES†

In many ways, silver and grey shades are the ideal colours for ground cover as they go so well with so many other shades.

♀ *Anaphalis triplinervis* 'Sommerschnee' Grey, felty; white heads.

♀ *Artemisia schmidtiana* 'Nana' Carpet of shimmering silver; sun.

♀ *Calluna vulgaris* 'Silver Queen' Silvery grey; mauve flowers.

Cerastium tomentosum Almost white mounds; white flowers.

♀ *Hebe pinguifolia* 'Pagei' Rounded silver leaves on flat stems.

♀* *Hosta sieboldiana var. elegans* Luxuriant bluish foliage; shade.

Juniperus sabina 'Tamariscifolia' Broad, grey-blue tabletop.

♀ *Lamium maculatum* 'White Nancy' Silver leaf; white flowers.

♀ *Pulmonaria saccharata* 'Argentea' Broad, silver leaf; shade.

Stachys byzantina 'Silver Carpet' Woolly leaves; no flowers.

PURPLE AND BRONZE LEAVES

Ground cover plants in these dark shades can look oppressive but make a wonderful background to flowers in brighter shades.

Acaena 'Kupferteppich' Bronzy green in shade; richer in sun.

Ajuga reptans 'Jungle Beauty' Huge leaf, bronzed in winter.

Berberis thunbergii 'Dart's Red Lady' Very dark; autumn colour.

♀ *Bergenia cordifolia* 'Purpurea' Colours in winter; sun or shade.

♀ *Erica carnea* 'Vivellii' Bronzy red in winter; deep pink flowers.

♀* *Heuchera micrantha* 'Palace Purple' Bronze leaves, dense clump.

Leptinella sqalida Ground-hugging bronzed lacy mat; vigorous.

Rheum palmatum 'Atrosanguineum' Dense; reddish; likes damp.

Tellima grandiflora 'Rubra' Reddish all year, best in winter.

Trifolium repens 'Quadrifolium Purpurascens' Four-leaf clover.

---

† Almost all those with hairy foliage are best in sunny places.

Good flowers and foliage

In small gardens particularly, ground cover plants which can provide both flower and foliage colour are indispensable.

♈ *Ajuga reptans 'Braunherz'* Deep shining bronze leaf; blue spikes.

♈ *Brachyglottis 'Sunshine'* Yellow daisies float over grey leaves.

Centaurea bella Fluffy mauve heads over grey and white leaves.

♈* *Dicentra 'Langtrees'* Fine, bluish leaves; pink and cream flowers.

Geranium 'Ann Folkard' Gold leaf; stunning magenta flowers.

♈ *Geranium 'Buxton's Variety'* Marbled leaf; white-eyed blue.

♈ *Geranium renardii* Sage green leaf; blue-veined white flowers.

Helichrysum 'Schweffellicht' Low silver carpet; yellow flowers.

Lamium galeobdolon 'Florentinum' Silver blotch; yellow flower.†

Lamium maculatum 'Pink Pewter' Silver leaf; pink flower.†

Other valuable features

Some ground cover plants have unusual flower or foliage colours or other valuable features, but do not fit into any of my categories.

♈ *Ajuga reptans 'Burgundy Glow'* Magenta, pink and cream leaf.

♈ *Alchemilla mollis* Clouds of tiny green flowers; soft green leaf.

♈* *Berberis wilsoniae* Coral berries; pink and orange autumn colour.

Cotoneaster cochleatus Red winter berries; ground-hugging.

♈ *Euphorbia robbiae* Very dark green leaves; vivid green flowers.

♈ *Hebe 'Red Edge'* Red-edged grey leaves; pale lilac flowers; sun.

Houttuynia cordata 'Chameleon' Leaf green, yellow, orange, red.

Lamium 'Hermann's Pride' Silver-veined leaf; yellow flower.†

♈ *Mahonia aquifolium 'Apollo'* Bronze leaf; red stem; yellow heads.

Symphoricarpus × chenaultii 'Hancock' Purple and pink berries.

---

† Lamiums come in a good range of other flower and leaf combinations.

Very vigorous

In some situations there is a need for really vigorous ground cover, but in small beds and small gardens this is the last thing required.

Anemone × *hybrida* White or pink; slow to settle, then runs freely.
Campanula poscharskyana Lax stems, blue upturned bells,
Campanula takesimana Long narrow white bells, tinted lilac.
Convolvulus altheoides Silver leaf; pink trumpets; runs in sun.
Dicentra 'Snowflakes' Dissected blue-grey leaf; white lockets.
Fallopia japonica Japanese knotweed; *please* don't plant this.†
Fragraria 'Pink Panda' Long runners which will take over lawn.
Glyceria maxima 'Variegata' Leaf striped white and yellow.
* *Lamium galeobdolon 'Florentinum'* Green leaf, blotched silver.
Petasites japonicus 'Giganteus' Weedproof; takes over in wet soil.

Best weed-suppressors

The very best weed-suppressors are very effective indeed, although they can also be very vigorous or only suited to certain situations.

Acanthus mollis 'Latifolius' Huge, dense, deep green clump; sun.
♈ *Choisya ternata* Evergreen shrub; sparse at first, very dense later.
♈ *Hosta 'Sum and Substance'* Dense; yellow; no scorch; slugproof.
Juniperus sabina 'Tamariscifolia' Smothers as it spreads out.
♈ *Mahonia aquifolium 'Apollo'* Suckering evergreen; yellow flower.
Persicaria campanulata Tall, dense and vigorous; unbeatable mix.
* *Prunus laurocerasus 'Zabeliana'* Spreading evergreen; for shade.
Rhododendron Hardy Hybrids Very effective once established.
Rubus 'Betty Ashburner' Steadily deepening mat smothers well.
Taxus baccata Yew; all good, 'Dovastonii' spreads well; for shade.

---

† This spreads into the countryside and smothers wild flowers.

HARDY ANNUALS†

Hardy annuals are raised from seed by sowing outside in the garden in spring; they flower and die later the same season. They are easy to grow, but seed in individual colours may be hard to find.

Flowers

Most hardy annuals are grown for their flowers rather than their foliage and can be very colourful, though their season may be short.

WHITE FLOWERS

This list includes hardy annuals with pure white flowers and cream flowers as well as some with contrasting throat colour or spotting.

    Amberboa moschata 'The Bride' Fluffy and white; fragrant. 2ft (60cm)

    Centaurea cyanus 'Florence White' Bushy white cornflower. 15in (38cm)

    Chrysanthemum 'Bridal Robe' Yellow-eyed, white double. 2ft (60cm)

    Chrysanthemum paludosum Pretty, yellow-eyed white daisies. 1ft (30cm)

    Clarkia pulchella 'Snowflake' Frilly, delicate, clean white. 15in (38cm)

    Convolvulus 'White Ensign' Like a tough white petunia. 8in (20cm)

    Crepis rubra 'Snowplume' White thistles; neat upright plants. 1ft (30cm)

    Cynoglossum 'Avalanche' A stylish summer forget-me-not. 15in (38cm)

    Delphinium 'Imperial White King' Impressive white larkspur. 4ft (1.2m)

    Dimorphotheca 'Glistening White' White dark-eyed daisies. 1ft (30cm)

    Eschscholtzia 'Milky White' Unusual white California poppy. 15in (38cm)

    Godetia 'Double White' Fully and semi-double flowers. 18in (45cm)

    Gypsophila 'Covent Garden White' Clouds of tiny flowers. 18in (45cm)

    Iberis 'Pinnacle' Dramatic scented candytuft; good for cutting. 15in (38cm)

*   *Lavatera 'Mont Blanc'* Clean white trumpets; dark green leaf. 2ft (60cm)

    Lobularia 'Snow Crystals' Large and long-flowering alyssum. 3in (7.5cm)

    Nemesia 'White Knight' Orange-eyed white; likes moisture. 10in (25cm)

    Nemophila menziesii 'Snowstorm' Pure white, dotted black. 6in (15cm)

♈ *Nigella 'Miss Jekyll Alba'* White, semi-double love-in-a-mist. 18in (45cm)

    Papaver 'Swansdown White' Huge double frilly poppy. 3ft (90cm)

---

†   Varieties come and go very quickly, so check catalogues.

PINK FLOWERS

Salmon, rose and blushed shades come here, some with darker marks and a few in a range of pink shades from one seed packet.

Agrostemma githago 'Milas' Soft, lilac-tinted pink trumpets. 3ft (90cm)
Centaurea cyanus 'Florence Pink' Bushy pink cornflower. 15in (38cm)
Centaurea cyanus 'Pink Ball' Fully double pink cornflower. 3ft (90cm)
Clarkia 'Apple Blossom' Double, salmon; good for cutting. 4ft (1.2m)
Clarkia 'Pink Joy' White-eyed, upward-facing pink bowls. 1ft (30cm)
Convolvulus 'Rose Ensign' Yellow-and white-throated; pretty. 8in (20cm)
Crepis rubra Pink thistles on sturdy upright plants; self-sows. 1ft (30cm)
Eschscholtzia 'Thai Silk Pink Shades' Fluted, silky petals. 9in (23cm)
Godetia 'Rosy Morn' Double coral-pink; good for cutting. 3ft (90cm)
* *Godetia* 'Sybil Sherwood' Single salmon-pink, edged white. 1ft (30cm)
Gypsophila 'Bright Rose' Clouds of tiny flowers; for cutting. 18in (45cm)
Lathyrus odoratus 'Cupid' Low, pink and white sweet pea. 6in (15cm)
Lavatera 'Silver Cup' Striking pink trumpets with dark veins. 3ft (90cm)
Leonorus sibiricum Unusual two-tone flowers in tight spires. 4ft (1.2m)
Lobularia 'Easter Bonnet Deep Pink' Pale alyssum, then deep. 3in (7.5cm)†
Malope 'Pink Queen' Shell-pink trumpets, dark veins and eye. 3ft (90cm)
Silene 'Peach Blossom' Rose buds, salmony then white flowers. 6in (15cm)
Tropaeolum 'Salmon Baby' Dark-eyed salmon nasturtium. 1ft (30cm)†
Vaccaria 'Florist Rose' Small rose flowers on straight stems. 18in (45cm)
Viscaria 'Rose Angel' Dark-eyed rose pink; deliacte but bold. 1ft (30cm)

---

† Look out for more varieties of this plant in unusual colours.

RED FLOWERS

These reds vary enormously, from dusky shades to vivid scarlet and orange as well as some startling red and white bicolours.

    Adonis aestivalis Black-eyed, deep scarlet; prettily cut leaf. 18in (45cm)

    Amaranthus caudatus Long, deepest pink, pendulous tassels. 3ft (90cm)

♀ *Amaranthus 'Pygmy Torch'* Deep, dusky red upright spikes. 18in (45cm)

    Centaurea cyanus 'Red Ball' Double deep red cornflower. 3ft (90cm)

    Convolvulus 'Red Ensign' Pink red trumpets on trailing plant. 8in (20cm)

    Emilia sonchifolia Fluffy orange-red balls on slender stems. 2ft (60cm)

♀ *Eschscholtzia 'Dalii'* Orange-eyed, red California poppy. 1ft (30cm)

    Eschscholtzia 'Red Chief' Brilliant and fiery orange-scarlet. 15in (38cm)

    Godetia 'Crimson Fire' Pale-eyed, crimson upturned flowers. 1ft (30cm)

    Helianthus 'Velvet Queen' Deep red sunflower; colour varies. 5ft (1.5m)†

♀ *Helichrysum 'Hot Bikini'* Fiery orange-red everlasting. 15in (38cm)

♀ *Linum grandiflorum* Bold, blood-red flower; slender plant. 15in (38cm)

    Lobularia 'New Red' Pale flowers darken with age; variable. 3in (7.5cm)

    Malope 'Vulcan' Shimmering red, dark-veined, green-eyed. 2ft (60cm)

    Nemesia 'National Ensign' Scarlet and white; short season. 9in (23cm)

    Papaver 'Danish Flag' Scarlet poppy with white basal blotches. 2ft (60cm)

    Papaver somniferum 'Laciniatum Crimson' Double poppy. 3ft (90cm)

    Phlox 'Beauty Scarlet' Fine bright red form of annual phlox. 1ft (30cm)

* *Tropaeolum 'Empress of India'* Deep scarlet; blue-green leaf. 1ft (30cm)

    Xeranthemum 'Lumina Red' Bushy everlasting; dries well. 18in (45cm)

---

†   Other unusual sunflowers are now becoming available.

YELLOW AND ORANGE FLOWERS

For many gardeners these bright and brilliant shades are the epitome of summer, but they need placing with the right neighbours.

Amberboa moschata 'Dairymaid' Gold-yellow puffs; scented. 2ft (60cm)

Argemone mexicana 'Yellow Lustre' Shining flowers; spiny. 18in (45cm)†

Bartonia aurea Golden bowls; cut back after flowering. 18in (45cm)†

Calendula 'Indian Prince' Intense double orange; red backs. 18in (45cm)

Calendula 'Yellow Gitana' Double yellow; prone to mildew. 9in (23cm)

Chrysanthemum 'Moonlight' Bold, all-gold daisies; spreading. 8in (20cm)

* *Chrysanthemum 'Primrose Gem'* Gold-eyed primrose. 18in (45cm)

Dicranostigma franchetianum Like yellow, cut-leaved poppy. 3ft (90cm)†

Eschscholtzia 'Orange King' Vivid orange California poppy. 15in (38cm)†

Eschscholtzia 'Sundew' Lemon yellow and scented; cut leaf. 6in (15cm)†

Helianthus 'Giant Yellow' Traditional monster sunflower. 6ft (1.8m)

Helianthus 'Sunspot' Huge 8in (20cm) sunflowers, dwarf plants! 2ft (60cm)

Hunnemannia fumariifolia Gold saucers; greyish cut leaf. 2ft (60cm)

♈ *Limnanthes douglasii* Yellow-eyed white; poached-egg plant. 9in (23cm)

Lobularia 'Creamery' Unusual cream alyssum; almost yellow. 6in (15cm)

Nemesia 'Orange Prince' Rich and intense; hates drought. 1ft (30cm)

Osteospermum 'Gaiety' Black-centred orange daisies; full sun. 2ft (60cm)†

Tropaeolum 'Peach Melba' Red-eyed, deep cream nasturtium. 1ft (30cm)

♈ *Tropaeolum 'Whirlybird Gold'* Semi-double gold nasturtium. 1ft (30cm)

Ursinia anethoides Red-eyed orange daisies; very prolific. 15in (38cm)†

† This does particularly well in a sunny, well-drained place.

BLUE FLOWERS

It's often said that there are few blue annuals, but while this may be true of half-hardy types, there are plenty of blue hardy annuals.

Anagallis 'Blue Light' Yellow-eyed gentian blue; low carpet. 6in (15cm)

Anchusa 'Blue Angel' Vivid ultramarine-blue; bushy habit. 9in (23cm)

Anchusa 'Blue Bird' Deep indigo, like giant forget-me-nots. 18in (45cm)

Asperula azurea Fragrant heads of tiny lavender-tinted flowers. 1ft (30cm)

♀ *Centaurea cyanus 'Blue Diadem'* Deep blue cornflower. 3ft (90cm)

Centaurea cyanus 'Ultra Dwarf Blue' Weird tiny cornflower. 9in (23cm)

♀ *Convolvulus 'Blue Ensign'* Bright blue, white and yellow eye. 8in (20cm)

Cynoglossum 'Blue Showers' Pale forget-me-nots; grey leaf. 15in (38cm)

Delphinium 'Imperial Blue Bell' Tall, elegant blue larkspur. 4ft (1.2m)†

Felicia bergeriana Orange-eyed blue daisies; spreading habit. 6in (15cm)

Linum usitatissimum Blue flax; flower short-lived but prolific. 2ft (60cm)

* *Nemesia 'Blue Gem'* Tiny blue flowers cover compact plants. 9in (23cm)

Nemesia 'KLM' Pretty blue and white bicolour; short season. 9in (23cm)

Nemophila menziesii White-eyed, sky-blue; hates drought. 6in (15cm)

Nicandra physaloides Pale, bell-shaped flowers; inflated pods. 3ft (90cm)

♀ *Nigella 'Miss Jekyll'* Classic pale love-in-a-mist; dries too. 18in (45cm)

Nigella 'Oxford Blue' Much deeper blue, taller with dark pods. 3ft (90cm)

Phacelia campanularia Bright bells; cut back for second flush. 9in (23cm)

Phacelia 'Royal Admiral' Deep purplish blue bells; loves sun. 18in (45cm)

Viscaria 'Blue Angel' Shining, dark-eyed blue; slender, elegant. 1ft (30cm)

---

†   Larkspur, in any colour, can be dried very successfully.

PURPLE FLOWERS

Here it is true that there are relatively few varieties; even when paler lavender and mauve shades are included, the list is short.

Centaurea cyanus 'Mauve Ball' Double mauve cornflower. 3ft (90cm)

Dracocephalum moldavica Violet, scented spikes; grey leaf. 18in (45cm)

* *Eschscholtzia 'Purple-Violet'* Rare purple California poppy. 15in (38cm)

♀ *Ionopsidium acaule* Tiny, white and violet flowers. 3in (7.5cm)

Lobularia 'Royal Carpet' Darkest purple alyssum; scented. 3in (7.5cm)

Nigella 'Mulberry Rose' Deep purple rose; striped seed-pods. 2ft (60cm)

♀ *Papaver somniferum* Opium poppy; pale mauve, dark blotch. 3ft (90cm)

Phacelia 'Lavender Lass' Lavender blue, white and cream eye. 1ft (30cm)

Senecio elegans Yellow-eyed lilac daisies; elegant, open habit. 2ft (60cm)

Specularia speculum White-centred, violet-blue bells; trailing. 1ft (30cm)

OTHER COLOURS

In the continuing quest for something new and different, hardy annuals in unusual colours and combinations have appeared.

Bupleurum rotundifolium 'Green Gold' Greeny gold heads. 18in (45cm)

Calendula 'Touch of Red' Many colours, all backed rusty red. 18in (45cm)

Centaurea cyanus 'Black Ball' Unusually deep black-purple. 3ft (90cm)

Coreopsis 'Mahogany Midget' Dark reddish mahogany. 10in (25cm)

* *Dimorphotheca 'Salmon Queen'* Dark and pale salmon shades. 1ft (30cm)

Linum grandiflorum 'Bright Eyes' White saucers, red centres. 1ft (30cm)

Lobularia 'Apricot Shades' Soft apricot alyssum, variable. 3in (7.5cm)

Lupinus 'Sunrise' Stunning blue, yellow and white spikes. 4ft (1.2m)†

Malva 'Bibor Fehlo' Sultry magenta flowers; purple veins. 6ft (1.8m)

Nemophila 'Pennie Black' Unique white-rimmed black bowls. 6in (15cm)

---

† The seedlings must not be disturbed or they will flower prematurely.

MIXTURES

Hardy annual mixtures provide the most dazzling and also the most surprising summer colours; give them a space of their own.

Centaurea cyanus 'Frosty Mixed' White-tipped cornflowers. 2½ ft (75cm)
🏆 *Chrysanthemum 'Court Jesters'* Bicolours and tricolours. 18in (45cm)
Delphinium 'Hyacinth Flowered Mixed' Pink, blues, white. 3ft (90cm)
Eschscholtzia 'Ballerina' Fiery and frilly California poppies. 9in (23cm)
Godetia 'Satin Mixed' Superb early mix; clear colours. 9in (23cm)
🏆 *Helichrysum 'Bright Bikini'* Dwarf, bushy everlasting mix. 15in (38cm)
Iberis 'Flash' Candytuft mix with widest possible colour range. 1ft (30cm)
Linaria 'Fairy Bouquet' Wide range of tiny snapdragons. 1ft (30cm)
Lobularia 'Morning Mist' Best colour range alyssum mix. 6in (15cm)
Lupinus 'Pixie Delight' Soft pinks, blues; happy in poor soil. 15in (38cm)
Mesembryanthemum 'Magic Carpet' Sparkly, sun-loving mix. 6in (15cm)
Nemesia 'Carnival' Large-flowered bright and fiery colours. 1ft (30cm)
Nemesia 'Pastel Mixed' Smaller flowers, softer pastel shades. 9in (23cm)
Nigella 'Persian Jewels' Love-in-a-mist in pinks, blues, white. 18in (45cm)
Papaver 'Angel Wings' Poppies in unusual pinks, lilacs, greys. 1ft (30cm)†
Papaver 'Peony Flowered Mixed' Huge fluffy double poppies. 3ft (90cm)
Papaver 'Summer Breeze' Yellow, orange, white; stunning. 1ft (30cm)
Phlox 'Coral Reef' Impressive new compact mix; pastel colours. 9in (23cm)
Scabiosa 'Double Mixed' Reds, purples, pinks and lavenders. 3ft (90cm)
* *Tropaeolum 'Whirlybird Mixed'* Semi-double nasturtiums. 1ft (30cm)

---

† Allow these poppies to self-sow but pull out any red-flowered seedlings.

DRYING

Although many half-hardy annuals for drying can be treated as hardy annuals in warm areas, these will be more widely successful.

℞ *Ammobium alatum 'Grandiflorum'* Pure white everlastings. 2ft (60cm)

* *Bracteantha 'Drakkar Pastel Mixture'* Pastel straw flowers. 3ft (90cm)

℞ *Carthamus tinctorius 'Orange and Gold'* Everlasting thistles. 3ft (90cm)

Chenopodium 'Andean Hybrids' Like gold, green, red millet. 4ft (1.2m)

Helipterum 'Double Mixed' Papery heads in red, pinks, white. 1ft (30cm)

Helipterum humboltianum Scented yellow, green when dry. 18in (45cm)

Lonas inodora Prolific golden yellow buttons in wide heads. 2ft (60cm)

Salvia horminum 'Claryssa' Stem leaves in best colour mix. 18in (45cm)

℞ *Scabious 'Drumstick'* Unusual spherical bronzed papery heads. 1ft (30cm)

Xeranthemum 'Lumina' Superb, prolific double; good colours. 1ft (30cm)

SCENTED FLOWERS

Scent is a scarce commodity among hardy annuals but in addition to the invaluable sweet peas there are a few exceptional varieties.

Amberboa moschata 'Mixed' Plums, pinks, yellows and white. 2ft (60cm)

Asperula azurea Slender, branched plants; lavender-blue heads. 1ft (30cm)

Dracocephalum moldavica Violet; leaf and flower scented. 18in (45cm)

Fagopyrum esculentum Pretty pink sprays; attracts hoverflies. 2ft (60cm)

* *Lathyrus odoratus* Most, but not all, sweet peas are scented. 6ft (1.8m)

Lobularia 'Sweet White' The sweetest-scented white alyssum. 9in (23cm)

Lupinus luteus Delicious sweet scent from bold yellow lupin. 2ft (60cm)

Lupinus nanus 'Pixie Delight' Mixed pale shades; good scent. 1ft (30cm)

Matthiola bicornis Night-scented stock; grow only for its scent. 1ft (30cm)†

Reseda odorata Distinctive heavy fragrance; green, tinted red. 1ft (30cm)

---

† The flowers are not colourful, sow behind more colourful plants.

HALF-HARDY ANNUALS AND BEDDING PLANTS

These are plants raised from seed each year in a warm environment then planted outside in late spring for a colourful summer display.

Flowers

One of the strengths of these plants is the enormous variety of shades in which they come; almost any shade you need is available.

WHITE FLOWERS

The purity of white bedding plants adds brilliance to summer schemes; they blend with pastels and contrast with bright colours.

Ageratum 'Summer Snow' Fluffy puffs; dead-head regularly. 8in (20cm)

Antirrhinum 'White Wonder' Yellow-throated snapdragon. 18in (45cm)

Aster 'Compliment White' Large and frilly; good for cutting. 2ft (60cm)

Begonia (fibrous) 'Olympia White' Pure white; green leaf. 6in (15cm)

Begonia (fibrous) 'Whisky' Pure white; dark bronze leaf. 6in (15cm)

Begonia (tuberous) 'Non Stop White' Full double; sow early. 1ft (30cm)

Campanula 'Kristal White' White bells; sow early; trailing habit.

*   *Cosmos 'Sonata White'* Stunning prolific dwarf; pure white. 2ft (60cm)

Dianthus 'White Charms' Single, fringed white; compact. 9in (23cm)

Gazania 'Mini Star White' Bold cream daisies; yellow centre. 9in (23cm)†

Geranium 'Gala White' Best pure white traditional geranium. 1ft (30cm)

Geranium 'Multibloom White' Smaller heads, very prolific. 9in (23cm)

Gilia 'Snow Queen' Yellow-throated, pure white; feathery leaf. 2ft (60cm)

Impatiens 'Tempo White' Large-flowered, bushy busy lizzie. 1ft (30cm)

Impatiens 'Accent White' Pure white; widely spreading habit. 6in (15cm)

Lobelia 'White Lady' Clear white; 10 per cent of plants always blue. 6in (15cm)

Nicotiana 'Domino White' Neat and prolific tobacco plant. 15in (38cm)

Petunia 'Mirage White' Prolific, bushy and weather-resistant. 1ft (30cm)

---

†   Gazania flowers tend to open in sun, but close on cool, shady days.

Petunia 'Supercascade White' Large flowers on trailing plants.

♀ Salvia farinacea 'White Victory' Flowers in silver spikes. 18in (45cm)

PINK FLOWERS

Seed companies have many words for pink shades but coral, blush, rose, salmon, orchid, salmon-blush and lipstick can be misleading.

Ageratum 'Pinky' Dusty rose fluffs fade to white; dead-head. 8in (20cm)

Antirrhinum 'Coral Monarch' Reliable traditional variety. 18in (45cm)

Aster 'Compliment Salmon' Open frilly flowers; lasts well cut. 2ft (60cm)

Begonia (fibrous) 'Gin' Bright rose; dark bronze leaf; lovely. 6in (15cm)

Begonia (fibrous) 'Olympia Pink' Strong pink; green leaves. 6in (15cm)

♀ Begonia (tuberous) 'Non Stop Pink' Dense double; sow early. 1ft (30cm)

Dianthus 'Colour Magician' Opens white, blushes to rose. 9in (23cm)

Dianthus 'Pink Flash' Dark-eyed rose pink; may overwinter. 9in (23cm)

Geranium 'Apple Blossom Orbit' Soft pink; dark-zoned leaf. 1ft (30cm)†

Geranium 'Sensation Blush Pink' Extraordinarily prolific. 1ft (30cm)

Geranium 'Shocking Susan' Unusually striking lurid pink. 1ft (30cm)

Impatiens 'Spectra Rose' New Guinea impatiens; colour varies. 9in (23cm)

♀ Impatiens 'Super Elfin Blush' Blushed white; low, spreading. 6in (15cm)

Impatiens 'Salmon Profusion' The most prolific busy lizzie. 9in (23cm)

* Nicotiana 'Domino Salmon Pink' Unique vibrant shade; 15in (38cm)

Petunia 'Mirage Rose' Bold pink; highly weather-resistant. 1ft (30cm)

Petunia 'Supercascade Pink' Bright pink; good in baskets; trails.

♀ Salvia 'Sizzler Salmon' Two-tone pink; unusual and effective. 9in (23cm)

Verbena 'Amour Light Pink' Pale-centred, bright pink. 9in (23cm)

Viola (pansy) 'Imperial Pink Shades' Plum, rose then blush. 6in (15cm)

---

† Seed is expensive, but this is a particularly impressive variety.

RED FLOWERS

From orange-scarlet to deepest blood-red is quite a range, and these diverse shades demand equally different neighbours in the border.

Alonsoa 'Scarlet Bedder' Like a slender, orange-red nemesia. 18in (45cm)

* *Antirrhinum 'Black Prince'* Deep blood-red; foliage bronzed. 18in (45cm)†

Antirrhinum 'Liberty Bright Red' Bright orange-scarlet. 18in (45cm)†

Aster 'Thunderball' Tight cushions of rich scarlet needles. 2ft (60cm)

Begonia (fibrous) 'Lotto Scarlet' Largest flowers; green leaf. 9in (23cm)

Begonia (fibrous) 'Volcano' Orange-scarlet; deep bronze leaf. 9in (23cm)

♔ *Begonia (tuberous) 'Non Stop Bright Red'* Double rich red. 1ft (30cm)

Dianthus 'Telstar Crimson' Deep red single; rich and prolific. 9in (23cm)

Gaillardia 'Red Plume' Fully double cushions; long season. 15in (38cm)

Geranium 'Horizon Deep Scarlet' Classic style; well zoned. 1ft (30cm)

Geranium 'Multibloom Flaming Scarlet' Bright and prolific. 1ft (30cm)

Impatiens 'Super Elfin Red' Deep red; dark green leaf; low. 6in (15cm)

Impatiens 'Tempo Burgundy' Rich colour; strong busy lizzie. 1ft (30cm)

Nicotiana 'Domino Crimson' The darkest red in the range. 15in (38cm)

Petunia 'Falcon Red' Very large flowers; appreciates shelter. 9in (23cm)

Petunia 'Ruby Horizon' Deep sultry red; weather-resistant. 9in (23cm)

Salvia 'Lady in Red' Tall, elegant; fits well into mixed borders. 2ft (60cm)

♔ *Salvia 'Red Arrow'* The best traditional scarlet salvia; dark leaf. 9in (23cm)

Verbena 'Sandy Scarlet' The most brilliant red; bushy plant. 1ft (30cm)

Viola (pansy) 'Imperial Blackberry Rose' Deep red; blotched. 6in (15cm)

---

†   These and all antirrhinums must be sprayed against rust disease.

YELLOW FLOWERS

Marigolds of various kinds provide the most brilliant of colours, although many other plants develop into more elegant plants.

Antirrhinum 'Yellow Monarch' Bright and piercing colour. 18in (45cm)

Aster 'Apricot Delight' Neat double; unusual and attractive. 2ft (60cm)

Begonia (tuberous) 'Non Stop Yellow' Bright, fully double. 1ft (30cm)

Calceolaria 'Midas' Fine bedding calceolaria; pretty slippers. 1ft (30cm)

Coreopsis 'Early Sunrise' Semi-double gold; good perennial. 18in (45cm)

Cosmos 'Sunny Gold' Semi-double gold; sow early; loves sun. 15in (38cm)

Gaillardia 'Yellow Plume' Rich yellow and fully double. 15in (38cm)

Matricaria 'Butterball' Bold yellow, lightly fringed white. 9in (23cm)

Mesembryanthemum 'Lunette' Sparkly sun-lover; dead-head. 3in (7.5cm)

Mimulus 'Malibu Orange' Monkey flower; quick to flower. 6in (15cm)†

Mimulus 'Malibu Yellow' Neat and bright; hates drought. 6in (15cm)†

Petunia 'Summer Sun' Best yellow petunia; demands sun. 9in (23cm)

Rudbeckia 'Marmalade' Bold golden, brown-eyed flowers. 18in (45cm)

Tagetes (African marigold) 'Perfection' Three shades. 15in (38cm)

Tagetes (Afro-French marigold) 'Zenith Yellow' Brightest. 1ft (30cm)

Tagetes (French marigold) 'Mischief Yellow' Prolific single. 1ft (30cm)

Tagetes 'Lemon Gem' Masses of lemon stars; aromatic leaves. 1ft (30cm)

Venidium fastuosum Like black-eyed orange sunflowers; sun. 2ft (60cm).

* *Viola (pansy) 'Imperial Gold Princess'* Yellow, red blotch. 6in (15cm)

Zinnia 'Orange Star' Small single flowers; spreading plant. 9in (23cm)

---

†   Mimulus are invaluable, as they can flower six weeks from sowing.

BLUE FLOWERS

Seed companies have a habit of using the term 'blue' to describe a variety of lilac shades as well as true blues; most of these *are* blue.

    Ageratum 'Blue Horizon' Fluffy heads; for border or cutting. 2ft (60cm)

    Ageratum 'Blue Swords' Clear colour; strong, mounded plants. 9in (23cm)

    Aster 'Blue Bedder' Tight hummocks; late, double flowers. 1ft (30cm)

    Brachyscome 'Blue Star' Quilled petals, purple-tinted; edging. 1ft (30cm)

    Campanula 'Krystal Blue' Blue bells; neat trailer; tiny seed. 9in (23cm)†

    Delphinium chinensis 'Sky Blue' Exquisite penetrating shade. 15in (38cm)†

    Heliophila longifolia Clouds of small, white-centred flowers. 18in (45cm)

♈ *Impatiens 'Super Elfin Blue Pearl'* Bluish, the nearest so far. 6in (15cm)

    Lobelia 'Cambridge Blue' Pale blue bushy lobelia; tiny seed. 6in (15cm)

    Lobelia 'Crystal Palace' Deep blue set against bronze leaves. 6in (15cm)

    Lobelia 'Sapphire' Dark blue with a white eye; trailing habit.

    Lobelia valida 'Blue Ribbons' White-eyed blue; upright habit. 1ft (30cm)

    Petunia 'Blue Daddy' Good blue with attractive dark veining. 1ft (30cm)

    Petunia 'Celebrity Sky Blue' The nearest to pale blue; lovely. 1ft (30cm)

    Salvia farinacea 'Strata' Slim silver stems; tight spikes. 18in (45cm)

♈ *Salvia patens 'Cambridge Blue'* Huge flowers, but sparse. 18in (45cm)†

    Solanum sisymbrifolium Rare, very spiny, but striking; pale. 3ft (90cm)

    Verbena 'Blue Lagoon' Good blue heads on spreading plants. 9in (23cm)

* *Viola (pansy) 'Blue Velour'* Small-flowered; very prolific. 6in (15cm)

    Viola (pansy) 'The Joker' Pretty-faced blue and white, yellow eye. 6in (15cm)

---

†   This may survive the winter in warm well-drained places.

PURPLE FLOWERS

Here, unfortunately, the numbers drop off, for even including the mauve and strongly lavender shades the choice is restricted.

Antirrhinum 'Lavender Monarch' Impressive pure colour. 18in (45cm)

Heliotropum 'Mini Marine' Deep purple, scented; bluish leaf. 15in (38cm)

Impatiens 'Deco Violet' Good deep violet; dark bronzed leaf. 9in (23cm)

Lobelia 'Lavender Lady' Unique shade of pale lavender; 6in (15cm)

Nicotiana 'Domino Purple' Rich purple tobacco plant; bushy. 15in (38cm)

Petunia 'Mirage Midnight' Deep, sultry, bluish purple. 1ft (30cm)

* *Petunia 'Supercascade Lilac'* Exquisite soft lilac; lax habit. 1ft (30cm)

Salvia 'Phoenix Purple' Traditional salvia in true deep purple. 1ft (30cm)

Salvia 'Sizzler Lavender' Clear lavender; surprsingly effective. 1ft (30cm)

Verbena 'Imagination' Small purple stars in prolific heads; trails.

OTHER COLOURS AND COMBINATIONS

Unusual colours can be very successful and attractive or create more bewilderment than excitement; these are the most appealing.

Ageratum 'Bavaria' White pads with blue filaments; pretty. 9in (23cm)

Aster 'Florette Champagne' Soft creamy pink; quilled petals. 2ft (60cm)

Geranium 'Orange Appeal' The purest orange geranium. 1ft (30cm)†

* *Nicotiana 'Unwins Lime Green'* Easily the best lime tobacco. 2ft (60cm)

Petunia 'Duo Mixed' Neat doubles in many colour pairings. 1ft (30cm)

Petunia 'Rose Flare' Cerise, white centre, rich cream throat. 1ft (30cm)

Salvia 'Sizzler Salmon' Pale salmon flowers in darker heads. 9in (23cm)

Tagetes 'Seven Star Red' Rich mahogany fading to orange. 9in (23cm)

Verbena 'Peaches and Cream' Pink and orange; love or hate. 1ft (30cm)

Viola (pansy) 'Imperial Antique Shades' Peachy, beige and pink. 6in (15cm)

---

† This thrives best in rich conditions and when dead-headed regularly.

BICOLOUR COMBINATIONS

Bicoloured flowers always seem to be popular, and in bedding plants the flow of these striking combinations continues.

Antirrhinum 'Brighton Rock' Old-fashioned striped mixture. 15in (38cm)†

Antirrhinum 'Floral Showers Lavender' Lavender and cream. 9in (23cm)

Antirrhinum 'Night and Day' White throat, crimson lips. 2ft (60cm)

Antirrhinum 'Princess' White with a bright rose lower lip. 18in (45cm)

Aster 'All Change' Tight, pale-edged, red or blue buttons. 15in (38cm)

Begonia (fibrous) 'Coco Ducolor' Pink-edged white; dark leaf. 6in (15cm)

♉* *Begonia (tuberous) 'Pin Up'* Huge, single, pink-edged white. 1ft (30cm)

Cosmidium 'Brunette' Orange daisies; bold mahogany centre. 3ft (90cm)

Dianthus 'Black & White Minstrels' Deep crimson and white. 1ft (30cm)

Dianthus 'Snow Fire' Startling, scarlet-centred, single white. 9in (23cm)

Geranium 'Multibloom Cherry Fizz' Red, with a white eye. 1ft (30cm)

Impatiens 'Mega Orange Star' Orange and white busy lizzie. 9in (23cm)

Impatiens 'Swirl Mixed' Pink shades with dark picotee edge. 6in (15cm)

Mimulus 'Viva' Large yellow flowers, boldy blotched in red. 1ft (30cm)

Nicotiana 'Domino Purple Bicolor' Deep purple, white eye. 15in (38cm)

Petunia 'Merlin Picotees' Red, rose and blue; clear white rim. 1ft (30cm)

Petunia 'Daddy' Prettily veined flowers in at least eight shades. 1ft (30cm)

Salvia 'Cherry Blossom' Pink and white; pretty and elegant. 18in (45cm)

Tagetes (French marigold) 'Harlequin' Rust/yellow striped. 2ft (60cm)

Viola (pansy) 'Jolly Joker' Orange with purple wings; extraordinary. 6in (15cm)

---

†   This always produces a small percentage of unstriped flowers.

MIXTURES

Mixtures can create a dazzling display, and it is worth remembering that they often contain extra colours in addition to those listed.

℞ *Antirrhinum 'Sonnet Mixed'* Prolific nine-colour mixture. 18in (45cm)†

Begonia (fibrous) 'Excel' Green/bronze leaf; eight shades. 6in (15cm)

Begonia (tuberous) 'Non Stop' Ten colours, all fully double. 1ft (30cm)

Cosmos 'Sea Shells' Unique fluted petals; reds, pinks, white. 3ft (90cm)

Dahlia 'Rigoletto' Bright semi-double mix; height may vary. 15in (38cm)

Dianthus 'Princess' Six prolific pure shades plus bicolours. 1ft (30cm)

Geranium 'Multibloom' Incredibly prolific; eight colours. 1ft (30cm)†

Impatiens 'Super Elfin Mixed' Eighteen colours; spreading. 6in (15cm)

Impatiens 'Super Elfin Mother of Pearl' Pastel shades only. 6in (15cm)

Lobelia 'Kaleidoscope' Blue, violet, mauve, rose, red, white. 6in (15cm)

Mesembryanthemum 'Harlequin' Stunning new mixture. 6in (15cm)

Mimulus 'Magic' Over ten colours; fast growing, hates drought. 8in (20cm)

Nicotiana 'Domino Mixed' Nine shades; the most colourful. 15in (38cm)

Nicotiana 'Sensation' Tall mix with unusual bicolours; scented. 3ft (90cm)

Petunia 'Daddy Mixed' Boldly veined; in at least six shades. 1ft (30cm)

Petunia 'Mirage Mixed' Eighteen weather resistant colours. 1ft (30cm)†

Salvia 'Phoenix Mixed' Scarlet, cream, two pinks, lilac, purple. 1ft (30cm)

* *Tagetes (Afro-French marigold) 'Caribbean Parade'* Best double mix. 1ft (30cm)

Tagetes (French marigold) 'Fantasia' Special blend of singles. 8in (20cm)

Verbena 'Romance' Up to eight colours; spreading habit. 9in (23cm)†

---

† This variety is an outstanding advance on previous varieties.

HALF-HARDIES AS YOUNG PLANTS

Some half-hardy annuals are less easy to raise from seed without special facilities, but seedlings and young plants are now available.

Begonia (fibrous) Tiny seed, very difficult to sow evenly.

Begonia (tuberous) Tiny seed, tricky to sow; very expensive.

Geranium (bushy) Expensive, very few seeds supplied.

Geranium (ivy-leaved) Cuttings raised types better than seed.

Impatiens (doubles) Only 50% double from seed; plants 100%.

Impatiens (singles) Expensive seed; difficult to start succesfully.

Lobelia Minute seed; seedlings rot easily when very young.

Petunia Small seed, difficult to sow thinly and raise successfully.

Salvia Not easy to grow well, seedlings often develop poorly.

Verbena Most varieties very difficult to germinate successfully.

SCENTED FLOWERS

In recent years most half-hardy annuals have been developed for colour and habit, scent has been ignored; some are still scented.

Cleome 'Helen Campbell' White spidery flowers; very elegant. 4ft (1.2m)†

Datura suaveolens Angel's trumpet; huge white lily-like bells. 6ft (1.8m)

Dianthus 'Chabaud Enchantment' Carnation; seven colours. 18in (45cm)

Dianthus 'Rainbow Loveliness' Frilly, scented, single mix. 18in (45cm)

Heliotropium 'Marine' Best vanilla-scented type from seed. 18in (45cm)

Ipomoea alba Moonflower; evening scented white climber 8ft (2.4m)

Mirabilis jalapa Evening-scented flowers in many colours. 2ft (60cm)

*   *Nicotiana affinis* The classic, tall white evening tobacco plant. 3ft (90cm)

Verbena 'Romance' Scent unpredictable; this mix seems best. 9in (23cm)

Zalusyanskia capensis Red-backed white stars; night-scented. 1ft (30cm)

---

†   Also available in carmine, violet and a five-colour mixture.

———————————————   **Attractive foliage**   ———————————————

These fall into two groups; some are grown only for their foliage and are good foils for other plants, others have good flowers too.

Amaranthus 'Joseph's Coat' Green, yellow, red; needs shelter. 15in (38cm)

* *Begonia (fibrous) 'Cocktail'* Bronze leaf; five flower colours. 6in (15cm)

Begonia (fibrous) 'Colour Queen' Spotted white; red flowers. 6in (15cm)

Begonia (tuberous) 'Ornament' Bronze leaf; five-colour mix. 1ft (30cm)

Beta 'Bulls Blood' Deep red foliage; good foil for hot colours. 1ft (30cm)†

Canna 'Tropical Rose' Green paddle-shaped leaf; pink flower. 2ft (60cm)

Euphorbia marginata Leaves edged white; good cut flower. 18in (45cm)

Hibiscus 'Coppertone' Bronzy purple, maple-like leaves. 2ft (60cm)

Humulus japonicus 'Variegatus' White splashed leaf; climbs. 8ft (2.4m)

Impatiens 'Deco' Darkest bronze-green busy lizzie; six colours. 8in (20cm)

Kochia trichophylla Dense feathery green bush, turning fiery. 2ft (60cm)

Ocimum basilicum 'Dark Opal' Purple-leaf basil; likes shelter. 1ft (30cm)†

Perilla 'Nankinensis Laciniata' Ruffled aromatic purple leaf. 18in (45cm)†

Ricinus 'Impala' Bold, bronze maple-like leaf; poisonous. 3ft (90cm)†

Ricinus 'Zanzibarensis' Huge, green-leaved castor oil plant. 8ft (2.4m)

Senecio cineraria 'Cirrus' Rounded, lobed, bright silver. 1ft (30cm)

Senecio cineraria 'Silverdust' Broadly cut pewtery silver. 6in (15cm)

Tanacetum parthenium 'Aureum' Clear yellow; white heads. 18in (45cm)

Tanacetum parthemium 'Golden Ball' Yellow aromatic ball. 4in (10cm)

Tanacetum ptarmiciflorum Leaves in upright, flat grey sprays. 1ft (30cm)

† This dark-leaved form is sometimes hard to find in catalogues and shops.

BIENNIALS

Biennials are sown in the summer to flower in spring and summer the next year. Some are good as bedding, taller varieties are best in borders.

Alcea 'Powder Puffs' Fluffy double flowers in five colours. 6ft (1.8m)

Bellis 'Habenera' Larger, blowsier daisy; red, pinks, white. 6in (15cm)

Bellis 'Pomponette Mixed' Neat, double, button-like daisies. 6in (15cm)

Calceolaria 'Sunset' Red, orange, yellow bicoloured slippers. 1ft (30cm)

Campanula 'Bell Tower' Cup-and-saucer Canterbury bells; 18in (45cm)

Cheiranthus 'Bedder Mixed' Dwarf bedding wallflower mix. 1ft (30cm)

Cheiranthus 'Fair Lady' Classic wallflowers; seven colours. 18in (45cm)

Digitalis 'Excelsior' Best range of colours in tall foxgloves. 6ft (1.8m)

Lunaria annua 'Mixed' Purples and white; everlasting pods. 2ft (60cm)

Lunaria annua 'Variegata' Purple flower; white-splashed leaf. 2ft (60cm)

Matthiola 'Legacy' Best biennial stock; seven colours. 15in (38cm)

Myosotis 'Rosie' Best pink-flowered forget-me-not; for edging. 6in (15cm)

Myosotis 'Royal Blue' Dark blue forget-me-not; not dumpy. 1ft (30cm)

Papaver 'Champagne Bubbles' Iceland poppy; superb colours. 2ft (60cm)†

Primula (polyanthus) 'Rainbow' Very hardy; eight colours. 1ft (30cm)

Primula (primrose) 'Wanda Supreme' Tough and colourful. 6in (15cm)

Viola (viola) 'Fanfare' Prolific, large-flowered; six colours. 6in (15cm)

Viola (viola) 'Princess' Small-flowered; five colours; lovely. 6in (15cm)

* *Viola (pansy) 'Ultima'* More colours than any other mix – 26. 6in (15cm)

Viola (pansy) 'Universal' Classic pansy; traditional colours. 6in (15cm)

---

† May suffer in cold, wet winters and in badly drained soil.

TENDER PERENNIALS

These are plants which will thrive outside in British summers but which are frost-tender so must be overwintered in warm conditions.

Flowers

Tender perennials are known for their generous display of flower, which often continues from planting time until the first frost.

WHITE FLOWERS

White flowers are usefully adaptable; in some situations they bring coolness to borders, in others they add contrast and brilliance.

Abutilon 'Boule de Neige' Large bells; good container centre. 6ft (1.8m)

* *Argyranthemum 'Edelweiss'* Anemone-centred; good dark leaf. 2ft (60cm)

Argyranthemum 'Snowstorm' White daisies; greyish foliage. 2ft (60cm)

Felicia 'Read's White' Large, bold, white daisies; vigorous. 1ft (30cm)

Nemesia 'Innocence' Prolific flat white snapdragons; twiggy. 9in (23cm)

Osteospermum 'Blue Streak' White daisies, blue petal backs. 2ft (60cm)

Pelargonium 'Snow Queen' Semi-double ivy-leaved geranium.

Petunia 'Surfinia White' Dark-throated pure white; trailing habit.

Salvia patens 'White Trophy' Hooked flowers, blue at base. 2ft (60cm)

Verbena 'Cleopatra White' Clean flowers; spreading habit. 6in (15cm)

PINK FLOWERS

Recently pink has become the most popular colour in summer bedding plants and more and more pink varieties have appeared.

Anisodontea capensis Twiggy, upright; small mallow flowers. 3ft (90cm)

Argyranthemum 'Gill's Pink' Small, single flowers; grey leaf. 2ft (60cm)

Begonia (fibrous) 'Gustav Lund' Double flowers, bronze leaf. 9in (23cm)†

Canna 'Orchid' Yellow-edged salmon; large bold green leaves. 4ft (1.2m)

Impatiens Enchantment Series Rosebud form; three shades. 1ft (30cm)

Nemesia umbonata Twiggy shrublet; smoky pink, yellow lip. 9in (23cm)

† This and other double fibrous begonias are listed under many names.

♈ *Osteospermum 'Pink Whirls'* Daisies wth spoon-shaped rays. 2ft (60cm)
 Pelargonium 'Salmon Queen' Semi-double, ivy-leaved, trailer.
* *Petunia Surfinia Series* Four pink shades; prolific trailing type.
♈* *Verbena 'Silver Ann'* Strong pink trailer, fading with age. 1ft (30cm)

RED FLOWERS

There is an unusual range of red shades, from the deepest crimson through
vivid scarlet to orangey and slightly pinkish shades.
 Abutilon 'Firebelle' Soft, orange-red bells; neat, compact habit. 3ft (90cm)
 Arctotis 'Wine' Deep red daisies; soft, grey leaves; needs sun. 1ft (30cm)
 Argyranthemum 'Rollison's Red' Single; best red, but pinkish. 2ft (60cm)
* *Dahlia 'Bishop of Llandaff'* Single scarlet; toothed bronze leaf. 3ft (90cm)
 Gazania 'Red Velvet' Deep red single; only opens in sun. 9in (23cm)
 Impatiens 'Enchantment Red' Deep red; 'rosebud' double. 1ft (30cm)†
 Impatiens New Guinea type Many reds, but names confused. 1ft (30cm)
♈ *Pelargonium 'Lord Bute'* Deep crimson regal; thrives in tubs. 1ft (30cm)
♈ *Pelargonium 'Yale'* Dark red, semi-double, ivy-leaved trailer.
♈ *Verbena 'Lawrence Johnston'* Brilliant deep scarlet spreader. 9in (23cm)

YELLOW FLOWERS

Marigolds are used too often in summer bedding, both in beds and borders
and in containers, so these yellow varieties are welcome.
♈ *Abutilon 'Canary Bird'* Big, bright yellow bells; black stems. 5ft (1.5m)
♈ *Argyranthemum 'Jamaica Primrose'* Bold daisies; ungainly. 2ft (60cm)
 Argyranthemum 'Yellow Star' Small daisies; feed well. 18in (45cm)
 Asteriscus 'Gold Coin' Bold yellow daisies; spreading habit. 1ft (30cm)
 Bidens aurea Small bright daisies on finely cut foliage. Trails.
 Euryops chrysanthemoides Neat daisies on dark leaved plant. 15in (38cm)
 Gazania uniflora Bright yellow daisies; bright silver leaves. 1ft (30cm)
♈ *Lotus maculatus* Large, dark-eyed parrot beaks; grey leaves. Trails.
 Lysimachia congestiflora Clusters of red-throated flowers; trails.
* *Osteospermum 'Anglia Yellow'* Rich golden daisies; upright. 2ft (60cm)

---

† Double-flowered busy lizzies are all good, but their names are muddled.

ORANGE FLOWERS

These fiery orange shades are especially successful when interplanted in borders or containers with purple and bronze foliage

    Arctotis 'Flame' Tangerine with a grey centre; rain tolerant. 1ft (30cm)

*   *Bracteantha 'Dargon Hill Monarch'* Orangey everlastings. 18in (45cm)

    Calceolaria 'Camden Hero' Rusty orange slipers; twiggy plant. 1ft (30cm)

    Canna 'King Humbert' Small flowers over rich bronze leaves. 4ft (1.2m)

    Cuphea cyanea Long season of slim flowers on a bushy plant. 15in (38cm)

    Gazania 'Tiger' Spiky, dark-eyed, rusty daisies; sun only. 1ft (30cm)

    Impatiens 'Enchantment Orange' Soft-coloured double. 1ft (30cm)

    Impatiens New Guinea type Orange shades; names confused. 1ft (30cm)

♀ *Streptosolen jamesonii* Pale orange; good in containers. 3ft (90cm)

♀ *Tropaeolum 'Hermine Grashof'* Double orange nasturtium; trails.

BLUE FLOWERS

There is something of a shortage of blue varieties among seed-raised summer flowers; these cuttings-raised types can fill the gap.

♀ *Felicia 'Santa Anita'* Yellow-eyed blue daisies; long season. 1ft (30cm)

    Heliotropium 'Mrs Lowther' Lavender-tinted, nearest to blue. 18in (45cm)

    Lobelia 'Kathleen Mallard' Bushy, double-flowered form. 6in (15cm)

    Lobelia richardii Large-flowered, white-eyed, pale blue trailer.

    Nemesia 'Joan Wilder' Pale violet-blue, white eyes; neat. 9in (23cm)

♀ *Osteospermum 'Whirligig'* White/blue spoon shaped daisies. 2ft (60cm)

*   *Petunia 'Surfinia Blue Vein'* Pale blue with dark veins; trailer.

    Scaevola aemula 'Blue Fan' Yellow-eyed, almost blue trailer.†

    Solenopsis axilliaris Pale blue stars on neat rounded plants. 1ft (30cm)

    Verbena 'Hidcote' Large, very deep blue starry flowers. 1ft (30cm)

---

†   The open habit of this plant makes it good with other plants.

PURPLE FLOWERS

Like blues, purple and mauve shades are not common among seed-raised
plants; the range of cuttings-raised varieties is small too.

Alogyne hiegelii 'Santa Cruz' Large, satin, deep mauve bells. 4ft (1.2m)
Brachyscome 'Harmony' Dark yellow eyes; rounded, compact. 6in (15cm)
Heliotropium 'Princess Marina' Rich purple, vanilla-scented. 9in (23cm)
Impatiens New Guinea type Lavender shades; names muddled. 1ft (30cm)
Lyacinthus rantonetti Golden-eyed purple-blue potato flowers. 3ft (90cm)
Osteospermum 'Tresco Purple' Black-eyed, purple daisies. 9in (23cm)
♀ *Pelargonium 'La France'* Dark-streaked mauve, ivy-leaved trailer.
* *Petunia Surfinia Series* Three purple shades; prolific trailer.
Salvia patens 'Chilcombe' Smoky mauve; parrot-beak flowers. 2ft (60cm)
Verbena 'Kemerton' Rich purple; spreading or trailing habit.

UNUSUAL COLOURS AND BICOLOURS

Now that more plant breeders are working on these plants, varieties in more
unusual colours and colour combinations are appearing.

Argyranthemum 'Peach Cheeks' Peachy pink; feed well. 18in (45cm)
Bracteantha 'Skynet' Pastel, pink-tinted orange; shrubby. 2ft (60cm)
Campanula isophylla 'Pamela' Blue and white bicolour; trails.
Canna 'Lucifer' Red and yellow bicolour; shorter than most. 3ft (90cm)†
Cosmos atrosanguineus Plain chocolate coloured and scented. 2ft (60cm)
Lotus jacobeus Small brown-eyed yellow pea flowers; bushy. 2ft (60cm).
Pelargonium 'Augusta' White with a deep pink eye; unusual. 1ft (30cm)
Pelargonium 'Rouletta' White ivy-leaved with red picotee; trails.
Verbena 'Aphrodite' Heads of white-striped mauve flowers; trails.
* *Verbena 'Pink Parfait'* Red and white bicolour; scented; trails.

---

†   The fat, iris-like roots are dug up in autumn and kept frost-free.

---------- **Attractive Foliage** ----------

In all summer schemes, be they in beds or containers, good foliage plants are
essential to provide a foil for the flamboyant flowers.

Abutilon pictum 'Thompsonii' Mottled yellow; orange bells. 6ft (1.8m)

Antirrhinum 'Taff's White' Cream-edged leaf; white flowers. 1ft (30cm)

♀ *Argyranthemum 'Chelsea Girl'* Threadlike leaf; white daisies. 3ft (90cm)

♀ *Argyranthemum 'Royal Haze'* Distinctive grey-blue leaves. 3ft (90cm)

Calocephalus brownii Compact, twiggy, grey-leaved shrublet. 1ft (30cm)

Canna 'General Eisenhower' Purple leaf; red-orange flowers. 5ft (1.5m)

Coleus Huge range of brilliant foliage colours; pinch out flowers.

Coprosma kirkii 'Variegata' Grey-green leaf, edged white; trails.

♀ *Gazania rigens 'Variegata'* Cream-edged leaf; orange daisies. 1ft (30cm)

Gazania uniflora Bright silver leaves; large yellow daisies. 1ft (30cm)

♀ *Helichrysum petiolare* Dependable vigorous grey-leaved sprawler.

* *Helichrysum petiolare 'Limelight'* Yellowish green sprawler.

Helichrysum petiolare 'Roundabout' Neat, cream and grey. 1ft (30cm)

♀ *Lotus berthelotii* Finely cut grey leaf; red parrot-bill flowers; trails.

Osteospermum 'Giles Gilbey' Gold-edged leaf; pink daisies. 1ft (30cm)

♀ *Pelargonium 'L'Élégante'* Grey-green/cream ivy-leaved; trails.

♀ *Pelargonium 'Mrs Henry Cox'* Magenta, pink, cream, green. 1ft (30cm)†

Pelargonium 'The Crocodile' Yellow-veined; red flowers; trails.

Plectranthus coleoides 'Variegatus' White-edged, vigorous, arches.

Plecostachys serpyllifolia Small grey leaves; bushy and trailing.

---

† This, and the many other coloured-leaved forms, need rich conditions.

Trailing habit †

Trailing plants, for flower and foliage, to tumble from tubs, window-boxes and hanging baskets are in great demand.

Bidens aurea Yellow daisies; lacy dark green foliage.

Coprosma kirkii 'Variegata' Greyish green leaves edged white.

♔* *Helichrysum petiolare* Vigorous all-grey trailer for larger tubs.

Helichrysum petiolare 'Goring Silver' Tight, compact and grey.

Helichrysum petiolare 'Limelight' Vigorous, limy yellow.

Helichrysum petiolare 'Roundabout' Silver and cream; compact.

♔ *Helichrysum petiolare 'Variegatum'* Silver and cream; vigorous.

Lobelia richardii Large, blue flowers; vigorous, open habit.

♔ *Lotus berthelotii* Thread-like grey leaves; red winter flowers.

♔ *Lotus maculatus* Fine, grey-green leaf; yellow winter flowers.

Lysimachia congestiflora Tight heads of yellow, red-eyed flowers.

Osteospermum 'Gweek Variegated' Cream edge; pink flowers.

Pelargionium (ivy-leaved) Huge range of colours and forms.

Petunia Surfinia Series Vigorous but hungry; nine colours.

Plectranthus hirtellus 'Variegata' Green, brightly edged cream.

Plecostachys serpyllifolia Small grey leaves on sprawling plant.

Scaevola 'Blue Fan' Blue, yellow-eyed; sparse but dramatic.

♔ *Senecio macroglossus 'Variegatus'* Like a classy trailing ivy.

Verbena 'Loveliness' Bluish purple flowers, strong colour.

Verbena 'Pink Parfait' Red and pink bicolour; scented; superb.

---

† No measurements are given as length of trailing depends on treatment.

BULBS

In this section I have taken a fairly relaxed view of what constitutes a bulb and included some plants with tubers or corms.

Spring

Bulbs are an essential feature of the spring garden; there are a few types like tulips and crocuses with very large numbers of different varieties and many smaller groups with only a few varieties.

WHITE FLOWERS

Many spring bulbs with white flowers have shading or flushing in other shades which makes them especially interesting.

Allium cowanii Pure white ornamental onion; sweet scent! 18in (45cm)

♈ *Anemone blanda* 'White Splendour' Strong; creeping; early. 6in (15cm)

Crocus 'Jeanne d'Arc' Best pure white Dutch crocus; prolific. 6in (15cm)

♈ *Crocus sieberi* 'Albus' Pure, globular flowers; late winter. 3in (7.5cm)

Crocus tommasinianus 'Albus' Elegant and early, naturalizes. 4in (10cm)

♈ *Erythronium* 'White Beauty' Cream, with red spotted throat. 10in (25cm)

♈* *Galanthus* 'Atkinsii' Vigorous, tall and early spring snowdrop. 8in (20cm)†

♈ *Galanthus nivalis* 'Flore Pleno' Double snowdrop; lasts well. 6in (15cm)†

Hyacinthus 'Carnegie' Pure white; scented, of course; sturdy. 9in (23cm)

Ipheion 'Alberto Castello' Pure white; greyish leaf; stunning. 9in (23cm)

Iris reticulata 'Natasha' Nearest to white in rock garden iris. 6in (15cm)

♈ *Leucojum aestivum* 'Gravetye Giant' Green tipped bells. 2ft (60cm)

♈ *Leucojum vernum* Like a large, bold, green-leaved snowdrop. 6in (15cm)

Muscari botryoides 'Album' Tight-packed spikes; sweet scent. 5in (13cm)

♈ *Narcissus* 'Jenny' Milky white; trumpet opens lemony; dainty. 15in (38cm)

Narcissus 'Mount Hood' Large trumpet daffodil; vigorous. 18in (45cm)

Narcissus poeticus White, swept-back petals; red eye; scented 18in (45cm)

Ornithogalum umbellatum Flat heads of green-striped flowers. 6in (15cm)

---

† Ordinary snowdrops are dainty but named sorts are more showy.

Tulipa 'Purissima' The best white tulip; very long-lasting. 18in (45cm)
Tulipa 'White Triumphator' Lily-flowered type; very elegant; 2ft (60cm)

PINK FLOWERS

As usual the pinks cover a wide range of shades, including some rather
unlikely ones, and occur in some unexpected plants.

Allium unifolium Sharp, candy pink onion; increases well. 9in (23cm).
Anemone blanda 'Pink Star' Rather variable in colour; creeps. 4in (10cm)†
Anemone nemarosa 'Pentre Pink' Best pink wood anemone. 4in (10cm)†
Chionodoxa forbesii 'Pink Giant' Soft pink, white centres. 5in (13cm)†
Convallaria majalis 'Rosea' Pink lily-of-the-valley! not strong. 6in (15cm)†
Crocus tommasinianus var. roseus Unusual old rose shade. 3in (7.5cm)
Cyclamen coum Rounded, in many pinks; leaves can be silver. 3in (7.5cm)
Cyclamen repandum Bright, twisted petals; for under shrubs. 3in (7.5cm)
Erythronium 'Pink Perfection' Good clear pink; damp shade. 5in (13cm)
Hyacinthoides hispanica 'Rosabella' Bold, pink 'bluebell'. 15in (38cm)
Hyacinthus 'Lady Derby' Soft shell-pink; intoxicating scent. 9in (23cm)
♀ *Hyacinthus 'Pink Pearl'* Stronger pink, pale edges to petals. 9in (23cm)
Narcissus 'Bell Song' White, pink cup; two flowers per head. 1ft (30cm)
♀ *Narcissus 'Passionale'* Large soft pink cup; white petals; bold. 18in (45cm)
Scilla bifolia 'Rosea' Unusual pink form of blue scilla; early. 6in (15cm)
♀ *Tulipa aucheriana* Deep rose with yellow base; prostrate leaves. 4in
   (10cm)
* *Tulipa 'Angélique'* Double; mix of pale and dark shades. 15in (38cm)
Tulipa 'Happy Family' Superb, multiheaded, rose pink; 18in (45cm)
♀ *Tulipa kauffmaniana 'Ancilla'* Pale pink with dark stripe; 8in (20cm)
Tulipa saxatalis Pale pink with yellow centres; good drainage. 1ft (30cm)

---

†   This is about the only pink variety of this plant actually worth growing.

RED FLOWERS

There seem very few good reds among the spring bulbs and some of those we have are closer to orange or magenta in colour.

♈ *Anemone blanda* 'Radar' Fierce magenta, white eye; creeps. 4in (10cm)

♈ *Corydalis solida* 'George Baker' Heads of brick red; shade. 6in (15cm)

Fritillaria imperialis Crown Imperial; orangey red; foxy smell. 2ft (60cm)†

Hyacinthus 'Hollyhock' Unusual double red on brown stem. 9in (23cm)

Hyacinthus 'Jan Bos' Deep rich red; heads well above leaves. 9in (23cm)

Narcissus 'Ambergate' Orange cup, pink-tinted orange petals. 15in (38cm)

Narcissus 'Jetfire' Gold reflexed petals, orangey red trumpet. 10in (25cm)

Tulipa 'Madame Lefeber' Fiery; black and yellow base. 18in (45cm)

♈* *Tulipa praestans* 'Fusilier' Multiheaded vermilion; superb. 1ft (30cm)

♈ *Tulipa* 'Red Riding Hood' Scarlet, black base; mottled leaf. 9in (23cm)

PURPLE FLOWERS

Many purple spring bulbs are rather too red or too black for inclusion here, so this leaves the list short and unusually mixed.

Allium rosenbachianum Dark violet balls with white stamens. 2ft (60cm)

♈ *Corydalis solida* Dense pinky-purple spikes; summer dormant. 6in (15cm)

Crocus 'Purpureus Grandiflorus' Huge, glossy purple goblets. 6in (15cm)

* *Crocus sieberi* 'Violet Queen' Bluish violet; rounded flower. 3in (7.5cm)

Hyacinthus 'Blue Magic' Deep violet flower with a white eye. 9in (23cm)

♈ *Ipheion uniflorum* 'Froyle Mill' Deep violet stars; long season. 6in (15cm)

Iris histrioides 'George' Bold, purple flowers; good scent. 6in (15cm)

Iris reticulata 'J. S. Dijt' Dark, reddish purple; sweet scent. 6in (15cm)

Muscari comosum Upper flowers pale blue; tall and bold. 9in (23cm)

Tulipa 'Dreaming Maid' Strong mauve, edged with white. 20in (50cm)

---

† Plant the hollow centred bulb upright, 6in (15cm) deep, on a bed of grit.

YELLOW FLOWERS

Yellow is the archetypal colour of spring, typified by the hundreds of different daffodils on the market; but there are many more.

℣ *Allium moly* Bright heads from ever increasing bulbs. 1ft (30cm)

℣ *Anemone ranunculoides* Yellow buttercups; creeps slowly. 8in (20cm)†

   Anemone × *lipsiensis* Primrose buttercups; bronzed foliage. 8in (20cm)†

   Crocus ancyrensis Orangey yellow; very prolific, very early. 2in (5cm)

℣ *Crocus angustifolius* Prolific golden yellow, bronze on outside. 3in (7.5cm)

   Crocus chrysanthus 'E. P. Bowles' Pure yellow, purple streaks. 3in (7.5cm)

℣ *Crocus* × *luteus 'Golden Yellow'* Bright, bold Dutch crocus. 5in (13cm)

   Eranthis hyemalis Winter aconite; very early; slow to settle. 3in (7.5cm)†

℣ *Erythronium 'Pagoda'* Sulphurous reflexed petals; vigorous. 9in (23cm)

℣ *Fritillaria imperialis 'Lutea Maxima'* Yellow crown imperial. 2ft (60cm)

℣ *Fritillaria pallidiflora* Large, straw-yellow, red spotted within. 1ft (30cm)

   Iris bucharica Cream with yellow blotches; luxuriant leaves. 1ft (30cm)

   Iris danfordiae Very early lemon yellow; often short-lived. 5in (13cm)

℣ *Narcissus 'February Gold'* Early, elegant, prolific and tough. 15in (38cm)

   Narcissus 'Golden Harvest' Best big, bright trumpet daffodil. 18in (45cm)

   Narcissus 'Hawera' Lemon with paler cup; very dainty. 10in (25cm)

℣ *Narcissus 'Tête à Tête'* Two miniature flowers on one stem. 6in (15cm)

   Tulipa 'Golden Appledoorn' Classic, simple deep yellow tulip. 2ft (60cm)

   Tulipa linifolia 'Apricot Jewel' Apricot flower, greyish leaf. 6in (15cm)

*   *Tulipa 'West Point'* Lily-flowered; good with forget-me-nots. 18in (45cm)

---

†   This plant makes a carpet of colour under deciduous shrubs.

BLUE FLOWERS

No surprises here, just a superb selection of familiar classic blue-flowered bulbs which look so good with other spring bulbs.

♥ *Anemone blanda 'Ingramii'* Intense deep blue; bold, strong. 4in (10cm)

♥ *Anemone nemorosa 'Robinsoniana'* Large-flowered, pale. 6in (15cm)

Chionodoxa forbesii Large, deep, white-eyed flowers; prolific. 6in (15cm)

♥ *Chionodoxa luciliae* Dainty, lavender-tinted blue, white eye. 5in (13cm)†

♥ *Crocus chrysanthus 'Blue Pearl'* Exquisite silvery blue; easy. 3in (7.5cm)

Crocus 'Queen of the Blues' Large pale blue, palest at edges. 5in (13cm)

Crocus sieberi ssp. atticus Soft blue, golden throat; prolific. 3in (7.5cm)

Hyacinthoides hispanica Spanish bluebell; tall and bold. 15in (38cm)†

♥ *Hyacinthus 'Delft Blue'* Familiar soft blue; heavily scented. 9in (23cm)

♥ *Ipheion uniflorum 'Wisley Blue'* Galaxies of clear blue stars. 6in (15cm)

Iris reticulata 'Cantab' Pale blue bulbous iris, yellow throat. 6in (15cm)

Iris reticulata 'Harmony' Brilliant gentian blue, yellow throat. 6in (15cm)

♥ *Muscari armeniacum* Cobalt blue, each flower white-rimmed. 6in (15cm)†

♥ *Muscari azureum* Dark-striped azure blue; crowded spikes. 5in (13cm)

Muscari latifolium Pale flowers turning blue-black; broad leaf. 9in (23cm)

♥ *Pushkinia scillioides var. libanotica* Green-striped; compact. 4in (10cm)

♥ *Scilla bifolia* Mauve-tinted; excellent for naturalizing in shade. 5in (13cm)

Scilla litardierei Tall, open spikes; only for full sun. 10in (25cm)

♥* *Scilla mischtschenkoana* Palest blue, dark-striped; very early. 6in (15cm)

Scilla siberica 'Spring Beauty' Very dark, almost violet blue. 6in (15cm)

---

† Spreads well by means of seedlings when happy.

UNUSUAL COLOURS AND BICOLOURS

There are many unusual shades and colour combinations among the spring
bulbs, but especially in the crocuses and fritillarias.

Anemone nemorosa 'Virescens' Green lacy flowers; unique. 4in (10cm)

Arisarum proboscoideum Flowers like purple mice with tails. 4in (10cm)

Arum dioscoridis Pale green with black blotches; foul smell. 1ft (30cm)†

Crocus 'Advance' Purple backs to petals, peachy inside. 3in (7.5cm)

♈ *Crocus imperatii* Violet inside, beige out with brown stripes. 3in (7.5cm)

Crocus sieberi 'Firefly' Outer petals white, inner sharp violet. 3in (7.5cm)

Erythronium 'Joanna' Petals pink on backs, yellow inside. 10in (25cm)

Fritillaria 'Martha Roderick' Cream-edged, brownish bells. 6in (15cm)

♈ *Fritillaria michailovskyi* Chocolate purple bells, yellow tips. 8in (20cm)

Fritillaria pontica Large shining green bells, tipped brown. 1ft (30cm)

Hermodactylus tuberosus Iris-like flowers, close to black. 1ft (30cm)†

Iris japonica 'Ledger's Variety' White, orange and blue. 2ft (60cm)

* *Iris 'Katherine Hodgkin'* Pale cream, yellow and palest blue. 4in (10cm)†

Muscari macrocarpum Opens violet, turns beige then yellow. 6in (15cm)†

Narcissus 'Tricollet' White, orange cup split and flattened. 15in (38cm)

Nectaroscordum siculum Allium relative; green and purple. 3ft (90cm)

♈ *Ornithogalum nutans* Spikes of silvery white, striped green. 1ft (30cm)

Tulipa 'Heart's Delight' Pink back; white, yellow, red inside. 8in (20cm)

♈ *Tulipa 'Stresa'* Yellow and red; attractive mottled foliage. 7in (17.5cm)

♈ *Tulipa turkestanica* White, shaded grey outside, yellow base. 4in (10cm)

---

† Requires a sunny, well-drained place to thrive. Add grit when planting.

---------- **Summer** ----------

The range of summer bulbs is far smaller than the spring selection; few are true bulbs but there are many, like dahlias, with tubers.

Agapanthus 'Isis' Dense, deep blue heads; full sun, light soil. 18in (45cm)

♀ *Allium christophii* Superb steely mauve heads like footballs. 2ft (60cm)

♀ *Allium flavum* Brilliant yellow flowers in heads like fireworks. 1ft (30cm)

Allium 'Purple Sensation' Tall, vivid, deep purple drumsticks. 3ft (90cm)

Camassia quamash Short spikes with large, deep blue stars. 1ft (30cm)

Cosmos atrosanguineus Dark chocolate colour and scent. 2ft (60cm)†

♀ *Crinum* × *powellii* Huge bulbs; lush leaf; big pink trumpets. 3ft (90cm)

Dahlia 'Bishop of Llandaff' Single scarlet; jagged bronze leaf. 3ft (90cm)†

Dahlia 'David Howard' Double orange; dark bronze foliage. 4ft (1.2m)†

Dahlia merckii Single mauve; tall, open plant, usually hardy. 4ft (1.2m)

Epipactis gigantea Vigorous hardy orchid; pink and green. 1ft (30cm)

Galtonia candicans Summer hyacinth; spires of white bells. 3ft (90cm)

♀ *Galtonia viridiflora* Large, pale green bells; broad leaf. 3ft (90cm)

Gladiolus byzantinus Rich, reddish purple; hardy and spreads. 2ft (60cm)

♀ *Gladiolus colvillei 'The Bride'* White, green marks; tender. 18in (45cm)†

Lilium martagon Elegant open spires of purple turkscaps. 4ft (1.2m)

♀* *Lilium regale* Huge white, purplish, heavily scented trumpets. 3ft (90cm)

Lilium tigrinum 'Splendens' Orange turkscaps spotted black. 4ft (1.2m)

♀ *Rhodohypoxis baurii* Pinks, reds and white; dry, acid soil. 4in (10cm)

Zantedeschia aethiopica 'Crowborough' Huge white arums. 3ft (90cm)

---

† Dig this up in the autumn and store in a frost-free place.

Autumn

Many newcomers to gardening are surprised to discover autumn bulbs, but they are among the most valuable plants of the season.

Allium tuberosum Russian chives; white heads from summer. 15in (38cm)

Amaryllis bella-donna Hardy relative of Christmas amaryllis. 18in (45cm)

Begonia evansiana Unusual, late, hardy begonia; pink or white. 2ft (60cm)

♈ *Colchicum speciosum* Pinkish mauve; weather-resistant. 9in (23cm)

♈ *Colchicum speciosum 'Album'* Lovely pure white goblets. 6in (15cm)

Colchicum 'Waterlily' Double pink "autumn crocus"; shelter. 6in (15cm)

♈ *Crocosmia 'Solfaterre'* Yellow spikes; flat smoky bronze leaf. 2ft (60cm)

♈ *Crocus goulimyi* Long-stemmed, lilac bowls; sun, light soil. 3in (7.5cm)

♈ *Crocus kotschyanus* Pale lilac with yellow throat; full sun. 3in (7.5cm)

♈ *Crocus speciosus* Dark-veined lilac flowers; naturalizes well. 5in (13cm)

♈ *Cyclamen hederifolium* Pink or white; marbled leaves later. 4in (10cm)

♈ *Cyclamen mirabile* Pink, dainty; leaf green, silver and pink. 3in (7.5cm)

Galanthus reginae-olgae Autumn snowdrop; amazes visitors. 4in (10cm)

♈ *Gladiolus callianthus* White, dark-centred flowers; scented. 3ft (90cm)

Gladiolus papilio Strange purple, green and white flowers. 3ft (90cm)

Iris unguicularis 'Mary Barnard' Purple, scented; winter. 15in (38cm)†

Iris unguicularis 'Walter Butt' Pale misty blue; large flowers. 18in (45cm)†

♈ *Nerine bowdenii* Flared pink flowers topping straight stems. 18in (45cm)

Sternbergia lutea Like a yellow crocus; full sun, gritty soil. 5in (13cm)

Zephyranthes candida White, crocus-like; slightly tender. 6in (15cm)

---

†   Cut the first autumn flowers for the house while still in bud.

ORNAMENTAL HERBS

In smaller gardens there is rarely space for a separate herb garden, but these ornamental herbs can be very effective in mixed borders.

Flowers

The flowers of most of these flowering herbs are used in the kitchen; in some cases they are simply attractive flowering plants.

    Angelica (*Angelica archangelica*) Greeny white, in huge flat heads.

    Bergamot (*Monarda* 'Adam') Red; better than 'Cambridge Scarlet'.

    Bergamot (*Monarda* 'Pisces') Pale rose-pink; mildew-resistant.

    Bergamot (*Monarda* 'Scorpio') Purple flowers; mildew-resistant.

    Bergamot (*Monarda* 'Sioux') Blushed white; mildew-resistant.

    Borage (*Borago officinalis*) Bright blue stars; easy hardy annual.

    Chives (*Allium schoenoprasum*) Pretty spherical mauve heads.†

    Chives (*Allium schoenoprasum* 'Corsican White') White form.†

*   *Chives* (*Allium schoenoprasum* 'Forescate') Bright rosy red.†

    Garlic chives (*Allium tuberosum*) Brilliant flat white heads.

    Hyssop (*Hyssopus officinalis*) Blue, pink or white; twiggy shrublet.

    Marigold (*Calendula* 'Art Shades') Soft and subtle; hardy annual.

    Nasturtium (*Tropaeolum* 'Alaska') Ten-colour mix; variegated.

    Nasturtium (*Tropaeolum* 'Empress of India') Scarlet; dark leaf.

♀   *Rosemary* (*Rosmarinus* 'Miss Jessopp's Upright') Upright habit.

♀   *Rosemary* (*Rosmarinus* 'Severn Sea') Very bright; neat, arching.

    Rosemary (*Rosmarinus* 'Tuscan Blue') Unusually deep colour.

    Sage (*Salvia officinalis*) Purple spikes; foliage forms less prolific.

    Viola (*Viola* 'Princess Mixed') Small, neat flowers; for summer.

    Viola (*Viola* 'Sorbet Mixed') Small, neat flowers; for spring.

---

†   The flowers of chives can go in salads as well as the leaves.

Foliage

Herbs with attractive foliage not only look interesting when used raw in salads, but bring long-lasting colour to garden borders.

Basil (*Ocimum basilicum* 'Purple Ruffles') Half-hardy annual.

♈ Bay (*Laurus nobilis* 'Aurea') Slower and less tough than the green.

Chives (*Allium schoenoprasum*) Forest of long slim oniony leaves.

* Fennel (*Foeniculum vulgare* 'Smoky') Fine, dusky bronze leaf.

Horseradish (*Armoracia rusticana* 'Variegata') Very invasive.

Lemon balm (*Melissa officinalis* 'Allgold') Best in partial shade.

Marjoram (*Origanum* 'Norton Gold') Yellow, with bluey sheen.

♈ Marjoram (*Origanum vulgare* 'Aureum') Yellow, scorches in sun.

Marjoram (*Origanum vulgare* 'Polyphant') Neat white variegation.

Mint (apple) (*Mentha suaveolens* 'Variegata') Pure white marks.

Mint (ginger) (*Mentha* × *gentilis* 'Variegata') Yellow-marked; slow.

Nasturtium (*Tropaeolum* 'Alaska') Small, neat mottled leaf.†

Parsley (*Petroselinum crispum* 'Curlina') Dark and tightly curled.

Rosemary (*Rosmarinus officinalis* 'Aureus') Yellow-splashed.

♈ Sage (*Salvia officinalis* 'Icterina') Gold and green mottling.

Sage (*Salvia officinalis* 'Kew Gold') Soft gold, red stems; slow.

♈ Sage (*Salvia officinalis* 'Purpurascens') Wonderful rich dark purple.

♈ Thyme (lemon) (*Thymus* × *citriodorus* 'Bertram Anderson') Yellow.

♈ Thyme (lemon) (*Thymus* × *citriodorus* 'Silver Queen') White-edged.

Thyme (*Thymus vulgaris* 'Silver Posie') White-edged, pink tips.

---

† Nasturtium leaves have a peppery taste, and they're the right size for sandwiches.

ROSES

Every garden needs roses, but the relentless stream of new introductions, combined with the continuing revival of older varieties, makes choosing the right variety increasingly difficult.

BUSH ROSES

Four groups are covered (see below†). In recent years there has been a move to replace the term Hybrid Teas with Large-flowered roses, and to rename Floribundas as Cluster-flowered roses.

WHITE FLOWERS

The purity of white flowers is always admired, and creamier colours are also included here; a few may blush slightly as they age.

- ♛ *'Alba Maxima'* OF Slightly untidy, blushed at first. Fine scent. 6ft (1.8m)
- *'Bianco'* D Pure white pompoms on neat and bushy plants. 18in (45cm)
- ♛ *'Blanc Double de Coubert'* OF Large flowers; long season. 6ft (1.8m)
- *'Boule de Neige'* OF Richly scented, camellia-like flowers. 5ft (1.5m)
- *'Evening Star'* HT Pure white, strong scent; dark foliage. 3ft (90cm)
- *'Florence Nightingale'* D Pink buds open pure white; scented. 2ft (60cm)
- *'Glamis Castle'* E Pure white, strongly scented cupped flowers. 3ft (90cm)
- ♛ *'Iceberg'* F Scented flowers blush with age; prone to mildew. 4ft (1.2m)
- ♛* *'Margaret Merrill'* F Wonderful scent and disease-resistant. 2½ ft (75cm)
- ♛ *'Mme Hardy'* OF Exquisite, scented flowers; vigorous, tough. 6ft (1.8m)
- ♛ *'Nevada'* OF Creamy; tumultuous flush then fewer; thin hard. 7ft (2.1m)
- *'Pascali'* HT Very shapely flowers; good to cut; poor scent. 3½ ft (1.05m)
- *'Polar Star'* HT Traditional HT shape; branches very well. 3½ ft (1.05m)
- *'Pour Toi'* D Full clusters of tiny flowers with creamier tints. 9in (23cm)
- *'Royal Smile'* HT Cream with pink tints; highly fragrant. 2ft (60cm)
- *'Sir Frederick Ashton'* HT Vigorous, dark-leaved; superb scent. 4ft (1.2m)
- *'Tear Drop'* D Semi-double, showy yellow centre; scented. 15in (38cm)

† In this section HT = Hybrid Teas; F = Floribundas, D = Dwarf roses of various kinds under 2ft (60cm); OF = Old fashioned shrub roses; E = English roses.

'Virgo' HT Shapely pure white, blushed pink; upright growth. $2\frac{1}{2}$ ft (75cm)

♀ 'White Pet' D Small, dense poms in a widely spreading mound. 2ft (60cm)

♀ 'Yvonne Rabier' F No scent, but prolific and almost thornless. 3ft (90cm)

YELLOW FLOWERS

Some of these yellow roses have additional tints in other shades but the majority are pure yellow or approaching gold in colour.

'Ann Harkness' F Saffron-orange, good cut flower; healthy. $3\frac{1}{2}$ ft (1.05m)

♀ 'Arthur Bell' F Bright yellow fading to cream; fragrant; tough. 3ft (90cm)

'Bright Smile' D Slim buds open flat to clear yellow; bushy 2ft (60cm)

♀ 'Canary Bird' OF Single, deep yellow on arching growth. 7ft (2.1m)

♀ 'Chinatown' F Fragrant clear yellow; unusually tall and healthy. 5ft (1.5m)

'Glenfiddich' F Golden amber, but poorly scented; healthy. $2\frac{1}{2}$ ft (75cm)

'Golden Years' F Copper tint; free and long-flowering; healthy. $2\frac{1}{2}$ ft (75cm)

♀* 'Graham Thomas' E Cupped, highly scented, rich yellow. 4ft (1.2m)†

'Grandpa Dickson' HT Very large lemony flowers; upright. 3ft (90cm)

'Korresia' F Good colour; prolific; healthy and fragrant. $2\frac{1}{2}$ ft (75cm)

'Lady Hillingdon' OF Waxy, apricot yellow; strong scent. 3ft (90cm)

♀ 'Mountbatten' F Elegant flowers; strong, bushy and healthy. 4ft (1.2m)

♀ 'Peace' HT Large, pale, with pink flushes; tough and easy. 4ft (1.2m)

'Peaudouce' HT Pale primrose in a classic shape; disease-free. 3ft (90cm)

♀ 'Remember Me' HT More copper and orange than yellow. $2\frac{1}{2}$ ft (75cm)

'Rise 'n' Shine' D Shapely, tightly double flowers; upright. 18in (45cm)

'Rosina' D Semi-double clear yellow; glossy leaf; bushy. 9in (23cm)

♀ 'Southampton' F Apricot and scented; vigorous and easy. $3\frac{1}{2}$ ft (1.05m)

♀ 'Sweet Dream' D Small, neat apricot cups; dense and upright. 18in (45cm)

'Yellow Doll' D Unusually narrow-petalled double; bushy. 1ft (30cm)

---

†   English roses are modern, long-season versions of old roses.

PINK FLOWERS

Pink roses come in so many shades that I could have produced about five lists, catalogues will reveal others as good as these.

'*Angela Rippon*' D Double coral ageing to salmon; good scent. 1ft (30cm)

♀ '*Anisley Dickson*' F Large deep salmon, paler on backs. 2½ ft (75cm)

♀ '*Ballerina*' OF Appleblossom-pink; neat, reliable and prolific. 4ft (1.2m)

♀ '*Blessings*' HT Salmon; healthy, fragrant, long season, reliable. 3ft (90cm)

'*Cecile Brunner*' OF Tiny, blush HT flowers; prolific; scented. 3ft (90cm)†

'*Celestial*' OF Shell pink, golden centre; scented, greyish leaf. 6ft (1.8m)

'*English Miss*' Crowded pale pink sprays; sweet scent; prolific. 2½ ft (75cm)

♀ '*Fantin-Latour*' OF Blush, deep centre; elegant flowers; tough. 6ft (1.8m)

'*Fragrant Cloud*' HT Highly scented, smoky deep coral; strong. 3ft (90cm)

♀ '*Gentle Touch*' D Shapely, pale rose-pink; spreading habit. 1ft (30cm)

* '*Heritage*' E Cupped soft pink; superb scent; long season. 4ft (1.2m)

'*Mary Rose*' E Loose, rose pink; good scent; long season. 4ft (1.2m)

'*Old Blush*' OF '*Monthly Rose*'. Pale; unusually long season. 4ft (1.2m)

♀ '*Paul Shirville*' HT Salmony; strong, spreading growth. 3ft (90cm)

♀ '*Queen Elizabeth*' F Clear pink; very tall and upright. 4–7ft (1.2–2.1m)

♀ '*Sexy Rexy*' F Very tight, soft pink flowers; bushy, little scent. 2ft (60cm)

♀ '*Silver Jubilee*' HT Well-formed, pink flowers shaded peach. 2½ ft (75cm)

♀ '*Stacey Sue*' D Soft pink, fully double; spreading growth. 9in (23cm)

'*Tip Top*' D Well-filled clusters of soft rosy salmon; dark leaf. 18in (45cm)

'*Wendy Cussons*' HT Dark rose pink; classic form; rich scent. 3ft (90cm)

† There is also a delightful climbing version of this dainty rose.

RED FLOWERS†

Roses in vermilion, scarlet, crimson and deep ruby are among the most popular of all but many have less scent than we would like.

'*Alec's Red*' HT Cherry-red, highly scented flowers; strong. 3ft (90cm)

'*Disco Dancer*' F Brilliant scarlet, with orange tints; vigorous. 3ft (90cm)

'*Dusky Maiden*' F Single, gold-centred, crimson; scented. 2ft (60cm)

'*Ena Harkness*' HT Deep velvety red; prolific but weak-necked. 2ft (60cm)

'*Ernest H. Morse*' HT Loose, crimson; dark leaf and stem. 3ft (90cm)

'*Evelyn Fison*' F Brilliant scarlet; little scent, but very healthy. 2½ ft (75cm)

'*Gipsy Boy*' OF Deep purplish crimson; highly fragrant. 6ft (1.8m)

*   '*L. D. Braithwaite*' E Cupped deep crimson; long season. 3½ ft (1.05m)

'*Lilli Marlene*' F Scarlet; vigorous, well-branched, prolific. 2½ ft (75cm)

'*Little Buckaroo*' D White-centred, bright red; bronzed leaf. 15in (38cm)

'*National Trust*' HT Bright red and very prolific, but little scent. 2ft (60cm)

'*Red Ace*' D Rather flat, deep red; little scent; neat, bushy. 1ft (30cm)

♀   '*Royal William*' HT Deep ruby, very well-scented; spreading. 3ft (90cm)

'*Super Star*' HT Brilliant vermilion; prolific but some mildew. 3ft (90cm)

'*The Prince*' E Deep crimson, fading rich purple; rich scent. 2½ ft (75cm)

♀   '*The Times Rose*' F Blood-red, in large heads; dark leaf. 2ft (60cm)

'*Topsi*' D Full clusters of orange-red flowers; bushy; no scent. 18in (45cm)

♀   '*Trumpeter*' F Bright red; long season and prolific; reliable. 2ft (60cm)

♀   '*Tuscany Superb*' OF Deep crimson, fading purple; scented. 5ft (1.5m)

'*Velvet Fragrance*' HT Deep crimson, shapely; superb scent. 3ft (90cm)

---

†   Unfortunately many dark red roses are prone to disease attack.

UNUSUAL COLOURS AND COLOUR COMBINATIONS

One recent trend has been the introduction of varieties in unusual colour combinations. Love them or hate them, there's no denying that they turn heads, but I prefer unusual colours without clashes.

'*Baby Masquerade*' D Yellow and red at first, then deep red. 18in (45cm)

♀ '*Buff Beauty*' OF Rich apricot paling with age; lush foliage. 5ft (1.5m)

'*Cardinal Hume*' E Rich deep purple, musky scent; spreading. 3ft (90cm)

'*Colibri*' D Buff, flushed orange; dark foliage, upright habit. 1ft (30cm)

'*Double Delight*' HT Creamy white with a bold cerise edge! 3ft (90cm)

'*Escapade*' F Semi-double rosy lavender, pale at base; scented. 3ft (90cm)

'*Eye Paint*' F Bold heads of white-eyed, single scarlet flowers. 3ft (90cm)

'*Harry Wheatcroft*' HT Orange-red, striped and splashed yellow. 2½ ft (75cm)

'*Joseph's Coat*' OF Bright pink with a yellow centre; vigorous. 7ft (2.1m)

♀ '*Just Joey*' HT Coppery orange, fading to pink at edges. 2ft (60cm)

'*Little Flirt*' D Pointed petals are orange, yellow on the backs. 15in (38cm)

'*Magic Carousel*' D Well-shaped white flowers tipped pink. 1ft (30cm)

'*Masquerade*' F Yellow, fading to pink and orange to deep red! 2½ ft (75cm)

'*Matangi*' F Vermilion with a white eye and white backs. 3ft (90cm)

'*Piccadilly*' HT Red, backed yellow, fading to orange; very thorny. 2½ ft (75cm)

* '*Rosa Mundi*' OF Crimson, striped with white; very dramatic. 4ft (1.2m)†

'*Rose Gaujard*' HT Silvery-tinted red, pale on backs; healthy. 4ft (1.2m)

'*Sutters Gold*' HT Deep yellow, tinted orange and pink; prolific. 3ft (90cm)

'*Variegata di Bologna*' OF White, striped crimson; cupped. 5ft (1.5m)†

♀ '*William Lobb*' OF Crimson fading to greyish purple; fragrant. 6ft (1.8m)

---

† These old striped roses hold a strong fascination for non-gardeners.

RAMBLING AND CLIMBING ROSES

Most roses have thorns because their wild ancestors needed them to grip as they scrambled through shrubs and trees. Some garden climbers and ramblers grow through shrubs, others need tying to supports.

Repeat-flowering

Climbing and rambling roses which flower all summer or in two colourful bursts give the most effective display in smaller gardens.

'Aloha' Large, cupped clear pink; highly scented; tough. 6ft (1.8m)

'Alister Stella Grey' Yellow rosette flowers all summer. 15ft (4.5m)

♧ 'Altissimo' Very large, deep red single flowers with gold centre. 8ft (2.4m)

'Breath of Life' Scented, apricot pink flowers of HT shape. 8ft (2.4m)

♧ 'Climbing Iceberg' Climbing version of familiar Floribunda. 10ft (3m)

♧ 'Compassion' Scented salmon-pink with orange tints; bushy. 10ft (3m)

'Danse du Feu' Bright orange-scarlet, fades purplish; no scent. 10ft (3m)

♧ 'Gloire de Dijon' Fluffy beigey pink with a wonderful scent. 15ft (4.5m)

♧ 'Golden Showers' Gold, then fading to cream; very prolific. 10ft (3m)

♧ 'Handel' Blushed cream, edged with stronger pink; vigorous. 12ft (3.6m)

♧ 'Mermaid' Large single yellow flowers; best on sunny wall. 25ft (7.5m)

♧ 'Mme Alfred Carrière' Highly fragrant, blushed white; tough. 20ft (6m)

♧ 'Morning Jewel' Fragrant, rich pink; unusually prolific. 10ft (3m)

♧* 'New Dawn' Scented silvery pink flowers in great abundance. 10ft (3m)

'Parkdirektor Riggers' Deep red single flowers; very healthy. 10ft (3m)

'Rosy Mantle' Spectacular, highly scented, silvery pink. 8ft (2.4m)

'Schoolgirl' Loose, highly scented, coppery orange flowers. 10ft (3m)

♧ 'Summer Wine' Large deep pink, red centre; nicely bushy. 10ft (3m)

'Swan Lake' Shapely buds open to blushed white; prolific. 8ft (2.4m)

♧ 'Zéphirine Drouhin' Prolific, scented, deep pink, thornless. 12ft (3.6m)†

---

† For more thornless climbers and bush roses, see page 261.

--------------------- **Once-flowering†** ---------------------

These varieties are spectacularly colourful when they're at their best in early summer, but only produce one brilliant burst of flower.

℣ *'Albertine'* Coppery pink, highly scented; a martyr to mildew. 20ft (6m)

'Bleu Magenta' Small crimson flowers fade to greyish violet. 15ft (4.5m)

'Emily Gray' Beigey yellow, fading to pale primrose; scented. 12ft (3.6m)

* *'Félicité Perpétue'* Tight-packed creamy pompoms; healthy. 20ft (6m)

'Francis E. Lester' Slightly blushed white; orange hips. 15ft (4.5m)

'Guinée' Deepest red rambler; large flowers, wonderful scent. 15ft (4.5m)

℣ *'Maigold'* Bronzy yellow; thorny, but good on poor soil. 12ft (3.6m)

℣ *'Mme Grégoire Staechelin'* Huge scented pink clusters. 20ft (6m)

℣ *'The Garland'* Creamy pink, scented, daisy-like flowers. 15ft (4.5m)

℣ *'Veilchenblau'* Magenta, fading to lilac; scented; thornless. 15ft (4.5m)

--------------------- **Roses to train into trees** ---------------------

The most effective way to grow vigorous rambling roses is to train them into trees, where they make spectacular curtains of colour.

℣ *'Albéric Barbier'* Creamy white, scented; small second flush. 25ft (7.5m)

℣* *'Bobbie James'* Huge heads of small, creamy, scented flowers. 30ft (9m)

℣ *'Climbing Cécile Brunner'* Tiny, pink HT flowers; healthy. 20ft (6m)

'Dr. W. Van Fleet' Shapely, scented, silvery pink; thorny. 20ft (6m)

℣ *'François Juranville'* Apple-scented, coral-pink; bronze leaf. 20ft (6m)

'Kew Rambler' Fragrant, white-centred, single pink; thorny. 20ft (6m)

℣ *'Kiftsgate'* Classic, sweetly scented, cream; very vigorous. 35ft (10.5m)

℣ *'Paul's Himalayan Musk'* Pink fading to blush; reliable. 30ft (9m)

℣ *'Rambling Rector'* Highly scented creamy white; autumn hips. 20ft (6m)

'Wedding Day' Pale yellow, opening white; very strong scent. 30ft (9m)

---

† When grown on a wall, these varieties may suffer from mildew.

Shorter varieties†

In small gardens, climbing roses of more modest growth are invaluable; these varieties can easily be kept smaller than about 8ft (2.4m).

 'Dortmund' Large, single, pink-centred crimson; very thorny.

 'Dreaming Spires' Yellow, fading rather paler with orange tints.

♀ *'Dublin Bay'* Blood-red; long season; even succeeds in containers.

♀ *'Golden Showers'* Large deep yellow flowers fading to cream.

 'Goldfinch' Prolific, small, gold and primrose; strong scent; bushy.

 'Kathleen Harrop' Prolific pale pink; scented and thornless.

♀* *'Mme Isaac Pereire'* Strongly scented, cupped, purplish pink.

♀ *'Phyllis Bide'* Creamy, with a pink edge; almost thornless.

 'Pink Perpétue' Prolific rich pink; vigorous, but can be kept small.

♀ *'White Cockade'* Pure white fully double; upright habit; thorny.

OTHER ROSES

This last section of roses covers a number of other groups which are worth considering independently when planning the garden.

Ground cover roses

This relatively new group is made up of varieties whose spread is greater than their height; some are mounded, some are almost flat.

℗ *'Bonica'* Soft pink semi-double; long season; healthy. 3ft × 6ft (90cm × 1.8m)

℗ *'Flower Carpet'* Broad trusses of deep pink flowers. 18in × 4ft (45cm × 1.2m)

'Francine Austin' Small, pure white pompoms; vigorous. 3ft × 4ft (90cm × 1.2m)

'Grouse' Fragrant, single, blushed white in mid summer. 2ft × 10ft (60cm × 3m)

'Norfolk' Neat, double, scented, bright yellow flowers. 18in × 2ft (45cm × 60m)

℗* *'Nozomi'* Small, single, blushed white; spreading growth. 2ft × 6ft (60cm × 1.8m)

℗ *'Snow Carpet'* Tightly double, pure white; low, spreading. 1ft × 3ft (30cm × 90cm)

℗ *'Surrey'* Long season of pale pink frilly double flowers. 2ft × 4ft (60cm × 1.2m)

℗ *'The Fairy'* Coral double; elegant arching shoots; tough. 2ft × 4ft (60cm × 1.2m)

† More advice in *Growing Roses for Small Gardens* by Michael Gibson.

Dwarf roses

In recent years shorter-growing roses have become popular; they may be called Patio or Miniature Roses; these are below 18in (45cm) tall.

'*Angela Rippon*' Large-flowered, coral pink; fragrant; bushy.†

♛ '*Anna Ford*' Bright orangey red with yellow centres; very healthy.

'*Baby Masquerade*' Yellow, turning red then darkening; twiggy.

'*Bright Smile*' Semi-double, rich bright yellow; very colourful.

'*Darling Flame*' Bright vermilion, good for cutting; disease-prone.

'*Easter Morning*' Like a miniature white HT, then opening flat.

♛* '*Gentle Touch*' Well-scented pale pink flowers; prolific; bushy.†

'*Hakuun*' Highly prolific buff-orange flowers fading to cream.

'*Magic Carousel*' White double with a pink edge; good for posies.

'*Peek-a-Boo*' Soft apricot pink; healthy but unscented; spreading.

'*Pour Toi*' Creamy white with yellow centres; rather large leaves.

'*Red Ace*' Well-shaped deep red flowers in large numbers; bushy.

'*Regensberg*' Pale pink, edged and eyed white; white petal backs.

'*Rise 'n' Shine*' Bright yellow double flowers; prone to blackspot.

♛ '*Stacey Sue*' Lightly scented, pale pink, fully double; good to cut.†

'*Starina*' Unexpectedly large, brilliant orange-red; well branched.

♛ '*Sweet Dream*' Peachy flowers in tight clusters; neat and bushy.

♛ '*Sweet Magic*' Tiny, golden tinted, orange flowers from neat buds.

'*Tip Top*' Semi-double, rosy salmon; needs regular spraying.

'*Topsi*' Exceptionally brilliant orange-scarlet; prone to disease.

---

†   Very few dwarf roses are scented; this is one of the few that is.

——————————————— **Scented roses** ———————————————

We demand scent in roses almost before anything else, and many gardeners feel that roses have now lost their scent. In truth there are thousands of scented roses; these are my pick across the types.

'*Alec's Red*' HT Almost black buds open deep red; thorny stems.

'*Anna Pavlova*' HT Blush with deeper tints; vigorous and tall.

♀ '*Cardinal de Richelieu*' OF Velvety darkest purple; feed well.

♀ '*Charles de Mills*' OF Large-flowered, deep crimson; feed well.

♀ '*Compassion*' C Shapely, HT-style, peach-tinted salmon; superb.

'*Denham*' HT Very prolific soft creamy yellow; vigorous, bushy.

'*Fragrant Cloud*' HT Rather variable shade of deep coral; classic.

♀ '*Gloire de Dijon*' C Prolific buff-pink; old cottage garden favourite.

'*Guinée*' C Large, deepest crimson; looks best on a pale wall.

'*Heritage*' E Captivating cupped blush-pink; climber or large shrub.

♀* '*Königin von Dänemark*' OF Pink quartered flowers; greyish leaf.

'*Louise Odier*' OF Cupped pink flowers, tinted lilac; long season.

♀ '*Margaret Merrill*' F White; exceptional relatively recent variety.

♀ '*Mme Isaac Pereire*' OF Pale crimson; short climber or shrub.

'*Papa Meilland*' HT Deep, rich crimson; lovely but unpredictable.

'*Prima Ballerina*' HT Large, rather blowsy deep rose-pink; thorny.

'*Reine des Violettes*' OF Violet, quartered flowers; few thorns.

'*Wendy Cussons*' HT Shapely, prolific cerisey red; inelegant plant.

'*Whisky Mac*' Pink tinted amber; disease-prone; poor in north.

♀ '*Zéphirine Drouhin*' OF Pink, thornless; climber or large shrub.

---

† In this section HT = Hybrid Teas; F = Floribundas, D = Dwarf roses of various kinds under 2ft (60cm); OF = Old fashioned shrub roses; E = English roses. Try to smell before you buy, as the type of scent varies between varieties.

Disease-resistant roses

Many gardeners worry about having to spray roses against diseases all season, but there are many varieties which are usefully resistant to diseases such as black spot and mildew in most gardens and seasons.†

℣   'Alexander' HT Prolific vermilion, creamy yellow centre; thorny.

'Cécile Brunner' OF Sweetheart rose; tiny, scented, blush flowers.

'Celestial' OF Shell-pink, yellow centre; greyish leaf; vigorous.

℣   'Golden Wings' OF Long season of large single yellow flowers.

'Grandpa Dickson' HT Long season of enormous lemony flowers.

'Korresia' F Semi-double yellow with a superb scent; long season.

'Lady Hillingdon' OF Soft apricot, scented; also climbing version.

℣   'Mermaid' C Huge, single yellow; vigorous; the healthiest climber.

'Paul's Scarlet' C Bright scarlet; dark leaf and almost thornless.

℣   'Peace' HT Large, heavy, yellow with pink tints; very reliable.

'Pink Favourite' HT Rose-pink; tough, adaptable and reliable.

℣   'Queen Elizabeth' F Tall, very vigorous pink; incredibly tough.

Rosa rugosa forms OF All are resistant, these are good:

℣*   'Blanc Double de Coubert' (double white),

℣   'Fru Dagmar Hartopp' (pale pink single),

℣   'Roseraie de l'Haÿ' (semi-double crimson).

'Rose Gaujard' HT Rich red, white on the backs; easy, reliable.

℣   'Silver Jubilee' HT Blowzy pink, shaded with peach; very tough.

℣   'Southampton' F Peachy orange; tall, strong and slightly scented.

℣   'The Fairy' GC Long season of small pink flowers; spreading.

'Wendy Cussons' HT Shapely rosy red; beautiful scent; bushy.

---

†   Mildew is worse in hot, dry seasons, black spot in wet seasons.

---------------- **Thornless roses** ----------------

Where there are children, by front doors and paths and tumbling over front fences thornless roses bring extra safety to the garden.

    'Blush Boursault' OF Double blush pink; tall and vigorous. 15ft (4.5m)

    'Duponti' OF Sweetly scented, pure white single; greyish leaf. 7ft (2.1m)

    'Goldfinch' R Small, tight yellow flowers fading to white. 10ft (3m)

*   *'Kathleen Harrup'* OF Soft pink climber; good as large shrub. 8ft (2.4m)

    'Mme Plantier' OF Prolific creamy poms on arching shoots. 6ft (1.8m)

    'Mrs John Laing' OF Cupped pink; little scent but greyish leaf. 3ft (90cm)

    'Reine des Violettes' OF Purple and lilac shades; greyish leaf. 4ft (1.2m)

    'Rose-Marie Viaud' R prolific purplish violet; late-flowering. 15ft (4.5m)

♀ *'Veilchenblau'* R Semi-double, white-eyed, pale purple; scented. 15ft (4.5m)

♀ *'Zéphirine Drouhin'* C Much loved, scented, strong pink. 12ft (3.6m)

---------------- **Roses for hips** ----------------

Many roses will produce some hips in some seasons, but the following roses are both more colourful and more dependable.†

    'Highdownensis' Large, reddish purple; single crimson flowers. 8ft (2.4m)

♀* *'Master Hugh'* Orange-red, unusually large; cerise flowers. 15ft (4.5m)

    'Ormiston Roy' Deep purple, almost black; very thorny. 4ft (1.2m)

    R. davidii Orange-red hips, prolific; late, pink, single flowers. 10ft (3m)

♀ *R. glauca* Masses of small, reddish-purple hips. grey-blue leaf. 6ft (1.8m)

    R. moyesii Most forms are pink or red with orange hips. 10ft (3m)

♀ *R. rugosa* 'Fru Dagmar Hartopp' Round red hips; pink single. 5ft (1.5m)

    R. rugosa 'Scabrosa' Big red round hips; huge crimson flowers. 4ft (1.2m)

    R. villosa Big, round, bristly, orange hips; scented pink flowers. 6ft (1.8m)

---

†   Of course to be sure of hips you must not dead-head these varieties.

English roses

The recently developed English Roses combine the flower shape and scent of the old roses with the long season of modern varieties.

'Evelyn' Shallow cupped rosette in apricot-yellow; rich scent. $3\frac{1}{2}$ ft (1.05m)

'Gertrude Jekyll' Elegant buds open to large rich pink rosettes. 4ft (1.2m)

'Glamis Castle' White with a touch of blush; myrrh scent. 3ft (90cm)

♀ 'Graham Thomas' Highly scented, pure deep yellow; vigorous. 4ft (1.2m)

* 'Heritage' Soft pink, beautiful cupped shape; wonderful scent. 4ft (1.2m)

'L. D. Braithwaite' Deep, bright crimson; very long season. $3\frac{1}{2}$ ft (1.05m)

'Mary Rose' Deep pink; unusually long season; well branched. 4ft (1.2m)

'Perdita' Apricot pink, quartered flowers; exceptional scent. $3\frac{1}{2}$ ft (1.05m)

'The Prince' Deep purple-tinted crimson; unusually neat habit. $2\frac{1}{2}$ ft (75cm)

'Winchester Cathedral' Pure white; very long season; bushy. 4ft (1.2m)

Roses for shade

No roses will thrive in full shade under trees, but some will do well in partial shade as long as they have no tree roots for competition.†

♀* 'Alba Maxima' Untidy white flowers; unusually tough. 6ft (1.8m)

♀ 'Félicité Parmentier' Tightly double pink, becoming creamy. 4ft (1.2m)

♀ 'Frühlingsgold' Yellow single flowers; strong scent; very tough. 7ft (2.1m)

♀ 'Königin von Dänemark' Elegant pink flowers; scent superb. 5ft (1.5m)

'Lady Penzance' Coppery salmon; red hips; fragrant foliage. 6ft (1.8m)

'Lord Penzance' Beigey yellow flowers; red hips; fragrant foliage. 7ft (2.1m)

'Maiden's Blush' Richly scented blush flowers; greyish leaf. 5ft (1.5m)

'Manning's Blush' Fragrant, blushed white; fragrant foliage too. 5ft (1.5m)

'Mme Legras de St Germain' White, camellia-like flowers. 6ft (1.8m)

'Shropshire Lass' Large, blushed white, scented single flowers. 8ft (2.4m)

---

† Old fashioned roses in the Alba group are generally best for shade.

CLEMATIS

Clematis are plants which confuse many gardeners, so I have singled them out for special treatment to help make them less bewildering.

Spring-flowering

SMALL-FLOWERED

The smaller-flowered species provide the main early spring clematis display and they vary greatly both in the vigour of their growth and in their colours. They are invaluable for gardens large and small.

♔* *alpina* 'Frances Rivis' Pale blue; the largest-flowered alpina. 8ft (2.4m)

alpina 'Frankie' Good blue with extra inner skirt of blue. 8ft (2.4m)

♔ *alpina* 'Helsinborg' Recent, unusually dark blue variety. 8ft (2.4m)

alpina 'Ruby' Nearest to true red; may flower in summer too. 10ft (3m)

alpina var. sibirica Old favourite, but still best creamy white. 8ft (2.4m)

alpina 'Willy' Pale pink, darker at the base of the petals. 8ft (2.4m)

alpina 'White Moth' Pure white; later than most forms. 6ft (1.8m)

armandii 'Apple Blossom' White, blushed pink; evergreen. 20ft (6m)

armandii 'Snowdrift' Pure white; fragrant; best on south wall. 20ft (6m)

macropetala The unimproved species is a lovely lavender-blue. 8ft (2.4m)

macropetala 'Jan Lindmark' Mauve; earliest macropetala. 10ft (3m)

macropetala 'Lincolnshire Lady' Deep purplish blue; frilly. 8ft (2.4m)

♔ *macropetala* 'Maidwell Hall' Deep blue; beware paler frauds. 8ft (2.4m)

♔ *montana* 'Elizabeth' Pale pink; slightly chocolate scent. 25ft (7.5m)†

♔ *montana* 'Grandiflora' White, scented, very free-flowering. 30ft (9m)†

montana 'Marjorie' Cream and pink, semi-double flowers. 30ft (9m)†

montana 'Picton's Variety' Deep pink; bronze foliage. 20ft (6m)†

♔ *montana var. sericea* Clouds of small white flowers. 20ft (6m)†

'Rosie O'Grady' Unusually large pinky mauve flowers. 8ft (2.4m)

'White Swan' Large, double, pure white; later than most. 10ft (3m)

---

† This is a very vigorous variety which needs plenty of space.

LARGE-FLOWERED†

Most of these large-flowered varieties start to flower towards the end of
spring and then continue into the summer; some varieties may then flower
again in late summer or early autumn.

'*Asao*' Bright rose with a white central stripe; prolific. 8ft (2.4m)

'*Barbara Jackman*' Deep purple, striped magenta; cream eye. 6ft (1.8m)

♀ '*Doctor Ruppel*' Carmine, paler along its wavy margins. 8ft (2.4m)

'*Étoile de Paris*' Dark eyed mauvy blue, red central stripe. 6ft (1.8m)

♀ '*Fireworks*' Bluish purple, deep red stripe; twisted petals. 10ft (3m)

♀ '*Henryi*' Slightly creamy white, purple-tinted eye; reliable. 8ft (2.4m).

♀ '*H. F. Young*' Large bright blue, cream eye; wavy edges. 8ft (2.4m)

'*James Mason*' Superb large white with dark maroon centre. 6ft (1.8m)

'*John Warren*' Large lilac pink, darker edges and centre. 8ft (2.4m)

'*Kakio*' Large pink flowers, white central stripe, yellow eye. 6ft (1.8m)

'*King Edward VII*' Huge puce-violet flowers, flushed red. 6ft (1.8m)

♀ '*Lasurstern*' Deep blue, cream centre; fades slightly; feed well. 8ft (2.4m)

'*Lincoln Star*' Raspberry pink; late flowers white, mottled pink. 5ft (1.5m)

♀ '*Miss Bateman*' White, cream stripe; one dramatic flush. 6ft (1.8m)

'*Moonlight*' The nearest to yellow; rather slow; shade only. 5ft (1.5m)

♀* '*Mrs Cholmondeley*' Lavender-blue, pale in centre; foolproof. 20ft (6m)

♀ '*Nelly Moser*' Rose, carmine central stripe; stunning in shade. 8ft (2.4m)

'*Snow Queen*' White, with a mauve tint at the wavy margins. 8ft (2.4m)

'*Vino*' Very large sultry purplish red flowers; cream centre. 8ft (2.4m)

'*W. E. Gladstone*' Lavender, red centre; flowers till autumn. 15ft (4.5m)

---

† In spring prune back the overwintered shoots to the first fat buds.

Summer-flowering

SMALL-FLOWERED

These small flowered clematis are more dainty, delicate and more manageable than the larger-flowered sorts, so they are especially useful for growing through shrubs and small trees.

♀ *'Bill MacKenzie'* Yellow 'orange peel' flowers; silky seeds. 15ft (4.5m)

campaniflora Small, pale blue bells; lacily cut foliage. 10ft (3m)

♀ × *durandii* Deep violet, cream centre; no clinging stems. 8ft (2.4m)

flammula Small, white, highly scented flowers; good in a tree. 25ft (7.5m)

florida 'Sieboldii' White, purple centre; best on warm wall. 8ft (2.4m)

'Helios' Flared, yellow 'orange peel' flowers but very short. 5ft (1.5m)

× *jouiniana 'Praecox'* Small, scented, milky blue; bold leaves. 10ft (3m)

tangutica 'Lambton Park' Large, rich yellow; good seeds. 15ft (4.5m)

texensis 'Étoile Rose' Deep pink with pale margins; nodding. 8ft (2.4m)

texensis 'Gravetye Beauty' Deep ruby red bell, opening star. 10ft (3m)

texensis 'Princess of Wales' Deep, rich but shining pink. 8ft (2.4m)

♀ *thibetana ssp. vernayi* Yellow flowers; blue-tinted leaves. 15ft (4.5m)

♀ × *triternata 'Rubromarginata'* Small, pink-edged white. 15ft (4.5m)

♀ *viticella 'Alba Luxurians'* White, with green tips to the petals. 20ft (6m)

♀* *viticella 'Madame Julia Correvon'* Wine red, twisted petals. 10ft (3m)

viticella 'Mary Rose' Deep smoky purple double; delightful. 12ft (3.6m)

♀ *viticella 'Polish Spirit'* Rich deep purple; early flowering. 10ft (3m)

♀ *viticella 'Purpurea Plena Elegans'* Small, purple, vigorous. 12ft (3.6m)

♀ *viticella 'Royal Velours'* Winy purple; exceptionally dark. 15ft (4.5m)

viticella 'Tango' White with a broad deep red edge and veins. 10ft (3m)

---

† If these varieties are pruned, they should be done in spring.

LARGE-FLOWERED†

These large-flowered clematis are best pruned hard in spring as they start to grow in order to promote the best summer display; many will also flower in spring on old wood if left unpruned.

Ⓐ *'Ascotiensis'* Good clear blue; flowers look you in the face. 12ft (3.6m)

Ⓐ *'Comtesse de Bouchaud'* Pink; one dramatic but short flush. 8ft (2.4m)

Ⓐ *'Ernest Markham'* Good warm red, gold eye; best in full sun. 15ft (4.5m)

Ⓐ *'Gipsy Queen'* Rich, sultry, deep violet-purple; vigorous. 12ft (3.6m)

'Hagley Hybrid' Mottled mauvy pink; good in containers. 8ft (2.4m)

'Jackmanii Superba' Deep bluey purple; one mad flush. 10ft (3m)

'John Huxtable' Impressive pure white; one snowy flush. 8ft (2.4m)

Ⓐ *'Madame Édouard André'* Wine red, fading gracefully. 8ft (2.4m)

Ⓐ *'Madame Grangé'* Purple, red streak, silver undersides. 10ft (3m)

'Maureen' Velvety purple with creamy eye; very full flower. 6ft (1.8m)

Ⓐ *'Mrs Cholmondeley'* Pale lavender-blue; vigorous and easy. 15ft (4.5m)

Ⓐ *'Niobe'* Rich ruby red; best in shade; can be tipped in spring. 8ft (2.4m)

Ⓐ* *'Perle d'Azur'* Light blue with a hint of pink; wonderful. 15ft (4.5m)

'Pink Fantasy' Soft pink with dark pink streak; best in shade. 8ft (2.4m)

'Rouge Cardinal' Deep crimson with paler hints; best in sun. 6ft (1.8m)

Ⓐ *'Star of India'* Purple with slightly reddish central streak. 12ft (3.6m)

'Victoria' Nodding flowers in pinky purple, fading to mauve. 10ft (3m)

'Ville de Lyon' Carmine, darker towards the edges; vigorous. 10ft (3m)

'Voluceau' Prolific reddish purple, yellow eye; twisted petals. 10ft (3m)

'W. E. Gladstone' Huge 10in (25cm) lavender flowers, red eye. 12ft (3.6m)

---

†   Clematis in this group are ideal for growing through shrubs.

DOUBLE-FLOWERED VARIETIES†

Most doubled varieties produce double flowers in the late spring and early summer, then follow with single flowers in the autumn.

'Belle of Woking' Mauve-tinted silver; late flowers also double. 6ft (1.8m)

'Countess of Lovelace' Lilac blue; single in autumn. 6ft (1.8m)

'Duchess of Edinburgh' Only fully double white; single later. 6ft (1.8m)

'Kiri Te Kanawa' Deep blue; double in autumn too; strong. 8ft (2.4m)

'Lilactime' Wisteria blue with deeper tints; semi-double. 6ft (1.8m)

'Mrs James Mason' Bright violet-blue, red streak; single later. 6ft (1.8m)

'Proteus ' Mauve with a touch of pink; slow to settle. 6ft (1.8m)

♔ 'Royalty' Rich velvety purple red; yellow centre; single later. 6ft (1.8m)

'Veronica's Choice' Lavender, paling in the centre; strong. 8ft (2.4m)

♔ 'Vyvyan Pennell' Violet-blue; lavender-blue singles later. 8ft (2.4m)

Autumn-flowering

Like many of these autumn lists this is a mix of plants still flowering well after starting in summer and autumn specialities.

♔* 'Bill MacKenzie' Prolific yellow alongside silver seeds. 20ft (6m)

♔ 'Gipsy Queen' Large, deep purple flowers; starts in August. 15ft (4.5m)

flammula Clouds of scented white stars; starts in August. 25ft (7.5m)

♔ × jouiniana 'Praecox' Small; blue and white; August till late. 10ft (3m)

'Huldine' Large white flowers, mauve-backed; starts in July. 20ft (6m)

'Lady Betty Balfour' Large, violet-blue, cream eye; full sun. 15ft (4.5m)

'Madame Baron Veillard' Large, rosy lilac, greeny white eye. 15ft (4.5m)

♔ 'Madame Grangé' Large, purple, silver-backed; starts August. 10ft (3m)

♔ rehderiana Small, yellow, cowslip-scented bells; likes sun. 15ft (4.5m)

texensis 'Gravetye Beauty' Deep red bells; starts in June. 10ft (3m)

---

† In early spring tip back the shoots as far as the first fat buds.

CONIFERS

Many gardeners are understandably confused by conifers, their rate of growth and their eventual size. Many of their names are also long and difficult. So, in this case, I've allowed a little extra space.

Size

Varieties described as dwarf may eventually grow very large, those described as quick may never stop; it's important to choose wisely

LARGE

These varieties make elegant specimens where there is space for them to develop but are generally unsuitable for small gardens.

Abies koreana Pyramid of dark green leaves, silver below, with bright blue cones, even on young plants. Grows about 1ft (30cm) per year.

Auracaria auracana Monkey puzzle. Stiff branches clothed with broad leaves. Often loses lower branches. Slow at first, then quicker.

♈ *Cedrus atlantica* 'Glauca' Blue cedar. Imposing specimen tree; best given space to develop and best viewed from a distance.

× *Cupressocyparis leylandii* Leyland Cypress. Notorious as the quickest conifer of all. Can be very useful – in the right place.

Gingko biloba Maidenhair tree. Unusual deciduous conifer with open habit and buttery autumn colour. Slow at first, then races.

♈ *Picea omorica* Exceptionally elegant tree with upcurved branches needing space to develop and to be viewed. Can grow 3ft (90cm) a year.

Picea pungens 'Glauca' Blue spruce. Conical tree, variable in colouring and vigour, 4–5in (10–13cm) per year or 1ft (30cm). 'Hoopsii' is very slow.

♈ *Pinus nigra subsp. larico* Corsican pine. Invaluable for shelter, tough, grows in most soils. Growth of 2–3ft (60–90cm) per year is common.

♈ *Taxodium distichum* Swamp cypress. Deciduous species with good autumn colour, making an elegant narrow cone in wet soil.

♈ *Thuya plicata* 'Atrovirens' A very tolerant and adaptable tree for all soils making a dark, glossy cone but growing at 3ft (90cm) per year.

†   Cypresses, thuya and some pines can be pruned; most conifers resent it.

SMALL

There are many less vigorous conifers which are suitable for smaller gardens, without being so small and slow-growing that they are best suited to specialized situations like raised beds or troughs.†

♈ *Chamaecyparis lawsoniana 'Ellwood's Gold'* Brilliant golden yellow in full sun, changing to a subdued yellowish green in winter.

♈ *Chamaecyparis pisifera 'Boulevard'* Soft, silvery blue, feathery dome but rather temperamental and best in rich, acid conditions.

Juniperus × media 'Gold Sovereign' Tight yellow, feathery mound remaining bright in full sun in winter; can be trimmed.

♈ *Juniperus × media 'Old Gold'* Rather slow, loose, feathery dome of arching shoots with bright yellow, slightly bronze-tinted foliage.

Juniperus scopulorum 'Skyrocket' Slim pillar of upward-slanted branches in attractive blue-green; especially bright in summer.

♈ *Picea pungens 'Globosa'* Tight set globe of grey-blue foliage, brighter blue in summer. Cut out any unnerving vigorous shoots.

Pinus pumila 'Globe' Slow, very attractive, open, spiky mound of long green needles whose silvery undersides show up well.

Taxus baccata 'Fastigiata Aurea' Yew making a slender pillar of upright branches. New tips gold, retaining a yellow cast in sun.

♈* *Thuya occidentalis 'Rheingold'* Makes a broad, rounded pyramid of feathery foliage, gold in summer then turning bronze for winter.

♈ *Thuya orientalis 'Aurea Nana'* Flat, vertical sprays of yellowish green leaves, golden yellow in midsummer, on a rounded cone.

---

† These varieties should never cause problems by growing too tall.

DWARF

In large troughs, in raised beds of alpines and in rock gardens, conifers provide structure and evergreen solidity especially in winter. Most of these will usually remain under 2ft (60cm) for a lifetime.

♀ *Chamaecyparis lawsoniana 'Aurea Densa'* Tight conical bush with dense stiff golden yellow foliage. Best in full sun.

Chamaecyparis lawsoniana 'Gnome' Makes a tight blue-green bun taking ten years to reach 8in (20cm). Cut out occasional strong shoots.

♀ *Chamaecyparis lawsoniana 'Minima Aurea'* Dense golden yellow foliage in vertical sprays; eventually makes a tight cone.

♀ *Chamaecyparis lawsoniana 'Pygmaea Argentea'* Broad dome of green foliage, all strongly tipped cream. Appreciates shelter.

♀ *Chamaecyparis obtusa 'Nana'* Attractive tiers of dense, dark green fans making a flat topped dome. 4in × 8in (10cm × 20cm) in ten years.

♀ *Juniperus communis 'Compressa'* Slow, very slender green column ideal for troughs. Likes shelter, especially when small.

♀ *Picea abies 'Little Gem'* Neat, dense, globular dome; fresh green in summer then rather paler in winter. Not for scorching dry sites.

Picea glauca 'Alberta Blue' Compact but not tight blue cone, especially silvery in early summer. Only grows about 1in (2.5cm) per year.

Pinus contorta 'Spaan's Dwarf' Rather spiky upward-swept branches densely set with dark green needles. May need thinning.†

Pinus mugo 'Humpy' About the tightest and most compact of all pines with closely set dark green needles. Reaches 1ft (30cm) in ten years.†

---

† Dwarf pines soon develop an attractive mature character.

--------------------------------- **Uses** ---------------------------------

CONIFERS FOR HEDGES†

Many conifers make excellent hedges. Being evergreen they provide shelter all
the year round, most can be clipped to almost any size and they provide a
good neutral background for the plants.

    Chamaecyparis lawsoniana 'Allumii' Soft, dense, bluish grey foliage in
        flattened sprays. An attractive change from dark green.

♈ *Chamaecyparis lawsoniana 'Fletcheri'* Bluish grey, but bronzed in winter.
        Slower than 'Alumii', so better for short hedges.

♈ *Chamaecyparis lawsoniana 'Green Hedger'* Classic rich green colouring
        which is the best background for perennials. Very dense.

♈ × *Cupressocyparis leylandii 'Haggerston Grey'* The usual variety, slightly
        greyish green. *Must* be topped at final height.

♈ × *Cupressocyparis leylandii 'Castlewellan'* Young shoots golden yellow,
        bronzed later. *Relatively* slow, but may seem too bright.

♈ *Cupressus macrocarpa 'Goldcrest'* Rich yellow, best in warmer areas. Think
        carefully before planting these bright yellow forms.

♈ *Pinus sylvestris* Scots pine. Unexpectedly successful as a 6–8ft (1.8–2.4m)
        hedge, and invaluable protection for cold and exposed gardens.

♈ *Taxus baccata* Yew. Rich dark green, the classic British garden hedge.
        Quicker growing than usually thought. Not for soggy soil.

♈ *Thuya occidentalis 'Smaragd'* Dense hedge of bright emerald green foliage.
        Regular clipping required to keep it windproof.

♈* *Thuya plicata 'Atrovirens'* Glossy green, one of the quickest after Leyland
        cypress, but easier to keep to the required size.

---

†   When first planted these appreciate shelter from winds.

CONIFERS FOR GROUND COVER†

Among heathers, interplanted with dwarf bulbs, around the edge of gravel drives or covering manholes, low spreading varieties offer a distinctive appearance and effective weed-smothering capability.

♀ *Juniperus communis 'Green Carpet'* Makes a dense carpet of bright green foliage, bronzing slightly in the winter. 3in × 3ft (7.5cm × 90cm)

♀ *Juniperus communis 'Hornbrookii'* More vigorous growth than 'Green Carpet' and eventually mounding in the centre. 1ft × 6ft (30cm × 1.8m)

Juniperus horizontalis 'Turquoise Spreader' Attractive bluish green foliage, which keeps its colour well in winter. 4in × 3ft (10cm × 90cm)

* *Juniperus sabina 'Tamariscifolia'* Makes a flat green table of horizontal branches striking out above ground level. 1ft × 3ft (30cm × 90cm)

♀ *Juniperus squamata 'Blue Star'* Bushier ground cover, the spiky leaves are deep blue in winter, more silvery in summer. 1ft × 2ft (30cm × 60cm)

♀ *Microbotia decussata* Bright green in summer, attractive rustier shade in winter. Dense but feathery; very hardy. 9in × 5ft (23cm × 1.5m)

Picea abies 'Procumbens' Unexpected form of familiar Christmas tree, layer of branches making a flat-topped plant. 1ft × 4ft (30cm × 1.2m)

Picea pungens 'Prostrata' Flat, silvery blue plant making a dramatic foil for heathers. Cut out any upright shoots. 18in × 6ft (45cm × 1.8m)

Taxus baccata 'Summergold' Dense but taller ground cover with yellow summer shoots and variegated winter foliage. 2ft × 5ft (60cm × 1.5m)

♀ *Tsuga canadensis 'Jeddeloh'* Less vigorous ground cover for smaller sites, green shoots raised in centre then trailing. 1ft × 18in (30 × 45cm)

---

†   As these conifers spread, be prepared to rescue choice plants nearby.

Foliage†

The colours of conifer foliage are one of their main attractions and they provide combinations of colours and habits of growth not seen in other plants. And they're doubly valuable for being evergreen.

YELLOW FOLIAGE

There are many shades of yellow conifers, including some which are genuinely gold. Some colour best in summer, others in winter.

Chamaecyparis lawsoniana 'Lane' Gold in summer, sharper yellow in winter. This is a vigorous plant and an ideal specimen. 8ft (2.4m)

Chamaecyparis obtusa 'Nana Lutea' Slow, broad cone, gold in summer then yellow in winter – always with some green. 18in (45cm)

♀ *Chamaecyparis pisifera 'Filifera Aurea'* A slow, broad mound of narrow leaves bright yellow all year. Growth faster eventually. 3ft (90cm)

× *Cupressocyparis leylandii 'Robinson's Gold'* Best gold Leyland; bronzed in spring, then gold, then lemony green. 30ft (9m)

Cupressus macrocarpa 'Goldcrest' One of the brightest of yellow conifers, a lovely specimen in the right place. 15ft (4.5m)

Juniperus communis 'Golden Showers' Upright habit but with drooping shoot tips; rich yellow in sumer, bronzed in winter. 4ft (1.2m)

* *Juniperus × media 'Gold Sovereign'* Low mound of slender foliage remains brilliant golden yellow all year; good in tubs. 2ft (60cm)

Pinus sylvestris 'Aurea' Startling yellow-leaved pine, greyish in summer but brilliantly coloured in winter. Rather variable. 10ft (3m)

Taxus baccata 'Standishii' An excellent emphatic plant making a slender pole; gold needle-tips in sun, summer and winter. 5ft (1.5m)

Thuya plicata 'Stoneham Gold' Bright yellowish gold foliage tipped with copper; colours best in full sun and exposure. 3ft (90cm)

---

† Most coloured conifers are good in Christmas table decorations.

BLUE FOLIAGE†

Blue foliage is generally relatively scarce, but among the conifers there are many varieties with bluish green, steely blue or silvery blue foliage which brings a whole new look to beds and borders.

♀ *Abies koreana 'Silberlocke'* Dark green leaves which twist to reveal their silver undersides. Slow at first, then a large tree. 6ft (1.8m)

♀ *Cedrus libani ssp. atlantica 'Glauca'* Spectacular silvery blue specimen tree for large gardens; sparse at first; do not crowd. 15ft (4.5m)

♀ *Chamaecyparis lawsoniana 'Chilworth Silver'* Feathery silvery blue foliage in a broad column. 'Ellwoodii' is similar but faster. 4ft (1.2m)

♀ *Chamaecyparis lawsoniana 'Pembury Blue'* Vigorous silvery blue, best in summer. Good in a shelterbelt or as a specimen. 8ft (2.4m)

♀* *Chamaecyparis pisifera 'Boulevard'* Temperamental and fussy, but soft leaves are a bright silvery blue. Best trimmed regularly. 6ft (1.8m)

Juniperus scopulorum 'Wichita Blue' Elegant narrow cone of silvery grey leaves all the year round. An ideal soft exclamation. 6ft (1.8m)

♀ *Juniperus virginiana 'Grey Owl'* Highly tolerant and adaptable grey leaved ground cover for almost any situation; resilient. 2ft (60cm)

♀ *Picea pungens 'Globosa'* Tight but irregular mound of shoots, greyish in winter then blue in summer; rather stiff and prickly. 18in (45cm)

♀ *Picea pungens 'Hoopsii'* Impressive tree with widely spaced branches, slow at first; grey in winter, silvery blue in summer. 6ft (1.8m)

Picea pungens 'Thomsen' Narrow tree with less spacious branches; superb silvery grey winter foliage, bluer in summer. 6ft (1.8m)

---

†   Some conifers look odd in mixed beds; blue-leaved varieties fit in best.

FOLIAGE WITH SEASONAL CHANGES†

Some gardeners complain that conifers look exactly the same all the year round, that they never seem to change. These varieties have a most valuable feature: they change colour with the seasons.

♡* *Chamaecyparis thyoides 'Ericoides'* Greyish green in summer but bronzed purple in winter. Snow may damage branches. 4ft (1.2m)

Chamaecyparis thyoides 'Rubicon' Slightly bronzed green foliage in summer, slightly silvery wine-red in winter. $2\frac{1}{2}$ ft (75cm)

♡ *Cryptomeria japonica 'Vilmoriniana'* Rounded ball of foliage, bright green in summer and bronze in winter. Best in open site. 18in (45cm)

Juniperus horizontalis 'Prince of Wales' Ground cover juniper with bright green feathery summer leaves, purple in winter. 4in × 3ft (10cm × 90cm)

Picea nigra 'Hornbrookiana' Green all year, but long reddish buds tipped with white sit in the tops of the shoots all winter. 2ft (60cm)

Pinus mugo 'Ophir' Green in summer, then turning brilliant yellow in the winter. Tough, and colours best in an open position. 2ft (60cm)

♡ *Thuya occidentalis 'Rheingold'* Soft, lacy golden yellow foliage in summer, turning a coppery yellow in winter. Best in open. 3ft (90cm)

♡ *Thuya orientalis 'Aurea Nana'* Yellowish green in spring, then increasingly gold and developing bronzed tints in autumn. 2ft (60cm)

Thuya orientalis 'Juniperoides' Greyish green in summer, dark purple in winter. Rather tender, likes a cosy sheltered spot. 18in (45cm)

Thuya orientalis 'Rosedalis' Pale or creamy yellow in spring, pale green in summer, then brown or purplish in winter. 2ft (60cm)

---

† Deciduous conifers like larch, taxodium and ginkgo have autumn colour.

AND FINALLY . . .

Requiring male and female plants to produce fruits

A number of fruiting plants will only produce berries on female plants and need male plants to ensure pollination.

Arisaema	*Rhamnus*
Aucuba	*Ruscus*
Gaultheria mucronata	*Skimmia*
Hippophaë	*Taxus*
Ilex	*Viburnum davidii*

Plants in this book that require acid soil

Many plants, especially shrubs, will not thrive on limy or chalky soils. Those marked † are less fussy than the others.

Camellia	*Gaultheria*	*Magnolia* (most)
Corylopsis†	*Halesia*	*Picea*†
Cryptomeria	*Hamamelis*	*Pieris*
Desfontainea	*Kalmia*	*Pinus*†
Enkianthus	*Kolreuteria*	*Rhododendron*
Erica (most)	*Larix*	*Skimmia* (most)
Fothergilla	*Liquidambar*	*Taxodium*

Short-lived plants

Some plants are naturally short lived. Pruning the shrubs regularly can prolong their life, as can dividing the perennials every two years.

Annuals (die in first year)	*Fremontodendron*
Biennials (die in second year)	*Lavatera* (shrubby)
Cistus (some)	*Lupinus arboreus*
Cytisus	*Primula vulgaris*
Diascia	*Spartium*
Euphorbia characias	Tender plants (killed by frost)

Harmful plants

While most plants are entirely safe both to adults and children, some are mildly poisonous and a few are deadly. Fortunately leaves and twigs, which can be highly poisonous, are the least likely to be eaten but fruits and ocasionally flowers can be poisonous too. Recent research has clarified the dangers and dangerous plants will soon be labelled in garden centres. The dangers of many plants are reduced by a bitter taste or by prompting vomiting. Assume that plants which may cause skin irritation or allergies will also be dangerous to the eyes. But consider the dangers realistically and consider whether children will be using the garden.

Aconitum All parts are highly poisonous and may cause an allergic reaction after handling.

Aesculus All parts are poisonous but rarely cause severe poisoning, especially as conkers are unpalatable.

Agrostemma All parts poisonous, especially the seeds, but the chances of poisoning are very slim.

Alstroemeria Contact may cause an allergic reaction.

Aquilegia All parts are poisonous, skin contact may cause irritation.

Arisaema All parts are poisonous, skin contact may cause irritation.

Arum All parts are poisonous, skin contact may cause irritation.

Berberis Contact with sap during pruning may cause skin irritation.

Borago Contact may cause skin irritation.

Caltha Contact may cause skin irritation.

Clematis Contact may cause skin irritation.

Colchicum All parts are highly toxic, fatalities have been reported.

Convallaria Seeds poisonous, but the attractive red berries taste foul and usually cause prompt vomiting.

Cornus Contact with sap during pruning may cause skin irritation.

× *Cupressocyparis* Contact with sap during pruning may cause skin irritation. This is especially likely with people sensitive to sticking plaster.

Daphne Foliage can cause a rash on a few susceptible people, the berries are toxic.

Datura All parts highly toxic and have been abused for their hallucinogenic effects; excessive consumption has led to death by respiratory paralysis.

Delphinium Contact may cause skin irritation.

Dendranthema Contact may cause skin irritation.

Dicentra Contact may cause skin irritation.

Digitalis Highly poisonous, but bitter taste and emetic qualities reduce risk.

Echium Contact may cause skin irritation.

Euonymus All parts highly toxic, eating the fruits is dangerous.

Euphorbia Contact with milky sap may cause severe skin irritation.

Fremontodendron Contact during pruning may cause skin irritation.

Gaultheria All parts, especially berries, of *Gaultheria mucronata*. Some other species may cause allergies in people allergic to aspirin.

Hedera Contact during pruning may cause severe skin irritation.

Heliotropium Contact may cause skin irritation.

Helleborus Contact may cause skin irritation.

Hyacinthus Handling bulbs may cause an allergic reaction.

Iris Handling plants may cause a severe allergic reaction.

Juniperus May cause irritation to people allergic to sticking plaster, fruits of *J. sabina* can cause severe poisoning.

Laburnum Seeds highly serious, but vomiting often prevents serious harm.

Ligustrum vulgare All parts poisonous, the main risk is from eating berries.

Myosotis Contact may cause skin irritation.

Narcissus Contact may cause skin irritation, bulbs are toxic if eaten.

Ornithogalum Contact may cause skin irritation.

Parthenocissus Contact may cause skin irritation.

Pentaglottis Contact may cause skin irritation.

Phytolacca Berries, especially unripe ones, can cause serious poisoning. Contact may cause skin irritation.

Polygonatum Berries are toxic but taste foul.

Primula Contact may cause skin irritation; most varieties of *P. obconica* cause an allergic reaction.

Prunus Fruits of *P. laurocerasus* are toxic, toxic leaves may be mistaken for bay leaves.

Pulmonaria Contact may cause skin irritation.

Ranunculus Contact may cause skin irritation.

Rhamnus Berries are highly toxic.

Ricinus The attractive seeds are poisonous but are rarely produced on garden plants so keep seed packets locked away from children.

Ruta Contact, especially in bright sunlight, can cause very severe skin blisters and even permanent scarring. Also toxic if eaten.

Sambucus Eating raw berries may cause digestive upsets.

Solanum The berries of some species are highly toxic, even fatal.

Taxus All parts except the fleshy covering of the seed are highly toxic; safest to assume all parts poisonous.

Thuya Contact during pruning or hedge clipping may cause an allergic reaction, usually in people allergic to sticking plaster.

Umbellularia The aroma from crushed leaves, while pleasant in small sniffs, can cause headaches and dizziness if overdone.

Veratrum Contact may cause skin irritation.

Wisteria Seeds highly toxic, but rarely produced in Britain.

Exceptionally spiny shrubs

Sometimes a spiny plant may be required to keep out wandering animals, but if you have children you might wish to avoid them.

Berberis All have spines at the base of the leaves and some also have spiny leaves, but *B. gagnepainii* and *B. julianae* with small yellow flowers are the most lethal and can be very dangerous.

Chaenomeles All forms are spiny but usually not excessively.

Elaeagnus angustifolia Sharp spines among silver leaves.

Genista hispanica Tight mass of spiny stems; yellow flowers.

Hippophaë rhamnoides Both sexes are spiny; silver leaves.

Ilex aquifolium Most hollies have at least a few spines on their leaves but 'Crassifolia' and 'Ferox' are especially brutal, while 'Camellifolia', 'J. C. van Thol', 'Golden van Thol', 'Lawsoniana' and 'Howick' are virtually spine-free.

Poncirus trifoliata Not evergreen, but looks it with its bright green stems and long, stout, sharp green spines on the stems.

Prunus spinosa 'Purpurea' Very stout and sharp spines.

Pyracantha All pyracanthas have stiff black spines at leaf joints.
Ribes speciosum Short sharp spines especially on young shoots.
Rosa pimpinellifolia Most roses are thorny, this is about the worst.
Rubus Fruiting blackberries and other rubus can be vicious.
Ulex europaeus Apparently without leaves but covered in spines instead.

Useful Latin†

There are many Latin words that occur commonly in plant names which tell us something useful about the nature of the plant. The endings of the words may change for different plants.

Flower colours

alba = white

aurantiaca = orange

aurea = gold

bicolor = two-coloured

caerulea = blue

carnea = flesh-coloured

coccinea = scarlet

flava = pale yellow

lilacina = lilac

lutea = yellow

nigra = black

punicea = crimson

purpurea = purple

rosea = pink

rubra = red

sanguinea = blood red

Leaves

aurea = gold

glauca = sea green

hirsuta = hairy

incana = downy grey

macrophylla = large-leaved

maculata = blotched

marginata = edged

microphylla = small leaved

sempervirens = evergreen

velutina = velvety

Size

arborea = tree-like

grandis = grand

major = greater

minima = the very smallest

minor = lesser

nana = dwarf

Growth habit

fastigiata = erect

horizontale = horizontal

humile = low growing

pendula = weeping

procumbens = creeping

prostrata = flat on ground

---

† For more information on the meanings of plant names, see *Plant Names Simplified* by A. T. Johnson and H. A. Smith.

Books and advice

In addition to the books mentioned occasionally in footnotes, the following titles should prove useful when choosing or buying plants.

The Complete Small Garden by Graham Rice (Papermac) A basic guide to planning, choosing plants, care and cultivation.

Plants for Problem Places by Graham Rice (Timber Press) Thirteen problems solved by adapting the situation then choosing the right plants which will thrive there.

Wisley Handbooks (RHS/Cassell) Sixty economical basic books on a wide variety of special topics.

Right Plant, Right Place by Nicola Ferguson (Pan) Plants chosen for the more common garden situations.

The Plant Finder by Tony Lord and Chris Phillip (RHS/Moorland) 60,000 plants (though not annuals) and the nurseries which stock each one. Every plant in *The Planting Planner* is in *The Plant Finder* – or it was when I finished the book.

Award of Garden Merit Plants (RHS) This book lists all the plants which have received the prestigious Award of Garden Merit from the Royal Horticultural Society and which are marked with this symbol ♥ in the book. These plant are also marked in *The Plant Finder* (see above)

Royal Horticultural Society

The RHS is the world's foremost gardening society and although the subscription is not cheap it provides excellent value for money if you take advantage of all their services. To mention just a few of the benefits membership can provide: a colourful monthly magazine, seed distribution scheme, information sheets on hundreds of subjects, free entry to three RHS gardens (Wisley, Surrey; Rosemoor, Devon; Hyde Hall, Essex) and some National Trust gardens; advice on solving pest and disease problems.

For details of membership, telephone the RHS on 0171 821 3000.

Name changes

In recent years, as botanical science has advanced, botantists have been forced to change a number of plant names. In this book the most widely accepted correct names have been used (here in **bold**) but here I give the more commonly used alternatives to avoid excessive bewilderment. Only in Aster and Geranium have I used the old, but incorrect names.

Acaena 'Kupferteppich' = *Acaena* 'Copper Carpet'

Acca sellowiana = *Feijoa selloana*

Acer palmatum 'Sengo-kaku' = *Acer palmatum* 'Senkaki'

Actinidia deliciosa = *Actinidia chinensis*

Allium christophii = *Allium albopilosum*

Aloysia triphylla = *Lippia citriodora*

Amberboa moschata = *Centaurea moschata*

Anacyclus pyrethrum var. depressus = *Anacyclus depressus*

Anaphalis margaritacea var. yedoensis = *Anaphalis yedoensis*

Anthemis punctata ssp. cupaniana = *Anthemis cupaniana*

Aristolochia durior = *Aristolochia macrophylla*

Aruncus dioiscus = *Aruncus sylvester*

Aster = Callistephus

Aurinia saxatilis = *Alyssum saxatile*

Borago pygmaea = *Borago laxiflora*

Brachyglottis 'Sunshine' = *Senecio* 'Sunshine'

Brachyscome = *Brachycome*

Bracteantha = *Helichrysum*

Buddleja = *Buddleia*

Citrus × sinensis 'Meyer' = *Citrus* 'Meyer's Lemon'

Clematis 'Kakio' = *Clematis* 'Pink Champagne'

Colletia paradoxa = *Colletia cruciata*

Coronilla valentina ssp. glauca = *Coronilla glauca*

Cotoneaster atropurpureus 'Variegatus' = *Cotoneaster horizontalis* 'Variegatus'

Crataegus laevigata = *Crataegus oxyacantha*

Crataegus persimilis 'Prunifolia' = *Crataegus prunifolia*

Darmara peltata = *Peltiphyllum peltatum*
Dendranthema = *Chrysanthemum*
Euphorbia amygdaloides ssp. robbiae = *Euphorbia robbiae*
Euphorbia polychroma = *Euphorbia epithymoides*
Fallopia baldschuanica = *Polygonum baldschuanicum*
Gaultheria mucronata = *Pernettya mucronata*
Geranium (half-hardy annuals) = **Pelargonium**
Geranium psilostemon = *Geranium armenum*
Gladiolus callianthus = *Acidanthera mureliae*
Hedera algeriensis = *H. canariensis* (usually!)
Hedera algeriensis 'Gloire de Marengo' = *Hedera canariensis* 'Gloire de Marengo'
Hedera colchica 'Sulphur Heart' = *Hedera colchica* 'Paddy's Pride'
Hedera helix 'Ori di Bogliasco' = *Hedera helix* 'Goldheart'
Helleborus Early Purple = *Helleborus atrorubens*
Hyacinthoides hispanica = *Scilla hispanica*
Hyacinthoides non-scripta = *Scilla non-scriptus*
Hydrangea anomala ssp. petiolaris = *Hydrangea petiolaris*
Iris unguicularis = *Iris stylosa*
Lamium galeobdolon = *Galeobdolon luteum*
Leptinella potentillina = *Cotula potentilloides*
Leptinella squalida = *Cotula squalida*
Leucanthella uliginosum = *Chrysanthemum uliginosum*
Leymus arenarius = *Elymus arenarius*
Lobularia = *Alyssum*
Lotus hirsutus = *Dorycnium hirsutum*
Luma apiculata = *Myrtus luma*
Lysimachia congestiflora = *Lysimachia* 'Lyssi'
Miscanthus sinensis 'Silberfeder' = *Miscanthus sinensis* 'Silver Feather'
Nectaroscordum = *Allium*
Paeonia delavayi var. ludlowii = *Paeonia ludlowii*
Penstemon 'Snowstorm' = *Penstemon* 'White Bedder'
Persicaria = *Polygonum*
Photinia 'Redstart' = × *Stravinia* 'Redstart'

Pinus nigra ssp. laricio = *Pinus nigra ssp. maritima*

Plecostachys serpyllifolia = *Helichrysum microphyllum*

Pleioblastus auricormis = *Arundinaria auricoma*

Primula 'Guinevere' = *Primula* 'Garryarde Guinevere'

Prunus laurocerasus 'Castlewellan' = *Prunus laurocerasus* 'Marbled White'

Prunus pendula 'Pendula Rubra' = *Prunus subhirtella* 'Pendula Rubra'

Pseudosasa japonica = *Arundinaria japonica*

Pseudowintera colorata = *Drimys colorata*

Rhodanthemum hosmariense = *Chrysanthemum hosmariense*

Rosa pimpinellifolia = *Rosa spinosissima*

Salix babylonica 'Tortuosa' = *Salix matsudana* 'Tortuosa'

Salix × sepulcralis 'Chrysosoma' = *Salix chrysocoma*

Sambucus nigra 'Guincho Purple' = *Sambucus nigra* 'Purpurea'

Saxifraga 'Gregor Mendel' = *Saxifraga × apiculata*

Scilla mischtschenkoana = *Scilla tubergeniana*

Sedum 'Herbstreude' = *Sedum* 'Autumn Joy'

Selinum wallichianum = *Selinum tenuifolium*

Seriophidium tridentatum = *Artemisia tridentata*

Stachys byzantina = *Stachys lanata*

Tamarix ramosissima = *Tamarix pentandra*

Viola riviniana 'Purpurea' = *Viola labradorica* 'Purpurea'

INDEX